Finding a Way in
International Development

Finding a Way in International Development

Options for Ethical and Effective Work

Sarah Parkinson

Kumarian Press

A Division of Lynne Rienner Publishers, Inc. • Boulder & London

Published in the United States of America in 2013 by
Kumarian Press
A division of Lynne Rienner Publishers, Inc.
1800 30th Street, Boulder, Colorado 80301
www.rienner.com
www.kpbooks.com

and in the United Kingdom by
Kumarian Press
A division of Lynne Rienner Publishers, Inc.
3 Henrietta Street, Covent Garden, London WC2E 8LU

© 2013 by Lynne Rienner Publishers. All rights reserved

Library of Congress Cataloging-in-Publication Data
Parkinson, Sarah, 1974–
    Finding a way in international development / Options for ethical and effective work /
      Sarah Parkinson.—1st ed.
    Includes bibliographical references and index.
    ISBN 978-1-56549-566-1 (alk. paper)
    ISBN 978-1-56549-567-8 (pbk.: alk. paper)
    1. Economic development. 2. Non-governmental organizations. I. Title.
    HD77.P37 2012
    338.91—dc23 2012034293

British Cataloguing in Publication Data
A Cataloguing in Publication record for this book
is available from the British Library.

Printed and bound in the United States of America

    The paper used in this publication meets the requirements
∞ of the American National Standard for Permanence of
    Paper for Printed Library Materials Z39.48-1992.

5 4 3 2 1

Contents

Acknowledgments

The preparation of this book has been a wonderful adventure, filled with many great characters. The initial idea came in part from regular conversations with friends and colleagues in Afghanistan, where we shared our experiences and mulled over big questions about ethics and effectiveness: Were we helping? What was the right thing to do? I was grateful for those conversations and the opportunity they provided to help me reflect on my own work. These gatherings also left me with the impression that we were all, in some sense, lost together, grappling with the same fundamental questions. That impression motivated my desire to broaden the conversation, and it led to this book. So I am particularly grateful to all those who kindly hosted and facilitated these friendly yet instructive meetings: Ian Holland, Semira Manaseki-Holland, Shumsa Tahseen, and Jasveen Ahluwalia. I also learned a tremendous amount from those who shared their thoughts and experiences during these times, and although they are too numerous to mention by name, I thank them all.

Once I began to broach the idea of this book and began pestering people for interviews, people were overwhelmingly supportive and generous with their time and participation. Friends, acquaintances, friends of friends, and often absolute strangers agreed to what was quite a personal process of reflecting on their work and their values. Most people were very frank, open, and thoughtful in their responses, which form the heart of the book. I am very grateful to every one of the 153 people that I interviewed, some of whom preferred to remain anonymous, and some of whom are named in the following pages. As readers will see for themselves, the interviewees' ideas and examples were often both insightful and instructive, and their efforts were often inspirational.

As I traveled to gather interviews, I had many generous hosts who supported my work in many ways. These include Tom Vincent in Afghanistan; Jenn Ball, Ricardo Ramirez, Adam Honsinger, Rain Bone, and Natalya Avakova in Canada; Anna-Marie Ball in Uganda; and John Gathuya in Kenya. I'm very lucky to know such kind and vibrant people: your support made my work not just possible but a great pleasure.

During the postinterview preparation and writing period, I was particularly lucky to take advantage of Len Milich's irresistible offer to avail myself of his breathtaking vacation home in Bali for several months. Such a beautiful and tranquil retreat must be every writer's dream. I also enjoyed the unique hospitality of Margaret McAuslan at UFO Studios in Bulgaria. It was a wonderful, creative environment and the place where I first drafted most of the chapters. And I must thank Suchi Rudra for her valiant, entertaining, and almost successful efforts to distract me from my self-imposed writing schedule!

I also owe a special vote of thanks to those who read various drafts of book chapters or the whole draft manuscript: Liz Parkinson, Laura Parkinson, Eleanor Augusteijn, Ashlee Consulo Willox, Sarah Cardey, Sheilagh Henry, Fabienne Glauser, and Naysan Adlparvar. Their feedback and suggestions were invaluable. I'd also like to thank Ian Smillie for his advice on publishing. Finally, I'd like to thank Jim Lance and Kumarian Press for working so positively and patiently with me to turn the manuscript into this book.

1

Introduction

On a searingly bright day in 2003, I sat on an upturned plastic milk crate on the floor of a one-room shack in the midst of a shanty settlement in Khayelitsha, a large black township on the sand flats thirty kilometers east of Cape Town in South Africa. I remember that day very clearly, sitting there on the milk crate, watching and listening while a woman in her early forties stood over a paraffin stove and worked as she spoke to Millicent, my research assistant.

"Khayelitsha" means "new home" in Xhosa, the language of most of its residents. But it isn't a particularly welcoming place to make a home. No vegetation, limited groundwater, just miles and miles of flat, bare sand. I could see it all from my vantage point on the crate because the door of the shack was wide open to let in the light. And all around us, on that sandy expanse, sprung up thousands of modest settlements, most put together from pieces of corrugated iron and sometimes wood. In that particular part, they were piled in almost on top of each other, so there was no sense of privacy, no particular order, no streets. We had wended our way through the maze of shacks, as people cooked and bathed and went about their lives in the open, outside their homes, or with the doors open to let in light.

Khayelitsha is sprawling and broken into sections. It boomed since apartheid ended, with an estimated population of about half a million by 2005.[1] Whole families came from the homelands to join the men who had been living there even as the postapartheid government tried to move people in from the already overpacked townships closer to Cape Town. Many of these people were unemployed, many of them children and youth. By 2003 there were some paved roads and social services in parts of it, and even a shopping center. The government had also instituted a program to provide people with modest but modern cement homes and to resettle them away from the shacks. But the program had run into problems of various sorts, including allegations of corruption and mismanagement. Khayelitsha's frustrated residents had vandalized many of the cement homes, their new glass windows smashed.

I was there because I was carrying out a small research project for the International Development Research Centre (IDRC), a Canadian agency funded directly through Canada's federal aid budget. IDRC had funded efforts to increase public access to new information and communication technologies (ICTs), mainly computers, telephones, and the Internet. I was studying community access to ICTs in South Africa and Uganda, in areas where IDRC had worked. So I had hired two young women who lived in Khayelitsha to help me, and we were carrying out, among other things, a small household survey. The results of all these efforts, which I carried out in select locations around the two countries, were later written and shared with the aim of improving universal access policy and strategy.

In a very weak, indirect way, this research may have been of some benefit to the woman who was answering our survey questions. We took about ten minutes of her time. Insofar as the results might play some modest role in influencing policy toward better public access, and insofar as this might help her or her family in their day-to-day efforts to communicate, to get information, to conduct business, and so forth, it could be helpful. Certainly not harmful. But probably not a pressing priority. Probably not anything that would ever make a felt difference in her life.

Sitting there, I had ample opportunity to reflect on all of this because the woman and Millicent were speaking in Xhosa, which I didn't understand. But then she switched to English, and turning from her stove, she looked at me as if she'd been sharing some of my thoughts and said, "You see how we are living here. It is not right. It is not good."

She spoke softly and deliberately with a melodious South African accent that made her sentences sound like a poem, beautiful and important. But the words, simple as they were, spoke to a truth that was not beautiful. Khayelitsha, its very existence, was a product of social injustice and seemed like a testament to the limitations of our humanity. She had a slightly wistful, expectant look on her face, as if she were vaguely hoping that I, a stranger with access to greater resources, to large institutions, had brought something more useful than the survey. I didn't know what to say; I had nothing to offer her. I just nodded.

We thanked her warmly for her time and stood up to leave. She'd already turned back to her work, away from us. But then she stopped, hesitating a few moments before calling to Millicent. They spoke in Xhosa. And then in

English: "Come, I will take you to the road; you are in danger here." And she walked with us back the way we came, back out of the settlement and to a paved main road, where she left us. Millicent explained to me that the woman had overheard a gang of young men talking. They had seen us. I was a white stranger; Millicent was from another part of Khayelitsha, also a stranger according to them. Khayelitsha could be a violent place, and order was kept through neighborhood protection groups and vigilantism. But we were out of our territory. They were waiting for us farther within the settlement, the direction we would have gone if the woman had not guided us. Their intentions were not good.

I had known some areas might be too dangerous to venture into, but I thought that place was okay because Millicent hadn't said anything, and she knew Khayelitsha. Millicent knew we might be in danger going too deep into that settlement, but she had not warned me because she thought I was the boss and should make the decisions. I didn't ask, so she didn't speak out. And so our unspoken assumptions led us unwittingly to what could have been a very bad situation.

Given the frequency of murder in South Africa at that time, the woman may well have saved our lives.[2] Police records show 2003–2004 to have been a particularly violent year for Khayelitsha, with 358 recorded murders, 395 attempted murders, and over 3,000 assaults with the intent to inflict grievous bodily harm.[3] I was doubtful that my efforts benefited her, but I am sure about what she did for me. I don't know her name. And I don't know, but I imagine her life hasn't gotten much easier since I saw her. I have often wondered what was in her mind as she hesitated. And I'm grateful for the kindness she showed to us that day.

When I think of that woman, I also think of the implicit question behind her words and looks: "What value does your work have for me?" I wonder, am I contributing to a broader, well-structured effort to address poverty, to address the causes of poverty that meant she was living in such conditions? Am I focusing my efforts in the best way? I was, after all, part of the international development system when I did that work; the funding came from Canada's aid budget. Perhaps it is rather simplistic or arrogant to think that there is anything much I should or could have done for her, but when she spoke, she spoke the truth. And I wasn't sure of an appropriate response. When I think of that day and that woman, I am aware foremost of all the uncertainties in my own understanding and the gaps between what I imagine international development to be, in some ideal parallel universe in my head, and the way I've experienced it playing out over the years I've worked in or around it.

The Rationale for International Development

Part of the reason for my wondering is that the purpose of international development is usually stated in terms of reducing, if not eradicating, poverty. International development can be loosely described as a global human effort to combat poverty and its concomitant suffering. The people at the World Bank claim to be "working for a world free of poverty."[4] The United Nations Development Programme explains itself as "the UN's global development network, advocating for change and connecting countries to knowledge, experience and resources to help people build a better life."[5] BRAC, the world's largest nongovernmental organization (NGO), is "dedicated to alleviating poverty by empowering the poor to bring about change in their own lives."[6] Oxfam, another well-known international development NGO, describes its work as "to find lasting solutions to poverty and injustice" through a combination of working directly with communities and seeking "to influence the powerful."[7] The Development Co-operation Directive of the Organisation for Economic Co-operation Development (OECD) claims its work is focused on helping to "ensure better lives for people in the developing world."[8] As a deliberate effort, it can be traced back to Harry Truman's 1949 inaugural address, as he became the president of the United States. Truman argued that the world, and particularly the West, had for the first time the capacity to address global poverty and hence the moral obligation to do so.

Since that time, the world's wealth has vastly increased, as has its interconnectedness through increased trade, travel, and communication. Official development assistance from rich nations to poor nations has increased, and some once-poor countries have become much wealthier. But poverty is still with us on the planet, and as the world's human population has increased from 2.5 billion at the time of Truman's speech to 7 billion in 2012, the numbers of people living in poverty have not diminished, even if the proportion has.[9] The depletion of natural resources, the consequences of climate change, and an increasing global population are putting ever-greater pressure on the ecosystems that ultimately sustain us. The growing prevalence and sophistication of transnational terrorist and criminal networks have provided further rationale for development assistance as a form of enlightened self-interest on the part of the wealthy. If large numbers of people are suffering in desperate poverty, knowing that others are living in comfort, and if they are given no other recourse, at least some are likely to resort to criminality or to radical political action.

Into the Looking Glass—Or How the Rationale Gets Lost in Practice

From the very beginning of international development's history, it has not been motivated solely, or even primarily, by the desire to rid the world of the scourge of human poverty and suffering. Rather, the international development effort has been as much political as humanitarian. Official development assistance often followed cold war politics more closely than it followed need, giving money to some horrific regimes for the sake of political alliances. The term "third world" was primarily a political designation for those postcolonial countries that had no clear alignment with either the United States or the Soviets. Former colonial powers such as France and Britain have used international development assistance as a way of maintaining trade and diplomatic links with former colonies. And aid has often been tied to the economic interests of big businesses within donor countries.

Although not secret, these other interests are not usually part of the official rhetoric about international development. And so there is a gap between what is said and what is done. This gap, visible at the broadest level of aid policy and international relations between donor and recipient countries, continues in various forms through every level of the aid system.

The donor agencies that provide official development aid may be influenced by the international political interests of their governments. This influence can filter down because those receiving aid from donors do so largely on the donors' terms. Although international development is justified in the name of the poor, it is accountable to those who pay. In one example from Georgia, an American working for a small development NGO there recalls that the United States insisted the World Food Programme temporarily stop food distribution to internally displaced people living in camps. Instead, prepackaged humanitarian daily rations supplied by the US military were given to agencies to distribute for about two weeks. The people receiving them complained that the rations were inedible, unfit even to feed their dogs. The United States' rationale for doing this was to send Russia a political message of "solidarity with Georgia."

Even without such overt political influence, aid institutions can be hobbled by their own management practices. Institutional accountability systems tend to focus on predictable, measurable outputs attributable to aid funds. Development theoretically aims at broader economic and social change, namely, the reduction of poverty, improvement of public health, improvement of other key services for people, and so forth. But it is hard to trace and attribute such changes to any three-year project or even a ten-year program.

There is an old story about a man who is looking for his keys under a street lamp one late evening. A friend who is passing by comes to help him but cannot see them anywhere. So the friend asks him, "Where exactly were you when you dropped them?" "Over there by my front door," the man replies, pointing to the door of his house, one hundred feet away. "Then why are you looking over here?" asks his friend in frustration. "Because it's too dark over there," he answers.

Efforts at monitoring and evaluation in international development often do the same thing—they focus on what is easy to measure rather than on what is important. And so the tools of development, the means by which some broader change is supposed to take place, become ends in themselves. Development becomes about how many workshops you had, how many people received training, compared to how many you said you would have in your funding proposal.[10] People living in squalor in places like Khayelitsha become almost invisible behind it all.

The tendency to measure rather than to understand reduces the possibilities to learn from experience. Even the most carefully planned development initiative may turn out quite different than expected. People have different views and interests that can make change more difficult. In Khayelitsha, the government plan to build better housing for people and move them out of the poorly constructed shacks seemed straightforward enough. But many people preferred to stay in their shacks and rent out the permanent housing they received for extra income, while profiteers diverted public funds to their own pockets, meaning construction was slow and quality was often lacking. The outcome was decidedly different from the original vision of the planners.

There is often a gap in perspective between those who are working in international development and those who are supposed to benefit. This gap is often wider when people come from different cultures, and it's wider still between citizens of donor countries and those of recipient countries. When I was doing research work in South Africa and Uganda, I would go back to visit Canada, and people would congratulate me for "helping" the Africans. I was conducting research that, realistically, was only of very marginal and indirect value to most of the people who kindly gave me their time and participated. I wasn't exactly out there saving lives, but many people back in Canada spoke as though I were. Given my experiences in Khayelitsha and elsewhere, that is quite ironic. People I met everywhere I went in South Africa and Uganda were continually helping me, informing me, looking out for me, and enlightening me. The assumption that Westerners are empowered and knowing and that Africans are passive and needy seems like a stale hangover from the colonial past, but it is still with us.

For anyone working in development, and particularly anyone from the West, we unfortunately carry the baggage of a collective historical heritage of paternalism and inequity. This could cause us to feel that our values, knowledge, and actions are more important than those of whom we purport to help. Even if we think we're free from that, the same history influences opportunities and relationships with others. In Khayelitsha, I wasn't trying to exercise power and silence Millicent from voicing her opinion. But still, with the history of the world, and the history of race relations in South Africa, Millicent was silent, and I wasn't perceptive enough in that moment to ask her explicitly for her advice.

Those coming to work in international development must contend not just with a gap between stated intent and actual practice but with countless gaps, from the grossest and most blatant political uses of development aid in support of war, to the most subtle psychological and interpersonal inconsistencies in their own practice. They must learn how to contend with and manage all of these gaps and try to be effective. Is it possible to be effective in such a topsy-turvy world? How do they adjust to this reality while holding on to whatever motivated them in the first place? What can they do?

What to Do?

The persistence of gaps and inconsistencies among words, actions, and results throughout the history of international development has not gone unnoticed. As early as the 1960s and 1970s, people were raising concerns about the effectiveness of development and voicing objections to the whole enterprise. Given the persistent use of development aid for political ends, some people argued that this was the only purpose of development, and so it was no surprise that development efforts routinely failed to achieve their stated goals. As David Mosse explains, "A now extensive literature argues that, like those of colonial rule, development's rational models achieve cognitive control and social regulation; they enhance state capacity and expand bureaucratic power (particularly over marginal areas and people); they reproduce hierarchies of knowledge (scientific over indigenous) and society (developer over the 'to be developed'), and they fragment, subjugate or silence the local," all while claiming to be benignly working on behalf of the poor.[11]

The staunchest critics of international development see the whole system as morally bankrupt and view the majority of people working within it as hypocrites, cynics, and self-important opportunists. In *The Lords of Poverty*, Graham Hancock documents the excesses of World Bank executives. He recounts, for example, how one donor employee proudly showed him a basement filled with a lifetime's supply of toilet paper, which he had supplied and shipped around the world several times at great expense, paid for with aid money.[12] Hancock is willing to exonerate many NGO workers as well intentioned, although he notes that by the age of thirty, many of them change tune and begin to show an interest in pursuing the coddled lifestyle of a UN or donor employee.

That greedy, indifferent, incompetent, and even villainous people are present in the aid system is incontrovertible. That they characterize it is not. Many of those who are attracted to work in international development do so because they are, at heart, idealists and humanists. Perhaps their initial understandings are limited, but they are capable of learning, of thinking critically, and of empathizing with other people. What happens to these people? Do they sell out, burn out, or drop out? Or are they at-large and at work? And if so, what are they doing, and how are they doing it?

The best-documented answers to these questions are held within the careful work of development ethnographers who have studied international development work and relationships, often as participant-observers. They are interested in how development operates through relationships and discourses and how people's actions are shaped by ideologies.[13] Their studies show that development practice is not nearly as clear-cut as it is presented by either the development policymakers, with their three-year plans and strategy documents that will lead to measurable progress through a logical sequence of actions, or the critics, with their equally deterministic analysis of how development processes are inevitably oppressive. The ethnographers argue instead that there are powerful tendencies within the system, especially the tendency to adopt and re-create certain prevalent ways of thinking. These ways of thinking in turn tend to re-create the system itself, including its gaps and inconsistencies. The only possible way out of this cycle is to understand one's role and learn to be reflective.

Everyone working in international development traverses a unique path through a broader system joined together by donors, aid funding, predominant ideologies, international conventions, institutions, and training. Although diverse, international development, or international aid, does have these broad commonalities, which means that certain patterns or tendencies are likely to occur across our experiences. Many people working in development, for example, have experienced the need to justify their work according to donor criteria that frame and prioritize issues in a different way than they would otherwise choose to. Their experiences in the system contribute to their ideas of what it is and what is possible within it. And because those development workers often share similar assumptions and understandings, they are likely to interpret their experiences and react in similar ways, contributing to the ongoing re-creation of the broader aid system.

As practitioners within the system, we can base our responses on fairly stock, superficial thinking or on deeper reflection. When we are able to reflect on our part in the system, we can begin to see spaces and opportunities for changing the system, or at least for a broader set of responses within it. This increases the power we have to renegotiate the rules.

Like the ripples that emanate from a stone thrown into the water, our power to act and effect change is strongest at the center, which in this case is our own assumptions and ourselves. Beyond ourselves, the next domain in which we can make some waves is our work environment. This includes the institution where we work and, more broadly, the international development system as a series of institutions. These institutions both condition and are conditioned by the actions and experiences of those working within them. As individual practitioners, we have power to choose where we work and some power to negotiate functions, culture, and policy within the workplace.

Finally, beyond the development system, we come to the political, social, and economic forces at play. These are as large and encompassing as an ocean. No matter the stones we throw, the waves we make, they are barely perturbed. It is difficult to expect we can change geopolitical realities as individuals, or even as a collective, although it may be possible to aspire to broader change on specific issues and practices. So these are most often seen as constraining forces on what we do.

It's the sum of all of these individual beliefs and actions, embedded in institutional dynamics and in broader social dynamics, that creates international development as we know it—a huge tangled web of the good, the bad, and the ugly. And it's through gaining a better understanding of these domains that we can maximize our own agency and come to terms with the limits we perhaps can't change.

At the heart of development's operation are knowledge framing and valuing, relationships, and relative power. We can understand these at an individual level, within our own professional practice. We share norms around them within our educational and professional development systems. Robert Chambers called for "reversals" that privilege the local and that see development professionals as facilitators of process rather than subject matter experts. But the international development system often requires people who are experts foremost in the international development system itself. That means being familiar with the particularities of donor reporting and audit systems, being able to speak English, knowing how to use computers, knowing the right jargon, and so forth. Uma Kothari has argued that the trend is toward a managerial view of professionalism in international development, one that reinforces the initial biases within international development—privileging the general and universal over the specific and local, the formal over the informal, the outside expert over the local.[14]

How can an individual practitioner navigate through these broad trends? Donald Schön argued that reflective practice can be learned and cultivated.[15] Those working in international development need to be reflective practitioners if they wish to be ethical and effective practitioners. They need to grapple with a system that is rife with internal contradictions. Most people coming to work in international development want and expect a logical, internally consistent system. But once we get over the shock that we don't have that, not even close, we can start to look at what is possible within what we do have. And the contention of this book is that for a reflective and dedicated practitioner, many possibilities exist. One possibility, which we consider in chapter 11, is to choose not to work in international development at all. Whether or not to work in international development is ultimately a personal decision. But it should, above all, be a conscious one.

Seeking Answers

The main concern of this book is to understand the various gaps and tensions between stated intent and actual practice and to understand the ways that individual development practitioners behave that may bridge, or fail to bridge, these gaps in their own work. By understanding this, we can improve our chances of being effective in our own work.

One obvious way to understand what people working in international development face and how they respond to it is to ask them about it. So I interviewed 153 people, mainly people working in international development, as well as professors who taught international development courses or programs, students studying development, and some people who studied development but never practiced it or people who decided to stop working in it. I asked them about their experiences, their thoughts about what international development was, what it should or could be, how their work related to it, how their ideas had changed over time, trends they saw within development, and the difficulties and achievements they'd experienced in their own work and seen in the sector more broadly.

Those interviewed are a diverse lot, working for different kinds of institutions in various positions, at different points in their careers, with different personalities and attitudes, coming from thirty-six different countries.[16] Some were seasoned hands who had already retired or were heading up major missions for a UN agency or a large development NGO; others were working in small independent initiatives or just starting out in their first job. In total, the people I spoke with have just about 2,000 years of collective experience working in international development. I spoke to people in Afghanistan, Kenya, Canada, and Uganda. But their work experience encompasses a much broader range of countries, upward of 107 in total, located all over the world. Some people had spent their whole career in one or a few countries, while others had worked in over thirty countries.

In terms of professional specializations, many people, especially those working in small or midsized NGOs, tend to be generalists, while others have very specific technical knowledge. Interviewees had worked on topics that included health, education, rural development, gender, agriculture, water and sanitation, emergency relief, disaster preparedness, governance and democratization, anticorruption, human rights, public administration and civil service development, refugee resettlement, security development, organizational development, national development planning, economic policy at a national level, drug control, peace building, private sector development, and research, policy, or advocacy related to any of these topics. Some people were primarily in administrative or support roles, while the majority of interviewees were in either programming or management positions and involved in setting overall policy and direction.

This gets back to the tricky question of what international development actually encompasses. Roles and positions are often classified as "international development" because of the nature of the funding and institutional arrangements—people working on education or sanitation in Canada might never consider themselves development workers, but individuals working on the same issues in Afghanistan or Bangladesh, especially if employed by an organization such as Save the Children or BRAC, might well classify themselves this way. Some government workers in countries such as Nepal or Uganda may end up implementing a donor or NGO program or partnering with such a program. Are they then part of the international development system if they are receiving funds from UNICEF and providing it with quarterly reports?

In selecting interview participants, I applied the term "international development" broadly and then asked people how they identified themselves professionally and if they felt the term "international development professional" applied to them. About two-thirds felt that it did apply to them. Some preferred other terms, such as "aid worker," or for those in the UN, "international civil servant." Many distinguish between long-term development and short-term humanitarian relief, but because many people have worked in both capacities or touch both issues in their work, I have included humanitarian work as a particular type of development work. This categorization may not be theoretically rigorous, but it seems to better reflect existing working realities. To refer to those working within the international development system, this book most often uses the terms "development worker" or "development practitioner."

Given the wide ranges of experiences and backgrounds, and the broad nature of some of the questions, the interviews were diverse. No doubt some of our conversations were a reflection of how someone's day had gone rather than someone's definitive viewpoint on issues of development. With that in mind, I viewed the interviews as snapshots of people's thoughts and feelings at a particular point in time, with the hope that from the larger collective, a broader gestalt would emerge. To frame and balance the often anecdotal and off-the-cuff nature of what was said during interviews, I have also considered various books and articles on international development, focusing on written firsthand accounts of working in development; work that analyzes international development as a sector, development ethnographies, and work examining particular kinds of institutions within international development, especially NGOs and donor agencies.[17]

Talking to so many people about their work and ideas on development has been a fascinating experience, and it was much more positive than I had ever expected. As I started interviewing people in Afghanistan, I was poised to be depressed given that international engagement in the country had been a "ten-year train wreck," as one friend observed. Effective work was hampered by deteriorating security and the overriding politicization of aid.[18] People would get frustrated and burned out fairly regularly, often choosing to leave after a relatively short period of time. And yet, many people were quite positive about their overall work experiences and what they had been able to do. Even those who faced grave doubts were, for the most part, so willing to engage with those doubts and seek ways forward, and so sincere about the work that they were doing that I was left feeling quite inspired and hopeful despite myself. The same held true when I interviewed people elsewhere. Certainly, many people I spoke with shared serious concerns about development, but for most these did not vanquish the value of what they had managed to do.

Some people interviewed for this book preferred to be completely anonymous, while some preferred to be acknowledged where their ideas are referred to or they are directly quoted. Understandably, most people did not want to go on public record speaking negatively about particular people, institutions, or programs, especially when they may have to work with them in the future. So with few exceptions, negative comments are anonymous. Where necessary to maintain participants' anonymity, I altered some details or removed them from such accounts.

I've tried to convey the heart of what I learned through the interviews in the following pages of this book. This book does not, however, convey the full depth or scope of those interviews and the thoughts and reflections that people expressed. It also cannot and does not attempt to reflect any definitive consensus emerging from the interviews. The overall tone and the assertions made in this book are based on my interpretation of what people told me, combined with my own experience and readings on the topic, and often may not reflect the opinions of those quoted.

This book, informed by these 153 interviews and secondary sources, seeks to answer the questions that have been raised in this introduction. Foremost among these, how can we reduce the gap between stated intention and actual practice, at least within our own work?

Given the great diversity of the work done under the title of "development," this book does not address any aspects of the "how-to" at a technical level. What we are concerned with here is understanding and working within the particular institutional context of international development and how to grapple with some of the practical and ethical challenges of international development work that are commonly faced by development workers.

We can learn, through the experiences of others, to better understand the institutional landscape. Development practitioners typically do this by extrapolating from their own immediate experiences and perhaps some incidents shared by friends and colleagues working in related areas. By casting the net widely and considering a much broader range of experience, we can gain some distance and objectivity in our thinking. This can deepen our understanding of both the international development system and our own part within it. We can learn about key strategies and choices that we can make over our careers and the potential consequences of these. Finally, seeing the diversity of approaches that people have taken in their work can both broaden our thinking and enable us to take greater responsibility for our actions.

Notes

1. Department of Social Services and Poverty Alleviation, *The Population Register Update: Khayelitsha 2005* (Cape Town: Government of the Western Cape, 2006).

2. South Africa has one of the highest murder rates in the world, at 39.5 homicides per 100,000 people (2004 figures). See "Global Homicide: Murder Rates Around the World," DataBlog, *The Guardian*, October 13, 2009, http://www.guardian.co.uk/news/datablog/2009/oct/13/homicide-rates-country-murder-data.

3. South African Police Service, *Crime in the Khayelitsha (Wc) Police Precinct From April to March: 2003/2004–2008/2009* (Cape Town: Government of Cape Town, 2009).

4. See their brochure, for example, World Bank, *World Bank Group: Working for a World Free of Poverty* (Washington, DC: World Bank, 2006).

5. United Nations Development Programme, *Overview: What We Do*, 2012, cited February 15, 2012, http://www.undp.org/content/undp/en/home/ourwork/overview.html.

6. BRAC, *BRAC*, 2012, cited February 15, 2012, http://www.brac.net/.

7. Oxfam, *Oxfam: About Us*, 2012, cited February 15, 2012, http://www.oxfam.org/en/about.

8. OEDC, *Development Co-operation Directorate (DCD-DAC)*, cited January 15, 2012, http://www.oecd.org.

9. Definitions of poverty may be given in relative or absolute terms, and there are various measures for this, which I will not go into here. Generally, though, global inequalities have increased, although patterns have changed with less clear inequalities between groups of nations (i.e., first world and third world), and even by absolute measures, the number of poor people has increased.

10. W. Easterly, "The Cartel of Good Intentions: The Problem of Bureaucracy in Foreign Aid," *Policy Reform* 5, no. 4 (2002).

11. David Mosse, *Cultivating Development: An Ethnography of Aid Policy and Practice* (London: Pluto Press, 2004), 4.

12. Graham Hancock, *The Lords of Poverty: The Power, Prestige, and Corruption of the International Aid Business* (New York: Atlantic Monthly Press, 1989), 80.

13. See, for example, David Lewis and David Mosse, eds., *Development Brokers and Translators: The Ethnography of Aid and Agencies* (Sterling, VA: Kumarian Press, 2006).

14. Uma Kothari, "Authority and Expertise: The Professionalisation of International Development and the Ordering of Dissent," *Antipode* 37, no. 3 (2005).

15. Donald A. Schön, *The Reflective Practitioner: How Professionals Think in Action* (New York: Basic Books, 1984).

16. This is counted based solely by where people were born; the number increases slightly more when national citizenships are included, as many interviewees hold multiple citizenships.

17. References to these works are made periodically throughout the book.

18. Ashley Jackson, *Quick Impact, Quick Collapse: The Dangers of Militarized Aid in Afghanistan* (Kabul: Oxfam, 2010).

Part 1

The International Development System

Ring the bells that still can ring
Forget your perfect offering
There is a crack in everything
That's how the light gets in.
—*Leonard Cohen,* "Anthem"

Familiarity breeds invisibility, as what becomes obvious recedes into the background. For those of us who have been working in international development for a while, the ideas, structures, and funding that hold together the international development system become like the air or the furniture. Although we make use of them every day, we largely take them for granted.

Those of us who are new to the world of international development have the gift of being able to see with fresh eyes, to question what others have long become habituated to. A consultant who has worked with a wide range of development organizations observes,

> If you spend more than six months in an organization, you get caught up in the culture, then you don't see it, like a fish in water . . . these people are in water all the time. I've learnt far more in a place from people who've just joined, because they're still going through the shock of, "This is the way they do things?" It's the nature of cultures . . . at a certain point you say, well, this is the way we do things around here.

In this first part of the book, we take a tour of the international development system. For readers who have already spent some time reading about and working in development, this may feel something akin to taking a tour of your home city because you have some out-of-town visitors you need to entertain. You'll be familiar with most of the stops and the key points, but you might not have visited them for a while or have forgotten a few details. Perhaps the tour operator will introduce some new trivia or have a different way of presenting one of your favorite spots. This is a good opportunity to revisit your familiar understandings.

For readers who are less familiar with international development, this tour provides an orientation to some of the key issues, ideas, and institutions. This begins to lay the foundation for the ideas and examples presented in parts 2 and 3 of this book.

The international development system is so much bigger than us that we are always more influenced by it than we are able to influence it. And yet at the same time, those of us who work within it also constitute it and revitalize it through our actions.

We may not be able to change the system, but we can pick where in the system we want to work, and even if we want to work in it at all. And we can start to ask what the system can do for us, how we can draw on it to pursue our own ideas of what effective development should be.

Radical critiques of the international development system charge that we cannot work effectively within it but should work on development issues through other channels. But one of the most interesting aspects of international development as a system is that it is often not in agreement with itself. For example, an NGO or group of NGOs may oppose key policies or practices of a big donor or of the multilateral banks. As individuals trying to leverage our own paths within the development system, understanding the ways that it is incoherent and contradictory is as important as understanding the ways it is coherent. It is in that incoherence, that contradiction, that our biggest range of choices, and hence our greatest opportunities, may lie.

And so it is time for the tour to begin. The following will orient you to the chapters ahead:

- In chapter 2 we take a look at the history of development and then discuss some of the key ideas that have influenced development practice.
- In chapter 3, we focus on how the international development system works in practice. Focusing on the ever-important issue

of money, this chapter devotes some attention to aid flows and relationships. We consider some of the contradictions and difficulties of international development through the case of Kenya, where aid appears to have abetted huge graft at the same time as it supported some fresh channels for democratic renewal.

- In chapter 4 we tour the major types of development institutions: donors, the United Nations, nongovernmental organizations, contractors, and consultants. For each, we consider what role it plays in the development system and what it is like to work for it.

2

The Idea of International Development

International development can be thought of in two very different ways. One is as an idea of the way the world should be and of how we can get there. The second way is as a system of practice, loosely tied together by shared ideas but also by a host of other interests and practical factors. This chapter examines international development principally as an idea. The next chapter will look at international development as a system.

Of course, we don't have to look very far to realize that development is not a single unitary idea but a whole cluster of ideas, some of which even contradict each other, and that there is very little general agreement on any of these ideas. One general agreement is that international development's main aim should be to reduce poverty. What does that mean, and how should it be done? There is no shortage of answers, although for many, these answers have all come up short. Mwambutsya Ndebesa, head of Development Studies at Makerere University in Uganda, comments,

> There's some intellectual anarchy with regard to development per-spectives—there are no clear contending ideologies of develop-ment. The forced triumph of neoliberalism has not been countered by another ideology, but all we know is it's not working, but we don't know the alternative, and that's frustrating.

While the ideas described in this chapter can often seem a world away from the practice described in the next chapter, it would be wrong to assume that the two are unrelated and that one has no influence on the other. In fact, both the ideas and the structures of international development have common beginnings, a common recent history. And so it is to this history that we first turn.

Beginnings

1949: The Speech

The start of international development as we think of it today can best be pinpointed to Harry Truman's "Four Point" speech, which he delivered at his inauguration on January 20, 1949. It was in his fourth point that he called for introducing a "bold new program" of international cooperation for development. He argued,

> More than half the people of the world are living in conditions approaching misery. Their food is inadequate. They are victims of disease. Their economic life is primitive and stagnant. Their poverty is a handicap and a threat both to them and to more prosperous areas. For the first time in history, humanity possesses the knowledge and the skill to relieve the suffering of these people.[1]

Truman went on to cast a vision of technical and financial support to the "free peoples of the world" and called on other nations to join in, in a world that should be ordered by democracy, to strengthen a system that was threatened by the communist philosophy.

And thus international development came into being at a very particular time in history, when the world was still reeling from two major wars, colonies were becoming independent countries, and the cold war between the United States and the Soviet Union had begun. It was also born into a world that firmly believed science and technology to be the answer to everything and, despite the recent horrors of the world wars, that believed firmly in modern progress.[2]

The Changing World

The decolonization of Africa began slowly in the 1950s as countries such as Libya (1951), Egypt (1953), Tunisia (1956), and Ghana (1957) gained independence. But it was in the early 1960s that the momentum really took off. In 1960 alone seventeen countries gained their independence, and most of the remainder followed soon after. While almost all of Africa, with the exception of Ethiopia, had been colonized, Asia and the Middle East had more mixed experiences. Some countries had not been colonized, and others gained independence right after World War II in the late 1940s, but the process of decolonization in these regions was largely over by the 1970s.

International development was a brand-new effort closely associated with the promise of these newly established and free nations. People who got involved in it in those early days recall a time that was filled with enthusiasm and optimism although also with naïveté.[3] The United Nations, heeding the call of American president John F. Kennedy, declared the 1960s the Development Decade.

The Institutions

The key international institutions associated with development today were established in the wake of World War II. The International Monetary Fund (IMF) and the International Bank for Reconstruction and Development (IBRD, now one of the World Bank institutions) were both established at the Bretton Woods Conference in 1944 by the countries that had allied to fight Nazi Germany. The purpose of the International Monetary Fund has always been to regulate global financial markets rather than to fund development per se, but development funds from the World Bank and others are in part conditional on IMF approval of national economic policy and practice. The IBRD was initially set up to help rebuild Europe.

The United Nations was established in 1945 with the central mandate of keeping peace between nations. It also provides a platform for dialogue and cooperation between nations in areas of international law, economic and social development, and human rights. The UN was envisaged as a worldwide federation of nations, although Western thinking drove its creation.

Most modern international development institutions were set up in the 1960s. The International Development Association (IDA), set up in the 1960s, is the part of the World Bank that provides loans at the most concessional rates, often interest free, to the poorest countries for development purposes. The IBRD continued to focus on slightly wealthier countries and providing loans at less concessional terms. The current US Agency for International Development (USAID) was established under the Foreign Assistance Act of 1961, replacing the earlier foreign aid system with one that was focused specifically on long-term economic and social development. Other Western countries did indeed follow Truman's call and established their own aid programs and agencies. The United Kingdom has gone through a number of configurations for its aid delivery, but the first purpose-created agencies, the Department of Technical Cooperation and the Ministry of Overseas Development, were established in 1961 and 1964, respectively. The Canadian International Development Agency (CIDA) opened its doors in 1968. The United Nations Development Programme (UNDP), the UN agency most central to long-term development efforts, was established by the UN General Assembly in 1968. The characteristics and tendencies of these institutions are described in further detail in the next two chapters.

The People

At first, international development was a dream, a blank slate. The people and institutions were mainly new. Those who were drawn to development were an eclectic lot; many were socially progressive and believed anything was possible. This was, after all, the 1960s. It was relatively easy to get a job in international development, it didn't necessarily require any formal credentials, and there were no formal development studies at that point.

Many Westerners from this time period onward got their first exposure to development and the "third world" through volunteer placements. The British Voluntary Services Overseas began in 1959. Canadian University Students Overseas (CUSO) began in 1960. John F. Kennedy started the Peace Corps in 1961. These programs all had similar goals of promoting mutual understanding between cultures and filling skills gaps in developing countries. Many of those who completed an overseas voluntary placement, typically for two years, came back wanting to continue with overseas development work. By the 1970s, these people were the first wave of students who returned to university to pursue further education related to development. Those who decided to go this route often ended up in Foreign Service Offices, the newly created state development agencies, within the UN, or in international NGOs, which were much fewer at that time. Some went on to start new NGOs.

Within former colonial powers, some of the first development workers were former colonial officers who had found that international development was the best fit with their skills in the newly emerging world order. Uma Kothari has interviewed some former British colonial officers turned international development experts. The continuities and discontinuities that she describes between colonial community development efforts and postcolonial international development efforts are fascinating.[4] Within the United Kingdom, British colonial officers were selected based on independence and character. They were posted in one place over the long term and were expected to learn the language and the context and to build relationships. International development, inspired from the very start by the idea of technology transfer from the West to the poor countries of the world, did not much value this particular knowledge so much as specialized expert knowledge that could be injected anywhere without much concern about context.

The Cycle: Hope, Disappointment, and Renewed Commitment

By the end of the 1960s, things had not moved quite as quickly as expected, and so the UN declared the 1970s as the Second Development Decade. While initial goals had been focused on increasing economic growth and large infrastructure projects, these didn't have the automatic transformative effects on poverty that had been expected, and questions and criticisms of development were already surfacing. It was time for a new idea. And so the "Basic Needs Approach" came to prominence with support from the World Bank, the International Labour Organization of the United Nations, and the Third World Forum.[5] Many were won over by the simplicity of the observation that all people need certain things such as food, clothing, housing, and transport. For the poorest people, struggling for survival, meeting such basic needs was surely a priority, and so development efforts should focus on these foremost. This led to various efforts to enumerate and quantify what basic human needs entailed, so that international development could ensure they were met. Gilbert Rist quotes a Food and Agriculture Organization (FAO) report that defines its "reference man" as a male weighing sixty-five kilograms and aged between twenty and twenty-nine years. It then goes on to detail his presumed lifestyle and working and leisure habits. As Rist sums up, "All this to demonstrate that the 'typical man' has to consume 3,000 calories and 17 grams of protein per day. But is this really an accurate identikit picture of a Third World peasant?"[6]

"Basic needs" was only one in a continuing chain of efforts to redefine development. When development efforts fail to meet expectations, theorists and practitioners try to reframe it in a new way, to improve and reform the institutions that deliver it, to find better ways to coordinate and manage efforts, and to call for renewed political will. This is a long recurring theme throughout development's history. And as better development requires new ideas, it is to the issue of development concepts that we now turn.

The Rhetoric: Ideas That Shape and Justify International Development

This section reminds us of some of the key ideas that have shaped approaches to international development. First, we look at two concepts that have endured throughout development's history up to the present day: modernization and transfer-of-technology. Then we consider the Western public's thoughts on international development and their influence on development operations. In the final part of this section, we touch on the ongoing proliferation of development ideas and where this may be leading.

Enduring Concepts: Modernization and Transfer-of-Technology[7]
Modern progress is a concept that is both foundational to and enduring within international development. This is the idea that some societies are more

advanced and others are less advanced, that the less advanced societies should try to catch up to the more advanced societies, and that development is the process by which they do so.

This idea implies that there is some standard or measure by which we decide what determines a nation's relative standing. The classic choice is the wealth of the economy, measured as per capita income. This is open to a lot of criticism, since having more money is not really synonymous with having a higher quality of life.[8] And what about societies that aren't based on money or in which money plays a minor role? According to the per capita income measure, nonmonetized societies are as undeveloped, and hence undesirable, as one can imagine. Development becomes essentially about integration into the formal global economy.

The idea of modernization—its definition, its desirability, and the various ways by which it can be measured—has been long debated and critiqued. Critics argue that societies can develop in very different ways, and so indicators of development need to be more diverse and possibly completely localized. Who can say what constitutes "development" within a given society or community other than those people who are its members? They should define development according to their priorities and decide on the indicators they want to monitor in its progress. Kerala state in India is a frequently cited example of a place that has fairly low monetary income but a high standard of living by other indicators.[9] The small mountain kingdom of Bhutan is another country often applauded for taking its own approach to development. The king there has declared that development should be pursued and measured not as "gross national income" but as "gross national happiness."[10]

In 1990, the UNDP began to rank countries based on a composite index called the "human development index," which includes per capita income but also considers the equity of income distribution, literacy rates, and life expectancy.[11] This was an attempt to move away from using purely economic indicators as proxies for development. However, it still includes them, and it still acts as a universal "one-size-fits-all" measure of development. It is now widely used, but it has supplemented rather than replaced the use of more traditional macroeconomic indicators.

In the family of development ideas, transfer-of-technology is the daughter of modernization theory. This is the idea that technological innovations and knowledge from more advanced societies can be transferred to less advanced societies, helping them to develop and "catch up." These can include medicines and medical knowledge, and knowledge and technology for accessing and purifying drinking water or for increasing the quantity and quality of food people can grow. Such items seem at first glance to be incontrovertibly beneficial, saving lives and possibly averting epidemics and famine.

Then what about engineering, education, road building, computers and telecommunications, economic theory, approaches to development, mining and the extraction of natural resources, the management of fisheries, the management of conflict, the justice system, the political system? All of these can be thought of as technologies; all can be "transferred" through the placement of foreign experts and the introduction of policies and laws, often written by foreign experts.

Transfer-of-technology is an idea that was in Truman's initial speech, when he spoke of the great expertise that the countries of the West, and especially the United States, had to share with the world. It is an idea that is relevant to international development professionals because it is a motivation and justification for many international jobs within the aid system. Taken at face value, it assumes a universal expertise that applies in any situation, and it assumes that technology is politically and culturally neutral.

The assumptions that technology is politically and culturally neutral are, of course, untrue. Almost any technology is a Pandora's box that carries cultural, social, economic, and environmental considerations. The way a technology will be used, who uses it, who does not, and the relative costs and benefits will vary from one context to another. Consider the Green Revolution in India. In the 1960s, the Indian government was concerned about looming food shortages. To increase agricultural productivity, the Ministry of Agriculture began to work with the American scientist Norman Borlaug and a series of agricultural research centers established by the Rockefeller Foundation. They introduced high-yielding wheat and rice varieties to regions with reliable sources of water, especially to the Punjab. Along with the new varieties, they introduced new agricultural practices, including monocropping, the use of new agricultural machinery, fertilizers and pesticides, and new forms of irrigation. The result was impressive: crop yields reportedly up to ten times higher than those of traditional varieties. India became a net exporter of food. Borlaug won the 1970 Nobel Peace Prize for his efforts and is credited with saving up to a billion people from starvation (not just in India but also in other countries). And yet there was also a great environmental and social cost. Vandana Shiva, one of the most outspoken critics of the Green Revolution, argues that the Punjab region, where Green Revolution approaches were first adopted in India, has consequently suffered from water scarcity and contamination, soil erosion and depletion, increased vulnerability to pests and crop diseases, increased rates of cancer, reduced availability of nutritious food to the local population, displacement of smallholder farmers, and social division and conflict.[12] And as the Green Revolution did not address problems of food distribution, it did not bring an end to hunger in the region.

As criticisms of the Green Revolution mounted, new transfer-of-technology theories were developed. These theories tried to remedy the early tendencies to simplify and universalize by taking local variables into account. Early farming systems theory recognized that smallholder farmers often had multiple crops and that different agroecosystems might require different approaches. Over time, farming systems approaches continued to incorporate more factors into their analysis, including social and economic variables.[13] Participatory approaches to farming innovation began to appear, on the basis that innovations originating from or adapted by farmers would be the ones best suited to their needs and preferences.[14]

Although many of these changes seemed potentially revolutionary, the initial assumptions of universality and neutrality are impressively resilient and are still at-large today. One obvious example is in the calls for a second Green Revolution for Africa. For a variety of reasons, the initial Green Revolution never made much of an impact in Africa, and crop yields have largely remained constant, while the population has grown. As Jeffrey Sachs explains,

> Food yields on the continent are roughly one metric ton of grain per hectare of cultivated land, a figure little changed from 50 years ago and roughly one third of the yields achieved on other continents. In low-income regions elsewhere in the world, the introduction of high-yield seeds, fertilizer and small-scale irrigation boosted food productivity beginning in the mid-1960s and opened the escape route from extreme poverty for huge populations. A similar takeoff in sub-Saharan Africa is both an urgent priority and a real possibility.[15]

The Alliance for a Green Revolution in Africa (AGRA) was founded in 2006, led by Kofi Annan as the chair of the board and with much of its funding from the Bill and Melinda Gates Foundation.[16] But many observers, especially among the NGOs, worry that the new Green Revolution will bring the same heavy social and environmental costs as the first one did.[17]

So there we have them—modernization and transfer-of-technology—two foundational ideas that have endured through the various fashions of development theory. They sometimes change their clothes, but they haven't gone away. We often see them within the logic of various development practices and initiatives.

Popular Wisdom and Public Support for International Development

Western taxpayers are the most important funding source for international development. The slogan of USAID, the world's largest bilateral donor, is "from the American people."[18] But the Western public's knowledge of the rest of the world is often limited and informed largely through media visions of deprivation, catastrophe, and failure. NGO appeals for personal donations often reinforce this by focusing their audience's attention on a pressing need and a simple and effective response that people can take to help. The complexities of context and the richness of a place and its history, culture, and politics are largely stripped away in these accounts, or used as selective garnishes to make an account more appealing.

A dramatic recent example of this is the Kony 2012 campaign by the California-based NGO Invisible Children. This small NGO has been impressively effective in bringing worldwide attention to the shocking atrocities of the rebel group the Lord's Resistance Army (LRA), which has been active in Uganda since the late 1980s. The group sought to create public pressure for US military intervention in Uganda to help capture the LRA's leader, Joseph Kony. In late 2011, attributed in large part to the group's lobbying, President Obama sent one hundred soldiers to Uganda to assist the Ugandan forces in tracking down Kony. Invisible Children then released the video *Kony 2012 Part II: Beyond Famous* on March 5, 2012. It immediately went viral on YouTube.[19] Before that month was over, it had reached 70 million views. But the campaign did not begin to capture the political complexities of the relationships between different groups in North and South Uganda and among the neighboring countries. Many people who understood the situation surrounding the conflict questioned the way the situation was represented and the wisdom of pushing for military intervention. As the journalist Michael Wilkerson put it, "Let's get two things straight: 1) Joseph Kony is not in Uganda and hasn't been for six years; 2) The LRA now numbers at most in the hundreds, and while it is still causing immense suffering, it is unclear how millions of well-meaning but misinformed people are going to help deal with the more complicated reality."[20]

The Kony 2012 campaign has stirred up controversy and plenty of discussion. While many people share Wilkerson's concern, many others argue that despite its limitations, it has still done a great service by putting the conflict in Northern Uganda into the global spotlight.[21]

The problem with a benign but poorly informed group is that it is not well situated to hold anyone to account. What kinds of interventions are helpful? When might they be harmful? Most Westerners just haven't thought of it too much. On the other hand, various scandals and debates periodically erupt in the media about international development and aid effectiveness. And again, it is really difficult for the Western public to make informed judgments about international development and whether their money is being used effectively. Campaigns that resonate with common understandings and have strong emotional appeal are best at rallying public support. Emergency appeals and child sponsorship schemes remain as crowd-pleasers because they seem like deserving causes, and the relationship between the money one gives and the good that will result seems straightforward.

The prevalence of overly simplistic ideas within international development is one that we will return to periodically throughout this book. The main point here, however, is that public understanding of international development acts like a gravitational force, pulling development discourse back down toward rather misleading notions that might otherwise have been discarded as naive or imperialistic. Despite this tendency, there is something fundamentally hopeful and optimistic about the fact that so many people feel connected to others throughout the globe and wish to help them and to find a shared future together. As the world globalizes and our relationships to each other continue to shift, popular wisdom about international development may well improve. People are more easily able to communicate with others around the planet and share messages, photographs, and videos. More people are traveling to different parts of the world and are being exposed to different cultures. Diasporas maintain connections to their countries of origin and often try to support people back home in different ways. So although old-fashioned ideas still linger, improvements in popular understandings of aid and development seem quite likely.

New Ideas: Increasing Diversity and Complexity

Since it began, international development has hosted a steady parade of "new and improved" theories and ideas about what it should do and how it should do it. People who have worked in development since the 1950s or 1960s have watched them all go by. Dirk Ullerich is a German national who has worked in international development for over forty years. He told me,

> I think I have witnessed all the different fashions of development.
> In the beginning, it was the time of the cold war, and as long as
> the government of a developing country was anticommunist, they

could get whatever they wanted. People like Mobutu in Zaire, real dictators, it didn't matter how bad they were, they could get whatever they wanted from the West. . . . Then there was the time when small is beautiful and the basic needs approach. Then there was the time of Thatcher and Reagan, and the market is the decisive sign of everything, what is not according to the market, you should just leave it. But then they saw some basic services, security, education and health—they can't work economically, and the system changed again. Then there was the environment issue that played a big role, and then again the big issue was sustainability—so you can do whatever you like; as long as it will continue once the program has closed down, it is good.

Why are there so many different ideas and approaches to development? And where do they come from?

To begin with, international development was theoretically light; it was a general idea—general enough, perhaps—that it could mean different things to different people. Economics was the academic discipline that initially had the biggest say about development, because development was essentially about economic growth of poor, and often newly independent, countries. But political science, sociology, agronomy, and other disciplines also had something to say about what development meant and how to go about achieving it. And as problems arose, this created space for debate and new ideas.

The international development system is fairly good at absorbing new ideas. It tends to do so by expanding. But it is harder to judge whether this has led to fruitful intellectual progress. There are many different, and often inconsistent, ideas within international development. Many of them don't get so much discarded as fade into obscurity. Ian Smillie, who has also watched development trends over the decades, cautions,

> I wouldn't get too carried away by the "trend of the day." I've seen lots of trends and they don't last. Integrated rural development was a favorite for a long time. The big one in recent years has been "putting the government in the driver's seat"—if I hear that one more time, I'll throw up. The donors who say this all remain firmly in the backseat, the quintessential backseat drivers.

There are at least three reasons to be skeptical about ideological trends in international development. First, as Ian alludes, sometimes the trends are just talk. We can see that when the practice doesn't match up. An aid agency can speak eloquently about fighting poverty, but that doesn't mean much if it is sending the lion's share of its budget to a middle-income ally in a strategic location or tying most of its funding to the hiring of its own nationals.

A second reason for skepticism is that sometimes the development sector has a propensity for wishful thinking. In adopting the latest new theory, it is like a fat person looking for a quick-fix diet. William Easterly has argued that there is no monolithic global problem that can be solved by a universal decree or policy or theory. Rather, there are a multitude of specific, localized issues that need to be understood and addressed in localized ways if they are going to work.[22]

The final reason for skepticism is that most large international development institutions are not great at learning about development. In fact, what they seem to be quite good at is forgetting. People who stay in the same position for more than two years can find that they start to become the institutional memory. Their colleagues are coming up with great new ideas—except those new ideas were already tried and didn't work a few years ago. This is an issue that we will return to in chapter 7.

Still, it would be simpleminded to say that none of the various development theories have had any enduring influence on international development practice or that there's been no change in thinking since development began. Rather, the constant change in ideas can become something of a distraction, almost an end in itself. But at least some of it appears to be evolutionary, rather than fad. There has been some progress on donor thinking about aid effectiveness and harmonization, described in the next chapter. And there has been broad agreement on what development should be focused on, encapsulated most explicitly in the Millennium Development Goals.

Conclusion

As David Mosse describes it,

> International development is characterised by a new managerialism, driven by two trends: on the one hand, a narrowing of the ends of development to quantified international development targets for the reduction of poverty, ill-health and illiteracy; but, on the other, a widening of its means. Whereas until the 1980s technology-led growth or the mechanisms of the market provided the instruments of development, today good government, prudent fiscal

policy, political pluralism, a vibrant civil society and democracy are also pre-requisites of poverty reduction.[23]

International development has grown and matured as a system. It has grown more complex, although it has not shown itself to be particularly well suited for handling complexity. Still, within the various agencies involved in development, different approaches and philosophies can find homes. Donor concerns provide the consistency behind it all, as they set the funding criteria. One of the most common buzzwords in recent years has been "sustainability," meaning, as Dirk explained, not environmental sustainability but sustainability of the development effort or effect after donor funding has stopped. Of course, development was always supposed to be about permanent change, so in many ways this is about the international development system realizing its own limitations and looking for better ideas and approaches.

Despite all the new ideas vying for attention, macroeconomic theories have remained very influential over three decades in determining how aid money should be spent and under what conditions. Since the debt crisis of the late 1970s and early 1980s, neoliberal principles of economic management dictated the lending policies of the IMF, the World Bank, and most of the bilateral donors. Neoliberal policies prescribed "structural adjustment" of governments as a condition of receiving soft loans and grants. This typically meant reducing public expenditures, expanding tax bases, privatizing public assets, opening markets, and reducing tariffs and trade barriers against foreign companies. These moves were publicly unpopular in countries where they were imposed, especially since they reduced government services to the public and increased fees and taxes. They were also controversial, not least because of the heavy-handed manner in which they were executed. During the Asian financial crisis in 1997, critics pointed out that the IMF and the World Bank, institutions that were not democratically elected, were directly dictating economic policy for a large segment of the world's population.[24]

Neoliberal policies have softened over the years, but they are still a major force in mainstream international development. We can see this when we look at Afghanistan post-2001. Donors brought in the same policies of rapid commercialization, privatization, and opening of markets that they had introduced in so many other countries, almost, it seemed, as a matter of reflex.[25]

To summarize, modernization remains a fundamental mainstay of international development thinking. Transfer-of-technology was a major approach for realizing modernization. And although transfer-of-technology has, in certain guises, become more refined in taking contextual factors into account, it remains central to many development efforts today. At the same time, development has also come to encompass many other new approaches and concerns—environmental issues, good governance, gender and development, human security, and so forth. Some pass through as fads, and some may perhaps have a more enduring influence. The constant influx of new ideas provides some energy and buzz that can give international development a sense of intellectual freshness. At the same time, contradictions between different ideas, and sometimes the abstracted nature of these ideas, can make international development seem theoretically shallow and unfocused. To the uninitiated, all this buzz can seem both exciting and a little confusing. To understand what the international development system is about, it can be more instructive to look at what it does. This is the topic of the next chapter.

Notes

1. For the full text of Truman's speech, see Halford Ross Ryan, *The Inaugural Addresses of Twentieth-Century American Presidents* (Santa Barbara, CA: Praeger, 1993).

2. Indeed, the belief in modernization was one of the few things that the Soviets and the Americans could agree on. James C. Scott describes, for example, how American agricultural experts advised their Russian counterparts on plans for huge modern communal monocropping farms. See James C. Scott, *Seeing Like a State: How Certain Schemes to Improve the Human Condition Have Failed* (New Haven, CT: Yale University Press, 1999).

3. Based on personal interviews conducted between October 2010 and August 2011.

4. Uma Kothari, "From Colonial Administration to Development Studies: A Post-Colonial Critique of the History of Development Studies," in *A Radical History of Development Studies: Individuals, Institutions and Ideologies*, ed. Uma Kothari (Cape Town: David Philip, 2005).

5. Gilbert Rist, *The History of Development: From Western Origins to Global Faith*, 3rd ed. (London: Zed Books, 2009), 162–69.

6. Ibid., 166–67.

7. Emma Crewe and Elizabeth Harrison, *Whose Development? An Ethnography of Aid* (London: Zed Books, 1999).

8. For a good discussion of this issue, see A. Sen, *Development as Freedom* (London: Oxford University Press, 1999).

9. R. Véron, "The 'New' Kerala Model: Lessons for Sustainable Development," *World Development* 29, no. 8 (2001).

10. Stefan Priesner, "Gross National Happiness—Bhutan's Vision of Development and Its Challenges," in *Gross National Happiness*, ed. Sonam Kinga et al. (Thimphu: Centre for Bhutan Studies, 1999); Karma Ura, *The Bhutanese Development Story* (Thimphu: Centre for Bhutan Studies, 2005).

11. United Nations Development Programme, *Human Development Report 1990: Concept and Measurement of Human Development* (New York: United Nations Development Programme, 1990).

12. Vandana Shiva, "The Green Revolution in the Punjab," *The Ecologist* 21, no. 2 (1991).

13. Food and Agriculture Organization, *The Farming Systems Approach to Development and Appropriate Technology Generation* (Rome: FAO, 1995).

14. J. Farrington and A. Martin, "Farmer Participation in Agricultural Research: A Review of Concepts and Practices," in *Agricultural Administration Unit Occasional Paper #9* (London: ODI, 1988).

15. Jeffrey Sachs, "The African Green Revolution," *Scientific American*, May 2008.

16. AGRA, *AGRA: Growing Africa's Agriculture*, cited February 2, 2012, www.agra-alliance.org.

17. Elenita C. Daño, *Unmasking the New Green Revolution in Africa: Motives, Players and Dynamics* (Penang, Malaysia: Church Development Service, Third World Network, African Centre for Biosafety, 2007); GRAIN, *A New Green Revolution for Africa?* (Barcelona, Spain: GRAIN, 2007).

18. OECD figures for 2011 show the United States is the top donor by volume with almost $30 billion in official development assistance for that year.

19. Invisible Children, *Kony 2012 Part II: Beyond Famous* [online video], Invisible Children, March 5, 2012, cited April 2, 2012, http://www.youtube.com/watch?v=Y4MnpzG5Sqc.

20. Polly Curtis and Tom McCarthy, "Kony 2012: What's the Real Story?" *The Guardian*, March 8, 2012.

21. Musa Okwonga, "Stop Kony, Yes. But Don't Stop Asking Questions," *The Independent*, March 7, 2012.

22. William Easterly, *The White Man's Burden: Why the West's Efforts to Aid the Rest Have Done So Much Ill and So Little Good* (New York: Penguin, 2007).

23. David Mosse, *Cultivating Development: An Ethnography of Aid Policy and Practice* (London: Pluto Press, 2004), 3.

24. Michael Richardson, "Q&A/Jeffrey Sachs: IMF Prescribes 'Wrong Medicine,'" *New York Times*, January 15, 1998.

25. Anna Paterson and James Blewett, *Putting the Cart Before the Horse? Privatisation and Economic Reform in Afghanistan* (Kabul: Afghanistan Research and Evaluation Unit, 2006).

3

The International Development System in Practice

As a system, international development is mainly funded by international aid, or overseas development assistance, which richer countries give to poor countries, either directly, through multilateral institutions, or sometimes through NGOs. The politics and administration of the aid system thus tend to shape international development practice. The international development system includes all aid institutions (donors and agencies entirely or primarily dependent on aid), as well as entities that have other funding sources: faith-based organizations, member-based organizations, and social enterprises.

The international development system doesn't have clear boundaries. Universities, for example, are not "aid institutions"; their mandate is not focused primarily on development, yet they play an important role in educating people who will work in development and in theorizing and critiquing what development is and how it should be. Many professors who teach development also work as consultants to aid agencies. Research centers and think tanks are also important contributors to development thinking and are lobbyists for various development ideas. The most important of these are probably the Consultive Group on International Agricultural Research (CGIAR) agricultural research centers. These are a consortium of fifteen agricultural research centers around the world with the mandate to improve food production and food security. They were primary actors in finding new varieties and technologies during the Green Revolution, described in chapter 2. Then there are churches and mission societies, which are some of the longest running development actors around. They are often the first ones to have set up schools and hospitals in areas that did not have them. Recipient governments receive the majority of aid funds and are central in creating national development plans and setting development priorities.

The next chapter considers some of the main aid institutions individually. First, however, it is worth looking at how the international development system, loose and sprawling as it is, operates as a whole. One common observation about international development as a system of practice, is that it often seems starkly contrary to any tidy ideas we have learned about it. As one seasoned development worker put it,

> I think that my concept of international development is focused around strengthening systems in order to make them work more efficiently and more effectively, even with finite resources. . . . That's what I believe in, but that's not what it actually is. . . . I think it's a mess, a monster that undermines itself, different agendas, mandates, everyone, NGOs, the UN, trying to chase a dollar from the donors; everyone with their own administrative structures and reporting structures.

In this chapter, we begin to peer into this mess. A reasonable first approach is to focus specifically on the role of aid. International development institutions, activities, and resources always inhabit and feed into larger international and national political, economic, and social relationships. Aid is the central resource of international development. In situations of scarce resources, it becomes an important player in larger unfolding dramas. Does it play a positive role or a negative role? And who holds it to account?

The answers to these questions depend very much on circumstance. A relevant example of this is the role that aid and development institutions have played in recent Kenyan history. We'll consider this example before turning back to the more general question of to whom development answers. Is it always the donors who get the final say? And what influences them?

The Example of Kenya

Most major power brokers within the Kenyan government have political links back to the preindependence era and have long managed to prosper as part of the tight-knit group of political elites. Although President Mwai Kibaki's government came into power in 2002 on a "new era" anticorruption platform, it quickly became apparent that the old bad habits had not been lost.

Michela Wrong's 2009 book *It's Our Turn to Eat: The Story of a Kenyan Whistle-Blower* tells the story of John Githongo. Hired by the Kenyan government to fight corruption, he soon uncovered a web of corruption implicating many senior politicians, all the way to the president. The government was spending huge portions of its budget, 16 percent of its 2003–2004 expenditures, on goods and services provided by a company called Anglo-Leasing. But Anglo-Leasing, as Githongo discovered, did not exist. High-level politicians were using its name as a facade to embezzle public funds. After documenting the fraud, Githongo fled to the United Kingdom and leaked the documents to the press.

While the fraud had not been fully documented and publicized before then, donor country diplomats were already aware of it. Aid providers were at best negligent in holding abusers of power to account, since they were providing them funds, and at worst complicit. Two successive country directors of the World Bank lived on land owned by Kibaki, and both failed to take any action in response to the evidence that the funds they were lending to the country for development were being stolen.

Donors were reluctant to make waves in standing up against the corruption of the Kenyan government. Even after Githongo released the documents and the full extent of the fraud was public, the Netherlands was the only country to freeze aid. Edward Clay, the British high commissioner to Kenya from 2001 to 2005, was exceptional in speaking out, which he did bluntly and frequently. He is best remembered for a speech in which he referred to Kenyan political leaders as gluttons who had eaten so much aid money that they were vomiting all over the donors' shoes.[1] This upset not only the Kenyan government, which later declared him persona non grata, but also the British government, which preferred to continue providing aid and did not appreciate such high-profile controversy.[2]

In an interview following the release of her book, Michela Wrong explained, "Essentially the story of Kenya has been a story where elites despoil the country for their own benefit. As a British citizen, I'm aware that the first elites to do that were my own compatriots when we colonized Kenya. The pattern you see being reproduced today began in the nineteenth century."[3] The Kenyan government has been democratically elected by its people.[4] What to do when there is compelling evidence that a government is not acting in the interest of the people? This is a question that donors have long been faced with but never satisfactorily answered. In the time of the cold war, it was purely about which side the leader was on. In these times, it is sometimes less clear what is staying the hand of the donors.

The story in Kenya is certainly not universal, but the patterns it illustrates do seem to run wide. For example, in post-Taliban Afghanistan, donors initially paid little attention to rampant graft. But by early 2011, the Kabul

Bank was on the verge of collapse, after various well-connected senior Afghan politicians were given millions of dollars in "dubious loans" that were never repaid.[5] Finally, in May, the IMF announced that foreign aid would be halted until the bank's management was cleaned up.[6] But in reality, the repercussions were limited. Although a $70 million payment was halted in June, by November, the IMF was back to approving projects almost double that amount.[7]

The same pattern is evident in Uganda. When I visited in spring of 2011, many people, including Ugandans and expats working for donor agencies, told me that the government had essentially looted its own treasury to pay bribes and military costs in the run-up to the recent presidential election. The situation was so dire that no civil servant had received a salary in the preceding six months. Despite this, only a few donors had officially spoken out about it, and, most shocking, the IMF had given Uganda a positive rating on its most recent financial assessment. Generally speaking, donors are reluctant to stop giving. They have quotas to meet and money to spend, and they often don't want to sour diplomatic relationships. They also argue, perhaps correctly, that stopping aid may be worse for the poor than providing it and having some of it disappear, as long as at least some of it is used for its designated purpose.

Such situations are rarely cut-and-dried. Although they can be incredibly frustrating, they are far from hopeless. To return to the example of Kenya, the same international aid system, over much the same time period, has also been an important source of funding to Kenyan civil society groups, including groups focusing on anticorruption and human rights. These groups are almost all quite new, as there was little space for this kind of civil activity under the heavy-handed Moi regime. Many of these groups were involved in a drive to draft a new Kenyan constitution. Their aims included enshrining a wide range of equal rights for women and for creating checks and balances on state power, so that it was less centered in the hands of the president. Sixty-six percent of Kenyans voted for the new constitution in a referendum, and it was passed as law on August 27, 2010.

Cecilia Kimani, who now works for the UN, was involved in the civil movement to draft a new constitution. She was the leader of a national women's rights organization at that time. She explains,

> I think it's quite exciting to be able to push an agenda that can improve people's lives. The new constitution we have for Kenya—it's been many years of work . . . and to see all the work we did, the language we used, in this very important document—is very fulfilling. The many forums we'd organized to talk about reproductive

health rights, and to say it's a poverty issue, it shouldn't be relegated to the sidelines, it's a critical issue and should be in the constitution. On the other hand we had another group that said no, you're bringing division and this shouldn't be in the constitution, it was quite challenging. . . . It was a long process . . . and there was a lot of civic education. We said what we need is reproductive health services and without them, women are dying . . . so the constitution passed by a very big margin.

John-Mark Ojang, another Kenyan activist who had also been engaged in the constitutional reform movement, agrees that it was a long journey. Beginning back in 1992, the activists' struggle went through several phases. Reformers came up against the entrenched political class who repeatedly attempted to resist and deflect reform. Over this time, civil society organizations strengthened themselves and were able for a time to unite together fairly effectively in a loose coalition. But Ojang also believes the international community played a crucial role as a "soft power" in the post-2008 period. Their presence contributed to the conditions that allowed the constitution to pass,

If you look at the debate after '08, something pushed the political elite toward achieving some consensus. . . . So in this phase, I would attribute the achievements made to a lot of efforts by the international community. . . . The Coalition Government provided the space for the international community to act—because this was a temporary government and the guarantors of that government were the international community, and so that was the invisible hand and soft power—so it was a government that was born out of an agreement that had milestones, and the creation of the new constitution was one of the milestones.

Many Kenyans I spoke with were excited about the new constitution, although they realized that its interpretation and implementation would be an ongoing challenge and its passing did not in itself guarantee a new political era. While donors have been largely unwilling to ask hard questions or really hold the Kenyan government to account for the abuse of funds they have given it, they have also played a key role following the 2008 election dispute to broker peace. And they have supported the growth of a Kenyan civil society that shows some promising signs of being able to hold the government to account.

Who Does Development Answer To?

It is pretty easy to look at the story of Kenya and say that politics has an influence on international development. Equally, international development, and particularly aid funds, can have some influence on politics—at least on the domestic politics of the country where aid is being spent. But it is very hard to look at Kenya's story and say that the political influence is all in one direction. On one hand, donors supported Kenya's political elites, who stole funds. On the other hand, they supported Kenyan civil society, which worked hard to push an agenda that would weaken the power of the old elites through constitutional reform.

Politics is a matter of relative power. So how does politics influence development practice? Whose voice gets heard, and who does development answer to? Most obvious are the donors themselves. They must answer, at least nominally, to their domestic constituents and also to lobby groups. Government officials receiving the funds also have some power to negotiate or, at the least, they have the power of refusal. But those receiving funds on behalf of a country may not necessarily have the same interests and perspectives as the people. For popular input into development, participatory approaches pioneered largely by NGOs have been the most important. We now consider each of these in more detail: donors and their constituents, recipient governments, and people in aid-receiving countries.

Donors and Their Domestic Constituents

"He who pays the piper calls the tune," so the saying goes. Most funding for international development activities comes from rich-country governments. The United States, Germany, France, the United Kingdom, and Japan were the top five donors, in terms of money given, for the year 2010, giving amounts ranging from $10.6 to $30 billion, according to OECD statistics.[8] The total aid given by all twenty-three OECD Development Assistance Council governments was $127.3 billion in 2010, and the total aid for the same year including private sources and sources from non-OECD countries was estimated by the OECD at just over $509 billion.[9] OECD official humanitarian aid accounted for an additional $11.7 billion. This does not fully account for all sources of aid, but it gives a good sense of the overall scale.

Citizens of donor countries generally want some of their taxes to go toward funding international development. Surveys consistently show about 80 percent and upward of Western populations support the existence of foreign aid programs.[10] But, unlike health care, national security, and the national economy, international development is unlikely to be a major issue during elections.

Since Western electorates are fairly passive when it comes to shaping an agenda for how aid is spent, what shapes a donor's international development policy? One factor is the way the aid administration is structured, and this varies greatly from country to country. In former colonial powers such as France and Britain, aid institutions are sometimes continuations of former colonial organizations. Often, they favor former colonies with greater amounts of aid money, as well as with preferential trade agreements. In the United States, political lobbyists have a lot of power over the aid budget as it gets debated through Congress. Congressmen, responding to lobby groups, can negotiate for part of the budget to be committed to certain countries or causes or to have other conditions placed on funds. In other countries, such as Japan, the aid bureaucracy has operated in relative secrecy and apparent independence.[11]

Domestic lobby groups can include business interests seeking new markets and subsidized sales, diaspora groups lobbying for economic or political assistance to their home countries, and NGO and civil society groups lobbying on various human rights and development issues. These lobbies are often competing with each other and are frequently at odds ideologically. Take, for instance, the issue of food aid. Cargill and other major agribusinesses have long managed to successfully lobby donors and receive subsidies to provide grain and rice to developing countries as "food aid."[12] Oxfam and other NGOs have lobbied against this practice, arguing that it artificially lowers the market prices of foods in the countries where it is dumped, putting local farmers out of business.[13] This can actually reduce the capacity of a country to produce food and increase dependence and food insecurity. Because donor governments are often susceptible to the influence of business lobbies, even when it clearly contravenes "good development," the watchdog function of NGOs on this front has become quite important, although their effectiveness is mixed.[14]

Governments Receiving Aid

How much say do recipient countries have in their own development? Well, first, the amount of aid they get is determined in part by how important they are seen by donors, whether politically or economically as emerging markets. This can also be influenced by their own lobbying efforts. For example, a major reason that Israel has been one of the United States' top aid recipients for many years has been because of its diaspora lobby in Washington, DC.[15] This is not to say that all aid-spending decisions are driven by political and economic interests. The Center for Global Development assesses wealthy countries using its Commitment to Development Index (CDI) that takes into consideration how much aid the country gives and how much the aid is based on development considerations (such as the level of poverty in the recipient country). In 2012, Denmark, Norway, and Sweden were the donor countries most committed to development according to this measure.[16]

When aid is being spent for purely political reasons, donors typically haven't cared very much about what the recipient government does with it, as long as it continues as a political ally. Some of the most well-known and blatant examples of this were during the cold war, when large quantities of aid money were sent to some pretty nasty regimes. It would have taken some willful ignorance for the donors to suppose that the elites receiving the money were doing anything with it that was likely to help their people. Mobutu Sese Seko, president of Zaire (now the Democratic Republic of Congo) from 1965 to 1997, stands as an exemplar of the worst excesses of the period. Supported politically and financially by the United States throughout his regime, Mobutu received large quantities of aid funds, largely because he presented himself as anticommunist. He stole about half of the money that his country received on loan from the IMF. When he was ousted in 1997, one of his enduring legacies was an immense national debt.[17]

As William Easterly points out, aid propping up dictators who have failed to serve their countries is not just a cold war phenomenon. It is still very much alive and kicking:

> Paul Biya, the dictator of Cameroon, is marking his twenty-eighth year in power in 2010 by receiving the latest in a never-ending series of loans from the International Monetary Fund with imaginative labels like "Poverty Reduction Growth Facilities." Biya, whose government also enjoys ample oil revenues, has received a total of $35 billion in foreign aid during his reign. There's been neither poverty reduction nor growth in his country: the average Cameroonian is poorer today than when Biya took power in 1982.[18]

The large quantities of aid money directed to Iraq and Afghanistan in recent years provide even more evidence that political and military factors remain paramount in aid spending and can weaken or directly conflict with development goals.[19]

With the introduction of structural adjustment in the early 1980s, aid was conditional on political and economic reforms.[20] Those receiving the money could take it and make the reforms, or they could refuse it. Most took it. The documentary *Life and Debt*[21] shows the negative impact that structural adjustment had in Jamaica. It includes a memorable interview with Michael Manley, the former prime minister of Jamaica.[22] He says that he disagreed with the measures but had no choice but to accept them, given the situation his country was facing. Graham Hancock, a staunch critic of the whole aid industry, is more skeptical. He has argued that structural adjustment allows for an ongoing collusion between the international financial institutions and the political elite receiving the money.[23] They make the reforms but then can do what they will with the money. After all, it does not require money to change policies or to sell off state assets.

Hancock made his observations over twenty years ago, and much has happened in the interim that might make us hopeful that the situation has improved. And yet we still see that the IMF, the World Bank, and other major donors are largely passive in the face of government corruption and misuse of aid funds, and Hancock's explanation still seems relevant.

The People

So where does that leave the citizens of countries receiving aid, who are the intended beneficiaries? How much say do they have in their own development? The short answer is that it varies quite a bit, but on the whole, there is great room for improvement.

People's ability to influence development decisions depends on what kind of government they have and on the relationship between the government and the people. It also depends on the presence and role of NGOs. Sometimes NGOs are major aid players, and some of them are very good at engaging people in decision making and in creating transparency in their own processes. For example, since the early 1980s, the Aga Khan Rural Support Program (AKRSP) in northern Pakistan has worked through member-based village organizations. Initially facilitated by AKRSP staff, each village organization discusses and decides what improvements they want to undertake in their village. These are typically initiatives such as building or repairing a road, a bridge, or an irrigation system or setting up a health clinic or school. The village organization also provides a contribution to the project in the form of money, labor, or materials.[24] AKRSP was pioneering in its use of this participatory approach. Through this approach, it claims to have contributed to the construction of hundreds of bridges and irrigation ditches, the reclamation of 90,000 hectares of degraded land, and improved incomes for 1.3 million villagers living in the isolated mountains of the Chitral and Gilgit regions. The Aga Khan Foundation has also set up similar programs in other countries, and other organizations have adopted or adapted its approaches.[25]

NGOs have been engaging in this sort of grassroots or "bottom-up" organizing since the 1970s. Since the 1990s, donor-funded government initiatives have increasingly included elements of participatory democracy. Some NGOs, such as ActionAid, have focused on informing people about their civil rights and act as watchdogs to create greater transparency in government programs.

For many people working in development, such bottom-up initiatives are some of the most inspiring examples of what is out there and what is possible. However, the majority of the international development system still tends to be oriented toward donor interests and requirements. Although the rhetorical commitment to beneficiaries is widespread, it can still be quickly relegated to an afterthought. This is a theme that we will revisit in later chapters. From the example of Kenya, we can see that much of development is fundamentally political, as it is about interests, perceptions, and relationships. It is about who is able to capture and leverage funds, to present ideas, and to convince those with control over resources that they are important, or worthy, or able to use those resources well.

The Expanding World of International Development

Although international development is just over fifty years old, it is already difficult to imagine the world without it. And throughout most of its brief history, the international aid system has been expanding. While the previous chapter touched on the expansion of development theories, the aid system has also expanded in terms of resources and actors. OECD figures on aid flows show that, other than a period in the 1990s when it looked like aid commitments were faltering, levels of aid funding have consistently risen, in rough parallel with the overall growth of the global economy. Back in 1960, total official development assistance (ODA) was US$36.2 billion (at 2009 prices), and in 2010 it was US$127.52 billion.[26] Recent OECD figures show year-on-year increases in aid flows from 1997 to 2010, although 2011 saw a 3 percent decrease in aid levels, attributed to global recession.[27]

Existing donors have largely maintained or expanded their commitments, and new donors are joining in. Emerging economic powers such as China and Brazil have established their own foreign aid programs. And there is also growth in private foundations funding international development, the largest being the Bill and Melinda Gates Foundation. The number of implementing agents and lobbyists, including NGOs, businesses, and consultants, has also expanded, as have the number of university programs and the number of students studying international development.

How Well Does the System Work?

All this sustained and expanded activity seems like a very strong de facto endorsement of international development. Surely we would not be doing all of this unless we were pretty sure that it worked. And so at this point, you may be wondering what have all these international development efforts resulted in so far?

The most recent comprehensive review of the evidence as to what degree aid can be judged successful was done in 2008 by Roger Riddell. Defining "success" is the first hurdle that such a study faces. Even the definition of what development is supposed to achieve is open to debate, beyond a loose consensus that it is about reducing poverty and improving human well-being.

Evidence suggests a substantial majority of funded development projects are successful in meeting their immediate objectives, while a lesser but still substantial percentage appears successful in achieving broader and more sustained gains. Longer term sustained change remains more elusive, and it is difficult to trace impacts of aid on a broader level.[28]

Riddell concludes that the overall aid system is hampered by serious structural issues on both the donor and recipient side. For example, Riddell estimates that about 60 percent of aid is still tied to conditions of purchasing goods and services from the donor country, which both increases the cost and reduces the likely relevance of aid. He argues that, with political will, these issues could be addressed, and the whole aid system could become much more effective. But that has always been true, and yet reform has remained elusive.

Trying to find answers about aid effectiveness writ large appears to be a bit of a wild goose chase. Donors have commissioned countless studies on whether aid works.[29] But specific success in one situation is not a reliable predictor of specific success in another situation. The studies also face methodological problems. Accurately measuring economic and social changes attributable to aid is fraught with difficulty. Riddell notes that the level of complexity involved, the multiplicity of possible goals and measures, the number of other factors that interact with aid, data shortages, and the fact that aid may not be the largest or most decisive element in shaping the socioeconomic future of a country and its citizens all limit what we can generalize about aid efforts.[30] There is plenty of evidence of both success and failure at project and program levels, less evidence of any decisive outcome at the country level, and inconclusive data and rhetoric beyond this. Riddell explains,

> More money has probably been spent and more research time allocated to examining the impact of aid on different macroeconomic variables across different aid-recipient countries than on any other aspect of the aid relationship. . . . One reason why so many studies have been carried out is that the conclusions (and the results) have continually been contested. . . . A small but growing number of researchers and aid specialists are beginning to question the value of these studies in helping to inform discussion about whether aid works.[31]

Rather than attempt to come up with a definitive assessment of a system so diverse and sprawling, a more fruitful approach is to consider the conditions under which aid is most likely to be effective. Or, conversely, the conditions under which it is least likely to work.

When the political influence is higher, the quantity of aid often tends to be higher, and the quality of aid spending tends to be lower. For example, we can look at the aid statistics and see that in the years following the US-led invasions of Afghanistan in 2001 and Iraq in 2003, those two countries have been among the top recipients of aid by OECD countries. This aid has been aimed at "state building," and much of it has been directed toward reforming and building up national armies and police forces. In Afghanistan, the international military has been directly involved in implementing "quick impact" aid projects expected to win the "hearts and minds" of the Afghan population, so that they support the Afghan government and its international allies rather than the insurgent Taliban. So this is essentially the use of aid as a military tool or, as counterinsurgency theorists coin it, "money as a weapons system."[32] In Afghanistan, it has meant that aid has gone to the least stable provinces rather than the poorest. Development efforts in the middle of war zones tend to be expensive and often ineffective. On the basis of extensive case study research, Andrew Wilder observes,

> Although more and more resources are being directed toward building roads because of their perceived stabilizing benefits, our research highlights the overwhelming importance of context. In areas where insecurity remained chronic and governance structures

broken, the road-building cash has tended to fuel corruption (both perceived and real), intercommunal strife, and competition between local warlords.[33]

Besides being a terrible way of approaching development, there is remarkably little evidence that this strategy is effective at winning over its target populations. On the contrary, the evidence shows that it can backfire by fueling corruption, which weakens the state and encourages war profiteers.[34]

It doesn't seem very surprising that development efforts don't work very well if the motivation behind them isn't really development. When the development goals of aid are overshadowed by political, military, or business interests on the part of those providing assistance or those receiving it, the quality of development tends to be low. Another very basic and yet endemic issue is poor coordination of efforts among various agencies working on similar development issues. Part of the problem behind coordination is again the problem of motivation. When various parties have interests other than achieving the best possible development outcomes, their drive to cooperate tends to be lower. For that reason, discussions about aid effectiveness often focus on trying to keep international development efforts focused on international development.

International Coordination of Aid

The term "international cooperation" came into development parlance to emphasize a more equal partnership between donors and recipients. Ideally, this means that both parties agree to overriding principles of good development and then hold each other to account for adhering to these. This concept of "mutual accountability" is part of the 2005 Paris Declaration on Aid Effectiveness, a nonbinding convention to improve aid. One person who has worked for a number of donors over his career expresses a common sentiment when he says, "I think the donors are operating in a much better way now, much more harmonized in theory and in practice. The Accra Agenda and the Paris Declaration, everyone's saying as a result of those the donors are behaving much better, and most of them are, much more."

Others are more skeptical. In Uganda, a close observer of the recent government misspending says,

I almost died when I heard the US government—which hardly gives budget support anywhere in the world—is thinking of going on-budget in Uganda. What does this say about commitment to accountability? It says we don't care that there's heavy evidence that this government steals 50 percent of its budget—here's more money! That just makes no sense—no thinking person would agree.

What's interesting is the Europeans are starting to fight hard against budget support—but they also need to explain how their money got stolen in the last three years. I mean part of this has to do with the global political cycle, right? The Europeans were really out in front on Paris Declaration principles much faster than the US, and I think in countries where they got burned, now they'd like to revisit the conversation. The US knows the other countries got burned, but they're also fed up of being maligned for being a nonplayer internationally.

Efforts including the Paris Declaration are attempts to change the nature of the relationship between donors and recipients to focus aid on development aims and release it from political cycles. These aid effectiveness agreements also focus on harmonizing aid so that it has a broader and sustained impact, as opposed to being delivered in discrete, uncoordinated projects of short duration, which has been the dominant mode of aid delivery for most of international development's history.[35]

Still, donor-recipient relations remain complex and uneven, as we saw in the example of Kenya. Giving money is inherently a political act because money is a resource that shifts or reinforces political relations based on who has access to it, who doesn't, and how it is used. Donors have some obligation to make sure that their funds are not misspent. Or, if the recipient government does something that donors feel is wrong for some reason, they can threaten to withhold aid as a political condition.

The Paris Declaration marked a shift in the previous trend for donors to channel aid outside of governments. In the first decades of international development, donors mainly gave aid to "third world" governments. But then NGOs became favored, as Anders Fange recalls:

You had a period in the '70s when there were quite a lot of scandals, white elephants—where Western aid agencies had gotten into huge development projects with governments which were not really capable, and there'd been huge, failed development projects. At least in Sweden, there was a lot of criticism. And then, during Biafra—it was the NGOs that went in and did the work . . . it was then the NGOs exploded. After Biafra, the donors saw—it's the NGOs that can do the work. That was the golden time for the NGOs, there were no questions asked. Just increasing amounts of money were thrown on NGOs.

This golden time of the NGOs didn't last. Donors grew more demanding in terms of reporting requirements, while the weaknesses and foibles of NGOs also became apparent. The bigger concern was that all the NGO efforts would fail to add up to long-term societal change. Coordinating NGO efforts is no easy feat when NGOs have independent philosophies and operations. The UN has often taken on the role of coordinating NGOs in humanitarian response situations, whereas in more politically stable situations, many argue that this should be done through the state. We return to some of these issues with NGOs in the next chapter.

Aid effectiveness forums held throughout the first decade of the 2000s have marked a resurgence in donor interest in working with national governments. Governments, after all, have the mandate to work on behalf of their people and the potential to build up a tax base so that whatever systems established through aid can be sustained. The jury is still out on whether this swing back represents a movement forward toward more effective, accountable aid systems rather than a temporary trend. The biggest challenge remains the risk that interests from both the donor side and the recipient side can easily subvert aid to nondevelopmental purposes.

Where Does All This Leave Those Working in Development?

The international development system is a reflection of the larger political state of the world. It is far from perfect, but it is also far from the worst possible scenario, and at least good things come from it some of the time. So it comes down to a very personal choice—whether this is something you can manage to work within or not.

For those working in international development, this "big picture" snapshot that we've encountered in this and the previous chapter is both bad news and good news. With the bad news first, there seem to be serious structural constraints on what international development can do overall. The very system delivering it is constantly subject to interests and influences that can weaken or entirely divert it from its declared objectives. Those who hope to reform it from within will find their work cut out for them. Many development bureaucracies can break their staff's spirits and entrap their energies.

What the international development system achieves overall is unclear, while some aspects of it appear downright dubious. And as far as broad social and economic change, international development is not the only means of change. Although it reaches high in its stated ambitions to eliminate global poverty, it is hard to argue that it is even the most important means of achieving this. Compared to the amount of money that passes through international trade, or is spent on international military exercises, it is a minor sideshow. And it's a sideshow that can often appear more like a cheap diversion than a genuine attempt at change when looking at the other actions taken by donor governments. For example, David Githaiga, a program specialist working on environmental issues for the UNDP in Kenya, observes,

> The developed countries have to [improve] also. . . . I'm concerned about them. They preach water but take wine. Like climate change—you know that Africa is only responsible for 3 percent of greenhouse gas emissions and 60 percent of that is South Africa, and yet we're the ones who are suffering most from climate change. But when you meet in all these international conferences, those developed countries are unwilling to reduce their emissions, but they're funding programs to help us reduce our emissions from here. Nuclear power—they'd be against us having nuclear power plants, but a country like France—a big part of it is dependent on nuclear power.

On the good news side, international development is far from being a coherent or cohesive system, and that does allow space for a lot of different ideas and approaches, even if they are often in contradiction with each other. We'll be encountering examples of various approaches to international development throughout this book, especially in chapters 8 to 11. Furthermore, on the basis of a review of documented evaluations at the project level, Riddell notes that "available evidence suggests, quite strongly, that the clear majority of official aid projects achieve their immediate objectives."[36] And all evidence confirms that context matters. The success or failure of specific projects and programs often rests on the decisions made by project planners and implementers. That means that individuals within international development often can and do find the space to work effectively and that the decisions that they make count. Indeed, it is only at this level that we really do have a clear view of aid effectiveness. Evidence at the more aggregate levels is scarce, and because development efforts are always so context bound, it is in some sense meaningless.[37] So as long as we can live with ambiguity, uncertainty, and imperfection, and as long as we are selective about where we put our energies and have a bit of luck, there are many opportunities to do effective work within international development on a small scale.

Are small-scale efforts drawing on aid funding enough to address the roots of widespread structural problems within human societies? For the most part, this is unlikely. The international development system may not be the best tool for achieving radical social change. An oft-quoted observation is that no country has ever lifted itself out of poverty because of international development. Strong political leadership, trade, and other factors, such as the absence of war, are more decisive in shaping the fate of a nation. While there are many small-scale projects that have drawn on the resources and structures of international development and succeeded in making a useful difference in some sense, not all small successes are equal. Some don't last long or reach far; Riddell notes that even on a project level, while a project can be a success on narrow terms, it often fails in terms of contributing to lasting change. Often, projects don't seem to get at the roots of structural problems occurring at a much broader level. Development practitioners can feel helpless when faced with these major structural problems, which often have horrendous consequences for large numbers of people. In the face of large-scale poverty, injustice, and suffering, the value of small-project success seems, well, small. Within all this, there is incredible variation in what people manage to achieve, in approaches taken, and in outcomes. And while momentum and the weight of the status quo are always formidable forces, there is no great master plan—whether for good or for bad—underpinning international development, or in the broader world, for that matter. As one analyst heading up an Afghan-based NGO puts it,

> The thing that always strikes me, growing up, I always used to think someone was in control, and as you grow up and take more control, you realize it's all in a big mess, we're all caught in the collective momentum of everyone else—which is weird and frightening, but good at the same time, because you realize there's no evil genius behind everything.

So, development practitioners can take heart in the observation that a big mess is preferable to an evil mastermind, and it seems like a big mess is closer to what we have. In the next chapter, we'll unpack the mayhem further by looking at some of the main categories of aid organization.

Notes

1. Michela Wrong, *It's Our Turn to Eat: The Story of a Kenyan Whistle-Blower* (New York: Harper, 2009).

2. Anne Penketh, "Kenya Tells Former Envoy Clay He Is 'Persona Non Grata,'" *The Independent*, February 6, 2008.

3. Jake Whitney, "Going Too Far: Jake Whitney Interviews Michela Wrong," *Guernica*, June 9, 2009.

4. Kenya has had multiparty elections since 1992.

5. Dexter Filkins, "The Afghan Bank Heist: A Secret Investigation May Implicate Dozens of High-Ranking Government Officials," *The New Yorker*, February 14, 2011.

6. Rod Nordland, "Afghan Bank Commission Absolves President's Brother in Fraud Case," *New York Times*, May 29, 2011.

7. Jon Gambrell, "IMF Stops Payment to Afghanistan due to Lax Financial Oversight," *Huffington Post*, June 17, 2011; IMF, *Program Note: Islamic Republic of Afghanistan*, April 9, 2012, cited April 20, 2012, http://www.imf.org/external/np/country/notes/afghanistan.htm.

8. OECD, *ODA by Country at 2009 Prices and Exchange Rates (Net Disbursements)*, 2011, cited August 16, 2011, http://www.oecd.org/dataoecd/31/35/47452831.xls.

9. OECD, *Development Aid: Total Official and Private Flows*, April 4, 2012, cited June 2, 2012, http://www.oecd-ilibrary.org/development/development-aid-total-official-and-private-flows_20743866-table5.

10. Roger C. Riddell, *Does Foreign Aid Really Work?* (New York: Oxford University Press, 2007); Ian Smillie, *The Alms Bazaar* (Ottawa: International Development Research Centre, 1995).

11. See Carol Lancaster, *Foreign Aid: Diplomacy, Development, Domestic Politics* (Chicago: University of Chicago Press, 2006), for a useful comparison of five major donors (the United States, Germany, France, Japan, and Denmark).

12. Brewster Kneen, *Invisible Giant: Cargill and Its Transnational Strategies*, 2nd ed. (London: Pluto Press, 2002).

13. See, for example, Oxfam, *Food Aid or Hidden Dumping? Separating Wheat From Chaff* (Oxfam, 2005), http://www.oxfam.org/sites/www.oxfam.org/files/bp71_food_aid.pdf.

14. Issues surrounding food aid are complex. See Christopher Barrett and Daniel Maxwell, *Food Aid After 50 Years: Recasting Its Role* (New York: Routledge, 2005).

15. Lancaster, *Foreign Aid*.

16. Center for Global Development, *2012 Commitment to Development Index*, cited October 28, 2012, http://www.cgdev.org/section/initiatives/_active/cdi/.

17. Charlotte Denny, "Suharto, Marcos and Mobutu Head Corruption Table With $50bn Scams," *The Guardian*, March 26, 2004.

18. William Easterly, "Foreign Aid for Scoundrels," *The New York Review of Books*, November 25, 2010.

19. Ashley Jackson, *Quick Impact, Quick Collapse: The Dangers of Militarized Aid in Afghanistan* (Kabul: Oxfam, 2010).

20. Refer back to chapter 2 for an explanation of structural adjustment.

21. Stephanie Black, *Life and Debt* (Tuff Gong Pictures, 2001).

22. Manley served two terms as prime minister: from March 1972 to November 1980, and from February 1989 to March 1992.

23. Graham Hancock, *The Lords of Poverty: The Power, Prestige, and Corruption of the International Aid Business* (New York: Atlantic Monthly Press, 1989).

24. N. Uphoff, M. Esman, and A. Krishna, *Reasons for Success: Learning From Instructive Experiences in Rural Development* (West Hartford, CT: Kumarian Press, 1998), 163.

25. Aga Khan Development Network, *Rural Development in Pakistan*, 2007, cited February 6, 2012, http://www.akdn.org/rural_development/pakistan.asp.

26. The same figures also show that ODA has declined since 1960 as a percentage of gross national income of donor countries, as their economies have grown. The UN has encouraged countries to commit 0.7 percent of their GNI to aid, but very few donors have achieved this. The average as of 2010 was 0.32, whereas in 1960 it was 0.49. OECD, "50 Years of Official Development Assistance," cited October 28, 2012, http://webnet.oecd.org/dcdgraphs/ODAhistory/.

27. OECD, *Development: Aid to Developing Countries Falls Because of Global Recession*, April 4, 2012, cited on May 8, 2012, http://www.oecd.org/newsroom/developmentaidtodeveloingcountriesfallsbecauseofglobalrecession.htm.

28. Riddell, *Does Foreign Aid Really Work?*

29. Ibid.

30. Ibid.

31. Ibid.

32. Center for Army Lessons Learned, *Commander's Guide to Money as a Weapons System: Tactics, Techniques and Procedures* (Fort Leavenworth, KS: US Army, 2009).

33. Andrew Wilder and Stuart Gordon, "Money Can't Buy America Love," *Foreign Policy*, December 1, 2009.

34. Andrew Wilder, "Losing Hearts and Minds in Afghanistan," *Middle East Institute Viewpoints*, 2009.

35. For a discussion on sectorwide approaches, see Riddell, *Does Foreign Aid Really Work?*

36. Ibid.

37. Ibid.

4

Development Organizations

"**That's just how development works.**" This is the world-weary exclamation of the development worker who has learned through experience, long years of it, that not all is as it first seems. Development organizations may say that they are focused on fighting poverty, improving basic health and literacy, and otherwise serving humanity in a noble manner. But that often isn't how they act.

So how does development work? What does it look like, what does it involve? How bad is it, really? The answer, of course, depends on where you are in the system.

In this chapter, we focus on the most prominent institutions in international development. These are the bilateral donors, the United Nations and its agencies, nongovernmental agencies, and for-profit development actors—namely, contractors and consultants. What role do these institutions claim, and how does this role play out in practice? And what do the people who have worked for these different institutions have to say? What is the view from the inside?

Donors

In the previous chapter, we looked at some length at the role and behavior of donors. Given their centrality in the development system, working for a donor provides an individual with the potential to input into mainstream development policy and practice, as well as some potential say in where and how to allocate resources. But at the same time, donors are closer to political influence and are often very bureaucratic. While a donor agency as a whole may be powerful, an individual within it might potentially feel very powerless, even in a relatively senior position. As Ian Smillie observes,

> A lot of people want to get into the development field to influence things. Many in my generation, including me, thought if they

could get in and up, they could fix it. One of my contemporaries eventually became a vice president of CIDA, but in the end became disillusioned and left.

But on the other hand, I spoke with people in relatively junior positions with some donors who reported having a reasonable amount of latitude in their work and who were generally satisfied with what they could accomplish. So let's examine a little further this relationship between the donor agency and the individuals working within it.

What Is It Like to Work for a Donor?

Donor countries vary in the way they administer aid. Most have one or several agencies purposed with spending development funds, but it is not unusual for multiple government departments and agencies to have a role in this.

While the bulk of a development portfolio is typically managed from the donor country, donors also have agency staff placed in country offices, usually located in embassies and consulates in countries where the donor has aid programs. In overseas country offices, donor staff tend to work closely with the recipient government's line ministry departments and other agencies.

The main work of an aid agency is to spend money. Each aid officer typically manages a portfolio of funded projects for a particular region or theme. In most aid agencies, the individual officer will not make unilateral decisions but will have a lot of discretionary power. This personal connection between the individual officer at the donor and the organizations receiving the grant money has a big influence, whether for good or for bad, on the whole donor-recipient relationship. A junior officer at the Swedish International Development Cooperation Agency (SIDA) explains,

> I'm managing my portfolio, and although the decision is made back in HQ, it's based on my recommendation. It's important to have a supportive boss in that, and I'm lucky that I do, so I do have that power.

Donor officers must assess project proposals and decide if they meet donor criteria and if they are likely to work. Of course, not all possible aid recipients are competent, and some may even be fraudulent. A project officer at one donor explains,

> I really don't believe that organizations that don't have the professional capacity should be mucking around in development just to

say they're doing something good. . . . Many of the proposals we've looked at in our section have major flaws in their approach to equality between women and men in a way that really makes you question the rationale of why they're even doing what they're doing.

Once an organization gets funding, the donor staff are supposed to monitor it, but many also try to take on a coordination and facilitation role in linking projects and partners, as well as providing advice in areas where they have expertise and introducing new ideas and theories about development into project designs.

However, not everyone working in a donor organization necessarily has a background or interest in development. Some people just see it as a job and don't put in the effort to research and learn about the possible risks and benefits of the projects they are funding. This is a problem because of the sheer complexity and variety of the projects. Sometimes aid recipients complain about donor representatives who don't bother to read their reports. One person on the receiving end of a USAID grant told me,

> I can't tell you how many times I get requests for information that they already have on file. We submit quarterly reports, but clearly our contact hasn't read any of it, or he wouldn't be as lost as he is.

On the other hand, aid recipients don't always appreciate overzealous project management from the donor side. As Ian Smillie notes, many people working for donors would rather be doing development than pushing paper, "so they tend to micromanage, so you get a lot of conflict and anxiety between the grantees and the people who have the cash."

Anders Fange explains how things have shifted as the donor bureaucracies, which twenty years ago were mainly hands-off and far away, have set up shop in Afghanistan:

> I remember when SIDA got their first civil servant in their embassy in Islamabad. . . . We took him for a tour to Afghanistan, and the teachers in the schools complained about low salaries, and he said of course we should give you higher salaries. So immediately he started to get involved in our business. . . . He created a lot of confusion.
>
> Now SIDA—they have four people with the Provincial Reconstruction Team [PRT] up in Mazar, and four down here in Kabul—

and it gets that they go into details, and they love to go into details. If you give them the opportunity to go into the details about a project, they jump for it. So it's a real art, how to keep them at arm's length. . . . They sit with their asses in Mazar, but their heads are in Stockholm. The problem is they come and stay here for a year, and then they go and new people come in—often young, inexperienced people—and they've never been to Afghanistan before.

As Anders notes, SIDA's behavior is typical of all the donor agencies. It is not just inexperience that hamstrings donor staff but the bureaucratic pressures and realities of the agencies they work for. As one SIDA worker explains,

At the end of the day, as donors in general, as much as we want to do the best for everyone, it's more about getting the money out the door—get the money, spend the money.

Many people who are interested in development issues find being part of a large bureaucracy less than scintillating. And somewhat ironically, they face the risk that as they move up the career ladder, the sense of distance from their interests will only increase. A senior staffer at CIDA explains,

When I joined the bureaucracy, it got less and less interesting—working with the government, for the government in Africa, it deals with managing a bureaucracy and it's very frustrating . . . [and] I don't want to get detached from that programming aspect. I'm forty-seven—there aren't that many my age at CIDA, and a lot don't want to move up, because they want to stay close to the projects, it's enjoyable, it's rewarding . . . you get good feedback once you get the relationship there—whereas if I'm promoted up a few levels, that information would be filtered and would usually be changed, depending on what they thought the boss wanted to hear.

Bureaucracy can sometimes get out of hand, especially when it is combined with continual restructuring because of changing politics. A former donor employee explained why he decided to quit:

I'll give you an example. . . . I wrote a country strategy every single year—these are supposed to be five-year strategies, but then the strategies or processes change every year, and they have to be redone;

the last year I had to revise it at least thirty times. . . . That was frustrating! And it felt like I wasn't doing development, these documents—how do they change people's lives in any way?

Wendy Quarry, who in the past worked for CIDA and the World Bank, has found these large aid bureaucracies value institutional loyalty over dedication to development work. There are certain donor practices that support her view. One is the constant rotation of staff from one place to another. A Danish aid official muses,

> The way the system works, they don't want you to be in place for more than three or four years max. . . . With the US it's two to three years. I don't know why . . . maybe it's because the more you move, the less you can be held accountable! That's a weakness of international development—so much of the work just disappears into space.

Because they change positions so often, donor staff frequently don't know the history of their own agency in a country more than two or three years back—forget about having a deeper historical understanding. Weak institutional memory and learning is a common complaint among people who have worked in or with these agencies for any length of time.

At the same time, donors face political pressure from their governments for accountability and results. They are on the front line of the aid system in terms of being exposed to changes in the domestic political climate. A Canadian aid official explains,

> You're always confronted with the challenges of how complex it is to do any kind of social development, and you have to accept high failure rates, which is difficult in [a] bureaucracy; you can't admit or accept failure, so it's difficult to stay positive and focused—but you can; look at some results and not get swallowed by the bureaucracy and negativity of working with an aid agency.

Although working in donors can be frustrating, people in donor agencies often have the opportunity to spend more time thinking about "big picture" issues than people who are more directly involved in programming and projects. Some donor staff are able to see and appreciate these big picture changes and their importance, as well as what they are able to achieve within their own sphere of influence. This is especially true when there is political commitment for development as an end to itself rather than just another foreign policy tool. Some people working for donors report great satisfaction with their work and are able to point toward specific projects they were involved in, as well as broader shifts that they see as positive.

The United Nations

The Role of the United Nations in International Development

Fifty-one nations founded the United Nations by charter in 1945. Its 193 member states include almost every country in the world, the only exceptions being the Vatican and politically contested states (Taiwan and Kosovo) that the UN does not recognize as sovereign.[1]

The four purposes guiding the UN are stated in Article One of its charter and have remained unchanged since it began. The first are (1) to solve conflicts and (2) to encourage universal peace through friendly relations among nations. The third purpose is, as stated in the charter,

> to achieve international co-operation in solving international problems of an economic, social, cultural, or humanitarian character, and in promoting and encouraging respect for human rights and for fundamental freedoms for all without distinction as to race, sex, language, or religion.

Its fourth purpose is to coordinate among all nations to achieve these things.

This unique mandate of the United Nations makes it central to international development efforts. While its composition of member states makes it an essentially political entity, it also seeks to transcend undue political influence by any one country by placing a ceiling on the maximum membership dues any country can contribute to its budget (currently 22 percent, which is assessed to the United States). The secretary-general is the most senior post within the UN and can be filled by a citizen from any of its member states. The General Assembly of the UN makes most decisions regarding the UN's development mandate, and it operates on a one-member, one-vote basis.

In its role of coordinating nations toward development, the UN's most notable recent effort is the declaration of the Millennium Development Goals (MDGs), eight goals with defined targets that all of its member countries agreed in 2000 that they would aim to achieve by 2015. These goals are as follows:

1. eradicate extreme poverty and hunger;
2. achieve universal primary education;
3. promote gender equality and empower women;
4. reduce child mortality;
5. improve maternal health;
6. combat HIV/AIDS, malaria, and other diseases;
7. ensure environmental sustainability; and
8. develop a global partnership for development.

With the deadline for the MDGs due to expire in 2015, most observers predict that they will be succeeded by similar or extended goals.[2] The UN has numerous agencies that provide grants for development or directly engage in development efforts themselves. Thirty of them are members of the United Nations Development Group. The largest of these is the United Nations Development Programme (UNDP), which is one of the biggest sources of development grants and technical assistance. Others are specialized agencies, some of the best known being the United Nations Children's Fund (UNICEF), the World Food Programme (WFP), the Food and Agriculture Organization (FAO), and the World Health Organization (WHO). Many of these deal with humanitarian relief and with development issues.

The World Bank and International Monetary Fund (IMF) were created shortly before the United Nations. Their mode of operation is quite different from that of other UN agencies, but they are also considered to be within the UN framework. A long-standing, informal agreement dating from the establishment of the World Bank in 1944 states that its president will be a US national, while the managing director of the IMF is a European national. While the IMF is an important player in terms of setting monetary policy and lending conditions, it is the World Bank that has a direct mandate to assist development through soft grants.

Not all UN agencies get their budgets covered through the assessed fees that UN member states are obliged to pay, and so they depend on additional voluntary contributions. Agencies like the World Food Programme put out emergency appeals to raise funds to address specific issues, but these often come up short. Some UN agencies, such as the United Nations Human Settlements Programme (UN-HABITAT), essentially end up competing for donor funds against NGOs so that they can run programs.

The UN also consists of numerous special missions, coordinating bodies, working groups, and other temporary and permanent structures, all of which tend to be subject to ongoing reform. Its institutional structure is labyrinthine and opaque. This leads to overlap between agency roles and mandates and sometimes to competition between them. It has also led to ongoing complaints about the UN's inefficiency and calls for reform. In 1989, Graham Hancock pointed out that the various committees and working groups created to streamline the UN had themselves got somewhat out of hand, while none had gotten very far in making the UN less bureaucratic.[3] That was over twenty years ago, and today the UN is as bureaucratic as ever, and calls for reform are no less strident. The UN convened a World Summit in 2005 that included UN reform on its agenda, and the General Assembly continues to pronounce new mandates for reform initiatives on a fairly regular basis.

It is indisputable that the UN fills a unique ideological need—it forwards a vision of a world united by the best of what human beings can imagine, rather than a world of war and competition between nations. But just as it is based on lofty dreams, it has a unique power to disappoint, when it is repeatedly apparent that the reality of the UN is quite far from these dreams. If international development is a land filled with contrasts and contradictions, the UN is its undisputed capital. Perhaps we aren't as surprised when a national donor acts according to political interest rather than on principle, but when the UN falls short of its stated mandate, many people take it hard. It is as though it has broken our most cherished hopes about humanity.

Those who work within the UN are at the front line of these contrasts, and they wear it in different ways.

What Is It Like to Work for the UN?
The whole UN system, including the secretariat and all its affiliated agencies, employs about 63,450 people.[4] Coming from almost all of its member countries (about 175 different nationalities), these individuals are considered international civil servants. Those who travel overseas are given special UN laissez-passer passports and associated limited diplomatic immunities.

There are two types of employment grade within the UN system: general services and professional. It is hard to switch from the former to the latter. The employment conditions for those hired on professional grade salaries are set to be internationally competitive. They are supposed to be equivalent to the wages of similarly skilled civil servants in the highest paid member state. This means that for most member countries, UN salaries are far above the wages they could ever hope to make through national employment. Benefits are also good, including health insurance, travel allowances, vacation time, and additional payment for "hardship" postings in countries where the security or living conditions are judged to be subpar. Hiring is done on a quota system based on citizenship, so that someone may be favored or disadvantaged based on whether the country is currently under- or overrepresented among UN staff. This system of hiring is unique among development institutions and means that the UN workforce is truly international.

Many people spend their whole careers within the UN. It can be hard to break in, but once people are there, job security is good. Perhaps because of this large cadre of lifetime international civil servants, the UN is also known to be somewhat self-important. Many parts of the UN get tangled up in internal politics that seem to become the overriding interest of some proportion of people working there. If you spend time socially with UN people, you will soon start learning about their grading system—the P3s and P4s and the various bonuses and allowances and so forth that different agencies allow. Comparing notes and grievances is a fairly common pastime.

One common complaint among UN staff is that the most useless people in the organization rise up, and some high appointments are entirely politically motivated. Because the UN has a lot of genuine talent in it, this means there is often a situation where highly skilled people find themselves under the management of someone who knows less than they do and who seems singularly unqualified for the position. One long-term UN staffer explains,

> There's a lot of deadwood in the UN, shuffled through the system, and around the system, and aren't serving and are just sucking huge salaries. . . . What's always surprised me, you work in an office with national staff, and they're the lowest, and at the whim of an international supervisor, they can be let go. But it seems to be that the senior staff—you can't get rid of them. People are terrified to let nonperforming staff go. There's too much hedging, and so many personal agendas and backstabbing. It becomes quite exhausting after a while.

The centrality of office politics within the UN is well captured in Michael Soussan's book *Backstabbing for Beginners*, about his experiences as a young aide within the UN's Iraq Oil-for-Food Programme.[5] The Oil-for-Food Programme was started in 1996 to provide relief to Iraqi civilians in the face of the UN trade sanctions against the regime. But senior Iraqi leaders used the program to make billions of dollars in kickbacks and illegally smuggled oil. Meanwhile, much of the food delivered through the program was judged, in later investigation, to have been unfit for human consumption. Senior UN officials charged with overseeing the program received bribes and allocations of oil and stonewalled efforts at investigation.[6] Soussan unwittingly gained a front-row seat to these events as a junior UN aide. His story captures how UN office politics can suck up much of the organization's energy and time. In the case of the Oil-for-Food Programme, it contributed to an atmosphere in which huge corruption flourished.

While most UN staffers can find parallels between Soussan's account and their own experience, the organizational culture of UN agencies is far from uniform. Staff of the WFP, for example, sometimes describe themselves as the "cowboys" of the UN, out on the front lines and active. The UNDP, by contrast, seems largely hands-off, and many of its staff say it is hard to know what impact their work is having.

While the UN bureaucracy has often been criticized by those outside the UN, it is also a major source of frustration for those working within it. One former UN staffer recalls being called to an appointment with a government minister. Her secretary told her to call him back and reschedule it because the UN required at least twenty-four hours' notice to book a car. For those who have little patience for bureaucracy, the UN can be a nightmare. In Nairobi, some hotels will no longer take bookings from the UNDP because the agency has taken over a year to pay its bills.

As one former UN worker says,

> I think the people who are effective in the UN are the ones who know how to go around the rules—then they're really powerful, because the UN has the biggest mandate and the most money. But you have to make the system serve the people instead of the bureaucracy.

Those who do manage to tap into the powers of the UN can do great things. James Grant, the former head of UNICEF, is one iconic example. He was able to persuade warring parties to call a temporary truce so that UNICEF could run child immunization campaigns.[7] UNICEF under his leadership ran effective campaigns for basic childhood health, which saved thousands upon thousands of lives.

Probably the biggest strength that the UN has is "convening power"— the power to bring governments together and have them listen to each other and to engage, and this is combined with a global reach. The UN has been responsible for some of the greatest and most celebrated successes in international development. Although food aid remains controversial, the World Food Programme has definitely saved lives through its services, as has the UN

Refugee Agency (UNHCR) in providing shelter and other basic services for refugees.

So while many within the UN seem to get caught up in the inner whirlwind of constant politicking and bureaucratization, others manage their work with the politics as a background noise or are lucky enough to inhabit some corner of the organization where such issues are less prevalent. Ricardo Ramirez used to work in the communication for development group of the FAO during the 1990s. He recalls the chief of the group was excellent at protecting the department from the broader politics of the FAO, allowing staff to do their work in relative freedom, operating "as though we were an NGO."

Many within the UN clearly care very passionately about the UN's mandate and the subject that they are working with, and they don't focus so much on the UN's shortcomings, or they just put up with them. Other people perhaps have that happy blend of political savvy combined with a sense of purpose that helps them to push through.

Nongovernmental Organizations

The Role of NGOs in International Development

Development NGOs have become increasingly important actors over the history of international development. The growth in the number of NGOs worldwide has been staggering. In 1951, there were 217 NGOs with special consultative status with the United Nations Economic and Social Council. This status allows NGOs to access many intergovernmental processes at the UN. By 1971, there were 469 NGOs with this status, and by 1991, there were 928.[8] Currently, about 3,500 NGOs have special consultative status, and the UN reports record numbers of new NGOs are registering.[9]

The number of international NGOs worldwide is much higher than this. Estimates vary as to the precise number, although 40,000 is a popular estimate. The Johns Hopkins Center estimated that in 2004, these NGOs hired a combined total of 140,000 employees and had total revenues of US$13 billion.[10] The numbers of national-based NGOs are even greater. In 2010, a study commissioned by the Indian government pegged the number of NGOs in that country at 3.3 million![11]

This widespread expansion of NGOs has been in part a response to the availability of funding and to the opening of political space that allows for such associations. As we saw in the previous chapter, political- and rights-oriented NGOs could not have existed in Kenya under the regime of President Moi (1978–2000). Since the fall of the Soviet Union and the end of the cold war, there has been a trend toward governments that allow NGOs, and some that encourage them. There has also been plenty of donor interest in promoting "civil society" as part of a healthy state.

NGOs have increased in size and scope as well. Many of the largest international development NGOs, such as Oxfam and CARE, have become almost household brands. Many of these have their origins as emergency relief foundations. They gradually expanded to longer term development and to advocating for policies and funds that would support their visions of social change.

Ideally, NGOs can play a watchdog role and counterbalance the authority of the state, advocating on behalf of citizens who are poor and otherwise disenfranchised from the political system. They are often seen as more efficient and effective in delivering services to people than a state too weak or corrupt to be effective. They can work effectively even in countries where the state is largely weak or absent, such as in Afghanistan during the Mujahadeen and Taliban eras from the late 1980s and throughout the 1990s. And because they are often small, nimble, and close to the people and the problems, they can be a source of innovative problem solving.

Lester Salamon has argued that the rise of NGOs is nothing short of an "associational revolution," representing an important alternative to both state-led development efforts, which have often been disappointing, and market-led solutions favored by neoliberals.[12] For many people working in NGOs, they are organizations that are driven by a belief in global citizenship and a common identity that transcends global boundaries. One NGO director explained,

> I associate myself with people according to their values, not the patch of earth on which I was born or live. . . . This isn't necessarily what I do, it's what I am. I need to justify to myself why I'm alive on this earth.

NGOs may claim high moral ground and universal principles, but not everyone is convinced. As NGOs are nonelected and often foreign entities, the source of NGO legitimacy is often contested. NGOs have gotten into conflict with governments in a number of countries where they have attempted to take a stand against government abuse of civilians—the Sudan and Sri Lanka being two countries where the governments highly criticized NGOs and at certain times expelled many of them. In many countries, governments view NGOs with suspicion as competitors for donor funds, impinging on their sovereignty by providing services directly to populations without government direction or engagement. Genuine concerns about the huge fragmentation and overlap of services provided by NGOs have helped fuel the drive back toward direct government funding.

NGOs also risk undermining their principles and priorities when they become overly dependent on donor funding. Some NGOs, such as Médecins Sans Frontières/Doctors Without Borders (MSF), do make financial independence a matter of policy and may depend on private contributions or avoid particularly politicized donors. Small NGOs often find it hard to diversify their funding base, and this makes them particularly vulnerable to changes in donor policy. In 2006, Gilbert Onyango was working at a Kenyan NGO called CRADLE that focused on child protection issues, and he recalls,

> In '06, we were on our knees, we didn't get money from Norway, they were putting their money into a basket according to the Paris Declaration—so we didn't get money for one year. That was a decision made within New York and Stockholm, without consulting with the beneficiaries. It affected us big-time, and we had to stop certain programs we were implementing.

International NGOs tend to have more options in terms of mixing up their funding and seeking direct financial support from individual sponsors. Some NGOs pursue income-generating activities to cover expenses and provide financial stability and independence. Still, many of them are tempted to chase donor money where it is plentiful. And donor money is most plentiful where political interests dominate. For example, post-9/11 Afghanistan became flooded with international NGOs. It was not because the need was greater than it had been under the Taliban regime, and it had been possible for NGOs to operate under the Taliban, as some did. The biggest change was the availability of funding. The same is true of Iraq, as Cedric Fedida discovered:

> I went to Iraq. That was 2003, just after the invasion. I started working in reconstruction programs for a French NGO in Baghdad. It was completely chaotic and crazy. We could hear bombs go off and would go up on the roof and see where the smoke was to see where the bomb went off. . . . In Madrid, in 2003, there was a big conference of donors regarding Iraq, a lot of money on the table, and some smaller NGOs thought they were depending on this money, both for their survival and for their program overheads in other countries. So basically, when the situation was getting more and more dangerous in Iraq, there were people from HQ telling

people in the field, "Guys, there's a lot of money on the table, we need to put in a lot of proposals, respond to RFPs." Basically just like a company would say, "We need the market share." And in the end we knew many of us had to leave . . . because it was getting too dangerous, especially after they blew up the UN in June. But other people in HQ wanted us to stay because of the money.

Whether an NGO manages to maintain a purpose other than its own survival seems to depend on the strength of its identity and leadership style. Many development NGOs that aim to maximize their "fundability" are very flexible in the type of work that they are willing to take on, raising questions about the quality of work. Many end up as generalist organizations doing much the same sorts of activities as each other.

Since it can be quite easy to start an NGO, many people choose to do so. Many of the NGOs they start are poorly run. Some are "briefcase NGOs" existing in name only for the sake of attracting funds. Some small NGOs may be well run but have problems connecting to funding sources. As the aid industry has developed, competition for grant money has become stronger, NGOs have tended to professionalize, some have expanded, and some have failed. Still, in poor places where NGOs seem to be one of the most common types of human enterprise, it is sometimes unclear what these fragmented efforts add up to.

Some NGOs have become giants. BRAC, a Bangladeshi NGO founded in 1972, is the world's largest NGO and is a major force in Bangladesh. In 2002, it began operations in Afghanistan and has since expanded to other Asian and African countries, as well as Haiti. As of 2007, it had an operating budget of $110 million and 110,000 employees.[13]

Although BRAC hails from Bangladesh, many of the largest NGOs have their origins and headquarters in the West. All of these big NGOs have operations that are truly international. Organizations such as CARE, Oxfam, World Vision, Caritas, and Save the Children are of such magnitude that Ian Smillie terms them "transnational NGOs," suggesting that in their management practices, they may have parallels to transnational corporations.[14]

As the number and size of NGOs have grown globally, collaborations and partnerships between Northern and Southern NGOs have also become common practice. Some large Northern NGOs, including World Vision, CARE, and Save the Children, continue to directly run programs, while others, such as Oxfam, work through "local partners" by identifying and funding locally based NGOs in the regions where they work. In one sense they have become middlemen between the donors and the local NGOs.

George Yap is the executive director for the Canadian NGO Water-Can.[15] Over his career, he's worked in both international NGOs and small local NGOs. He believes the local NGOs have an edge:

> Over the last twenty years, I've come to the conclusion that there's a lot of great development that can be done much more efficiently through local NGOs, rather than through large international NGO bureaucracy—I'm not saying that large NGOs can't be good, but there can be comparative advantages, cost-effectiveness being one of them.

He's been with WaterCan since 2001, and he's brought his philosophy to its work:

> I would say ten to fifteen years ago, we'd mainly fund Canadian NGOs—the CAREs and Oxfams of the world. Today, our delivery model is very different—we do not provide funding for international NGOs, our funding is exclusively with local NGOs. These are NGOs that are registered locally and have no head office elsewhere they report to. Some more, some less, but one of their biggest challenges is access to resources so they can deliver services. It's a good approach, as long as you understand what the implications are working with a local NGO.

As NGOs have increased in number and have linked together, they have increased their collective ability to advocate at the global level. Many NGOs have official consultative status at the UN. They are not voting members, but they are able to input into various processes. They have also sought to mobilize public opinion and to present issues to different national governments. To cite some prominent examples, the NGO lobby has been an important voice in arguing against structural adjustment, for increased consultation with development beneficiaries, for debt relief, and for increased and untied development funding. In all of these efforts, they have been at least partially successful.

What Is It Like to Work for an NGO?

The range of NGOs, and hence the range of experiences people have working in them, is huge. This means that those thinking to join an NGO need to critically assess whether it is well run, ethical, and in line with their own values and objectives.

NGOs operating internationally also vary in terms of their ethos and approach to development. People who have worked in different NGOs usually find that some of them are consistent with their own values and ideas about how development should be approached, and some are not. Sheilagh Henry recalls one large NGO she worked with:

> They were the type of NGO I never wanted to work for. . . . You have an impact, just by being there—but [this NGO] didn't take that into account at all; it was all about hugging that black baby and getting the best famine photo. And the people they had attracted were very good people, thank God, but with no idea [about international development] and were just thrown into it, and they were doing poor development.

When NGOs, especially international NGOs, engage in poor development, the results can be tragic. Sheilagh learned this early on in her experiences, as she witnessed the consequences of a paternalistic development effort:

> In about 1996 I went to work in Honduras with a missionary society. They were working in a beautiful village of eighteen houses, a wonderful village. Honduras is relatively Catholic in the first place, but the missionary society was Episcopalian, and they came and built this church, and everyone in the village was expected to go to this church. The programs that they were running were things that Episcopalians in Texas could put their hands on—they were buying goats and rabbits for the village. And the villagers didn't know what to do with the rabbits—they didn't eat them. This one little boy who was about eight—I loved him—he didn't go to school because he had to look after the rabbits, his brother had to look after the goats. They didn't do livestock, they were subsistence farmers, and they got into this commercial livestock that was a burden for them. The only nice development was the guesthouses and structures for the mission—and they had these lovely flush toilets that flushed into the neighbors' farm.

Not all development looks like this. But the fact of its existence and persistence, that NGOs can operate this way with relatively few checks and balances on their behavior, means that individuals looking to work in development have to stay critical and question what they see. NGO incompetence and misconduct can also endanger the staff, especially those working in insecure areas. As a young aid worker recounts,

> In South Sudan, I was country representative, had 160 national staff and 16 expats, and the funds earmarked for our projects that we had to justify, but they were sent off [by our head office] to other places, and we suddenly had no liquidity and a lot of projects ongoing. . . . I had debt collectors coming around, I was held up at gunpoint many times. . . . That was an Italian NGO, but I've seen it with many NGOs. I think it's unforgiveable.

Given these tales of weakness and incompetence, the general trend of professionalization across NGOs is not a bad thing. As master's degrees in development-related topics are now often required for NGO posts, and as reporting and accountability measures tighten up, we can hope that these horror stories will become rarer.

However, the flipside to the professionalization is an increase in "managerialism" as larger NGOs become more corporate. With improved communications technologies, it is easier for overseas head offices to increase their level of oversight and control. Tom Vincent, an American who has worked in the field for international NGOs for many years, fears that these trends will make things worse, as people with PhDs but little or no experience take the rein from "home offices" and reduce the amount of discretionary power that field staff have on the ground. His worry is that this trend essentially increases upward accountability to donors at the expense of the work.

Trying to navigate the space between accountability, financial stability, and effective work is not easy for NGOs or those working in them. Because NGOs have to keep a positive public face, their staff sometimes find that it is hard to have open and frank discussions about the problems and pitfalls they face. The Internet is hosting an increasing number of critical, and often anonymous, blogs about aid and development written by development workers, many of whom work for NGOs. This is good news for those who feel like there needs to be greater transparency and frank discussion about some of the difficulties, dilemmas, and dark spots that NGOs face.

Although the world of NGOs is not a perfect sanctuary for the development idealist, when the balance is right, working for an NGO can be a deeply rewarding experience. One person working with women's programs through a large international NGO in Afghanistan reflects,

It's amazing seeing the resilience and strength that women here have, despite everything they've had to undergo. And even now, to see the passion in women for change and the drive to bring that about—for themselves, for their families, for their communities. For me it's important—I see my role in most of these situations as a kind of facilitator.

Another NGO worker, also in Afghanistan, describes his experiences as challenging but ultimately satisfying:

It's been much more difficult in the beginning than I expected, a much more complex world to get into. On the side of making a difference, it has actually met my expectations; I feel that I make a difference, that my work contributes to the work of the organization I work for, and that the organization is changing people's lives for the better.

Compared to staff at donors and large multilateral agencies, those working in NGOs tend to be much closer to the people that their efforts are expected to benefit. This also means, crucially, that they are often in a much better position to see the results of their efforts and thus learn from them than those in large, hands-off bureaucracies. This topic of learning is one we return to in part 2.

Contractors

The Role of Contractors in International Development

Over the past fifteen years or so, private aid contractors have become more prominent in development as donors, particularly USAID, have increasingly turned to them to implement aid programs. This is due mainly to changes in USAID itself: staff numbers have decreased even as its budget has increased.[16] Aid contracting allows USAID to outsource development work while maintaining ownership and control. Other donors such as AusAID, Department for International Development (DFID), CIDA, and the EU also make use of private development contractors, although less extensively.

The use of private contractors has been most prevalent and most controversial in hot spots such as Afghanistan and Iraq, where they have been contracted mainly by USAID to deliver a wide variety of development and state-building projects, aiming to expand commercial agriculture, build up the civil service and judiciary, expand and train the police and military, build roads and infrastructure, deliver cash-for-work projects in the most conflicted areas of the country, and support the growth of civil society and a wide variety of other projects. In Afghanistan, private contractors carry out development projects in areas and under conditions that NGOs largely refuse, collaborating with the military in some of the most insecure areas of the country. Charges of opacity in the awarding and oversight of contracts, windfall profits, and strong links to the American administration have tainted many of these contracts with scandal. A 2009 memo issued by the US Senate's Subcommittee on Contracting Oversight noted that USAID had about 14,000 contractors in Afghanistan in 2009 and had spent billions of dollars. To quote from the memo,

> In October 2009, the USAID Inspector General concluded that the lack of contract management and oversight personnel has "significantly" impaired USAID's mission in Afghanistan. In April 2009, Michael Walsh, the former director of USAID's Office of Acquisition and Assistance and Chief Acquisition Officer, testified that many USAID staff are "administering huge awards with limited knowledge of or experience with the rules and regulations." According to one USAID official, the agency is "sending too much money, too fast with too few people looking over how it is spent." As a result, the agency does not "know . . . where the money is going."[17]

Some companies are largely or entirely dependent on USAID contracts for their existence. These "beltway bandits" are usually located within the Washington, DC, area. The emphasis in the contracting game is on pleasing USAID or the incumbent ambassador where the project is carried out. High salaries and inflated costs are quite common. Many of these companies prefer to hire as many expatriates as possible, rather than local people, because they make a profit on each person's salary.[18] In this climate, the company has a perverse incentive to waste money and create dependency.

As an increasingly visible element in the aid landscape, aid contractors often spark controversy and are viewed with suspicion by those working in NGOs. While they are not all crooks, the nature of the contracts means they have less independence and flexibility than NGOs to make sure that their work is done in the best possible way. The rise of for-profit contractors also arguably makes it harder for NGOs to assert their own independence to donors and still secure funds.

What Is It Like to Work for a Contractor?

Some people working for or with aid contractors have found them to be efficient and fairly straightforward places to work, where the results are liable to be as good or bad as the contracts they sign. Others have found them to be profligate spenders with questionable results. Across everyone's experiences, a common reality is that the contractor works for the client—which is the donor. If the donor's interest is more politically driven than driven by the motive to carry out high-quality development work, this will affect the whole enterprise. As a senior employee at an AID contractor in Afghanistan explained,

> There's so much emphasis on pleasing AID, as a contractor. If I think back to [my previous employer, an NGO], there were conversations about how our work could help Afghanistan, the country, the Afghan staff. Among senior staff here, I don't think I've ever had a conversation about that—it is all about pleasing AID. I get a lot of respect from our AID people at the embassy, but they have their people to report to. . . . A lot of things they [AID] want of us aren't good for the project. . . . It's easy to tick the boxes, but it's a lot harder to have an impact.

A worker at another USAID contractor focused on infrastructure development reached similar conclusions about the value of his work:

> I tell people this when they're interested in working in Afghanistan: first I ask them, what do you think development is? . . . You can throw that out of the window. It's about what Congress can show—how many schools are built this year that will fall apart next year. There's no long-term vision—if you want real development, go to Zambia. But there's too much money here, too much politics; the military is involved. We build roads with the support of the community, with the idea that they're the beneficiaries, but the forces also go down the roads—and they benefit, and guess what happens when a tank goes down a gravel road? It damages it; it becomes useless. And then it is also a target for the Taliban. . . . That's where the cynicism comes in, where you think you're doing something good, and you realize you're not.

Most NGOs refuse to work with the military, and those adhering to principle would refuse to do work with a likely negative impact. But contractors tend to ask fewer questions and operate according to the donor's specifications, usually at a much higher cost than an NGO.

With their different mandates and organizational cultures, aid contractors tend to attract and select different people than NGOs do. More people working at contractors do it primarily for the money. Fewer people in the private sector have studied development. As someone at one large contractor explained, "Certainly the general thought in my company is 'never hire anyone with a degree in international development'—because you have to get an MBA or experience, or something a bit more practical than international development—it's not seen as a practical degree."

Still, many people who have worked for both NGOs and for-profit contractors argue that the practical distinction between the two is minimal. Cedric Fedida, who has worked for both, reflected,

> I'd say twenty years ago, there was a big difference. NGOs were made up of mainly volunteers working for very low salaries, but now they're highly qualified professionals, salaries have gone up also in many of the big organizations, even if of course there are still some volunteers around, but they remain volunteers for less time. We all come from the same sort of programs or schools or master's degrees, or whatever, so we can all get the same salaries in the end, and sometimes we do exactly the same job.

Not all private companies working in development extract huge overheads. Some are smaller and leaner and operate more like . . . well, like companies. Some pay attention to the quality of work, even when they don't profit from doing so. Some people who have moved from the private sector to NGOs find the latter to be more inefficient. Astrid de Valon appreciated the greater administrative efficiency she found working with a private contractor:

> I went to Bunia in the Eastern Congo, to work for Chemonics, which is a for-profit organization. . . . We were taking over a project that had been started by an international NGO but didn't work well, so USAID did not extend the original contract and gave it to Chemonics. I remember when I did that, my friends said in horror that I was going to the evil capitalists, making money from humanitarian interventions. But I really enjoyed it— the structure was super efficient, the administrative part was functioning really well like in a private company, and then you could

focus on the job; all the problems with headquarters that you'd have [with NGOs] you didn't, so it was really simple to focus on your job.

Those who work for development contractors often question the "holier than thou" attitude espoused by many NGOs, which they point out are still part of the same development system, often competing for the same money to do the same type of work, and who may not always know better. For those who shift from development NGOs to development companies, making peace with for-profit contracting is making peace with the reality of aid work. Marielle Rowan, who now does social impact assessments for Mott MacDonald, muses, "I think I'm more practical, more realistic. I've always been a practical person, but this idea of it being a business, it's important to accept and recognize, and see how the pieces fit together."

Consultants

The Role of Consultants in International Development

International development organizations often hire consultants to meet short-term work requirements of a specialized nature that fit outside the remit of their regular staff. External evaluations, workshop facilitation, short-term research, and expert input into policy, programming, or project design at key periods are all common requirements for which consultants are hired. People work as consultants in international development both within their own country (as "nationals") and internationally, with the latter commanding much higher rates. It is not unusual for an international consultant to be paid in one day what a midlevel national employee would get paid in a month for the same organization.

Some people fall into consulting when they find they have a skill for which there is high demand, and many people consult in between or in addition to other jobs. University professors, for example, may often take on short-term consultancies.

Unfortunately, many consultants are hired based on an expertise assumed to be universally applicable. Because this assumption is often untrue, and the time permitted for their work is often minimal, there is widespread skepticism about the value of fly-in consultants. It is particularly painful for those who know the area well but who are lower down in the implicit hierarchy of international development to watch consultants fly in and get paid high rates for useless work. One former NGO staffer from Tajikistan recalls,

At one point they hired an international consultant, I don't re-member where she came from, but somewhere from the West. She didn't know too much about Tajikistan before she came there, and the recommendations that she wanted to make—everyone knew they wouldn't work.

Not all fly-in consultants are hopeless. Some are "area experts" who may have worked in a particular context for many years before becoming a consul-tant and hence have connections and an understanding of the situation that could more than compensate for the fact that the work duration itself is quite brief. Some consultants are also quite stringent in their own decisions about whether or not to take on a work assignment and consider what they may bring to it and whether or not they can do it well.

What Is It Like to Work as a Consultant?

For those who find the bureaucracy and internal politics of large aid bureau-cracies too stifling, consultancy offers an alternative. As long as work is plenti-ful enough, it can also be very lucrative.

Some sorts of skills and activities are well suited to short-term consultan-cies. Well-designed evaluations are best done by outsiders with an appropriate awareness of the context and enough time. Harry Cummings, who is a profes-sor at the University of Guelph in addition to running a consultancy specializ-ing in monitoring and evaluation, spends considerable attention and effort in educating his clients on various aspects of research design necessary to acquire meaningful results. Likewise, facilitation and organizational development ac-tivities seem suited to consultancies.

However, consulting work also has drawbacks. Continually having to chase after the next contract is an experience that some find unappealing. Naysan Adlparvar recalls of his brief stint consulting, "Three months as a con-sultant full-time was too much, because I'd have to constantly think, when meeting people, can this person give me a job? I got sick of myself, couldn't do it anymore."

Consultancy work often doesn't have much impact, and consultants have limited opportunity to follow up. Consultants often write reports and make recommendations that the commissioning institutions then seem to ignore. One person with extensive consulting experience explains,

> I worked as a consultant for a bunch of years—in different roles, as a researcher, on post-harvest, etc. I'd make recommendations and

they'd say, "Oh, these are great ideas—never heard of that," but when I went back, no one had ever implemented what I'd recommended. I realized that they just hire consultants because that's a requirement; they confuse events with accomplishments. There was only one organization that had me back as a consultant enough times that they followed my recommendations.

And then I see so many consultants out there, it's shocking to me the kind of shoddy work they do, the reports they produce, and they just get hired over and over, and it's just part of development that it doesn't matter, hiring a consultant is an end in itself, so whether they produce anything of use, it's irrelevant. When I was a consultant, I worked fourteen hours a day every day, and sometimes I thought, "Why work so hard? Whatever junk I produce is the same anyway." It's disheartening, because I could just join the crowd, and it's a good thing I'm a conscientious person.

When consultants are brought in to contribute to weak organizations dealing with complex issues, it is unlikely that they are going to be of much benefit. Likewise, if neither the consultants nor those hiring them are realistic about what consultants can do and how their work can be used, their main value becomes as a checkbox filled for donors and to achieve the vague sense that "something has been done." Although sadly common, this misuse of consultants is by no means inevitable. For those who want to work as consultants and who want their work to be useful, the onus is on them to work for organizations that are in a position to benefit, on topics where they have something to bring, and under realistic terms.

Conclusion

Each kind of aid institution has its own tendencies and characteristics, but at the same time each tends to be very interdependent, and the boundaries between institutions often blur. Take the example of the Karamoja Livelihoods Programme (KALIP). A fairly new program in the Karamoja region of Uganda, KALIP is being funded mainly by the European Union. It is run out of the prime minister's office, and its Ugandan staff are considered to be government employees, although they are hired on contract. It also has a small number of foreign staff, and they are technically employees of Cardno, a private international agency. However, most of the employees, Ugandan and international, were hired specifically for the program—they have no history with Cardno or the prime minister's office. KALIP's biggest function is to provide funding under a number of different streams to NGOs working in the area. The NGOs will compete for the funding, do the work, and report back to KALIP.

This real-life blurring between different categories of development organization supports the argument that different types of development institutions often have as many similarities as differences. Development is often driven by the business of bidding and contracting and pleasing the donor, and somewhere in that process, it is hoped that some work of social benefit will be done.

When we look within each category of institution—the UN, the donors, the NGOs, and the notorious aid contractors—we find that none can claim a medal for untainted virtue and purity (notwithstanding that an increasing number of NGOs and development actors have won Nobel Prizes for their work in the past ten years or so). Perhaps with bilateral donors, aid contractors, and the international financial institutions, we are not very shocked to see that they can be political, discriminatory, and self-interested. But for the UN and NGOs, the ideals they embody, the hope for a more peaceful, truly just, and mutually prosperous global society . . . when we are confronted with the extent of their shortcomings, many of us take it personally.

The good news is that just as we can't find any kind of aid organization that lives up perfectly to our collective hopes, we can't find one that is entirely hopeless. The World Bank, for example, is one organization that many people associate with the word "evil." That's a very strong word but one that comes up repeatedly when people talk about the World Bank.[19] For many, it has a reputation as the heavy hand of the status quo imposing itself on helpless countries in their time of weakness and destroying everything good that they had. It has a reputation as one of the ugliest faces of political power and blind technocratic arrogance that the modern world has manifested. And there are reasons for this. Graham Hancock explains the World Bank's funding of very expensive and ecologically and socially disastrous resettlement schemes in Brazil and Indonesia.[20] Michela Wrong recounts the World Bank's complicity in the theft of loans made to the government by the political elite of Kenya.[21] Jim Shute recalled a 1981 meeting in Nigeria with a senior official of the World Bank for Africa and finding him to be an openly racist white man from Southern Africa whom the bank had proudly appointed as an "Africa expert." The list is long, and much of it is well documented.

And yet the World Bank is the single largest donor behind the National Solidarity Programme, which is widely judged to have been one of the best-designed development efforts in Afghanistan. Although many aid projects in Afghanistan have been viewed with skepticism by Afghans, one independent study found that "a notable exception to this was the Ministry of Rural Reconstruction and Development's National Solidarity Program, which was viewed more positively for the greater role that local communities played in the planning, design, implementation, monitoring, and evaluation of the projects."[22] After much lobbying by NGOs, the World Bank has put stringent environmental criteria in place for development lending.[23] It is also a major source of information on development, and it puts much of its research into the public domain.

My point is not that the World Bank is good or that it is evil. The point is that some people within the bank have managed to support efforts at development that seem quite positive and well conceived, so it is at the least possible to do it. Just as some people have managed to negotiate the space to do decent work within aid contractors. And just as some people who go to work in NGOs do work that can actually be damaging.

None of this impinges on arguments for institutional reform. Such arguments have been made; many of them are sound. Most of them have not resulted in change and will continue to stall, because too many people are comfortable with the way things are now and are in some way or another benefiting from existing arrangements. And in the meanwhile, those of us who want to work in development and try to be effective must work with what we have. It's not the best, but it's far from hopeless.

In trying to be effective then, we depend on our own discretion, discernment, and ability to make trade-offs. We have to find the balance between pragmatism and idealism. By doing this, we can start to see all the spaces, all the opportunities, within the existing system to act in ways that are meaningful. This depends critically on our own relationship to the larger development system, which is the topic of part 2 of this book.

Notes

1. United Nations, "Growth in United Nations Membership, 1945–Present," 2012, cited October, 20 2012, http://www.un.org/en/members/growth.shtml.

2. Frans Bieckmann and Anna Meijer van Putten, "Goalposts: What Next for the MDGs?" *The Broker*, October 6, 2010, cited February 3, 2012, http://www.thebrokeronline.eu/Articles/Goalposts-What-next-for-the-MDGs.

3. Graham Hancock, *The Lords of Poverty: The Power, Prestige, and Corruption of the International Aid Business* (New York: Atlantic Monthly Press, 1989).

4. United Nations, *United Nations Website*, cited February 8, 2012, http://www.un.org/en/.

5. Michael Soussan, *Backstabbing for Beginners: My Crash Course in International Diplomacy* (New York: Nation Books, 2008).

6. See also the report from the official investigation into the scandal: Independent Inquiry Committee Into the United Nations Oil-for-Food Programme, *Report on Programme Manipulation* (Washington, DC: Independent Inquiry Committee Into the United Nations Oil-for-Food Programme, 2005).

7. David Bornstein, *How to Change the World: Social Entrepreneurs and the Power of New Ideas* (Oxford: Oxford University Press, 2007).

8. Peter Willetts, *The Growth in the Number of NGOs in Consultative Status With the Economic and Social Council of the United Nations*, City University, 2002, cited November 6, 2011, http://www.staff.city.ac.uk/p.willetts/NGOS/NGO-GRPH.HTM#graph.

9. NGO Branch of the United Nations Department of Economic and Social Affairs, *At Your Service*, 2012, cited June 10, 2012, http://csonet.org/; United Nations Department of Economic and Social Affairs, *Record Number of NGOs Seeking Participation in the UN*, January 31, 2011, cited January 6, 2012, http://www.un.org/en/development/desa/news/ecosoc/ngos -applications-ecosoc.html.

10. IDA Resource Mobilisation, *Aid Architecture: An Overview of the Main Trends in Official Development Assistance Flows* (Washington, DC: International Development Association, 2007), 31.

11. Archna Shukla, "First Official Estimate: An NGO for Every 400 People in India," *Indian Express*, July 7, 2010.

12. Lester M. Salamon, "The Rise of the Nonprofit Sector: A Global Associational Revolution," *Foreign Affairs*, July/August 1994.

13. "The List: The World's Most Powerful Development NGOs," *Foreign Policy*, July 1, 2008.

14. Ian Smillie, *The Alms Bazaar* (Ottawa: International Development Research Centre, 1995).

15. At the time of the interview, he was program director; he was appointed as executive director in late 2011.

16. In 1970 it had 4,300 full-time employees, and in 2007 this number had reduced to 2,417, with an additional 908 on limited appointment. Over the same time period, USAID's budget has continuously increased.

17. Homeland Security and Governmental Affairs Subcommittee on Contracting Oversight, *Memorandum Re. Hearing: "Afghanistan Contracts: An Overview"* (Washington, DC: Homeland Security and Governmental Affairs, December 16, 2009), 5.

18. William Easterly and Laura Freschi, *Save the Poor Beltway Bandits!* NYU Development Research Institute, May 7, 2012, cited October 20, 2012, http://nyudri.org/2012/05/07/ save-the-poor-beltway-bandits/.

19. For example, a number of people I interviewed casually referred to the World Bank as an evil institution, while one former World Bank employee I spoke with felt the need to state that the World Bank was not evil, in defense against the many people who think it is.

20. Hancock, *The Lords of Poverty*.

21. Michela Wrong, *It's Our Turn to Eat: The Story of a Kenyan Whistle-Blower* (New York: Harper, 2009).

22. Andrew Wilder and Stuart Gordon, "Money Can't Buy America Love," *Foreign Policy*, December 1, 2009.

23. "The World Bank and the Environment: When the Learning Curve Is Long," *The Economist*, June 25, 2009.

Part 2

Learning to Fit

The world as we have created it is a product of our thinking.
It cannot be changed without changing our thinking.
  —*Albert Einstein*

I'm starting with the man in the mirror
I'm asking him to change his ways
And no message could have been any clearer
If you wanna make the world a better place
take a look at yourself and then make a change.
  —*Michael Jackson* ("Man in the Mirror")

It may be that we are puppets—puppets controlled by the strings
of society. But at least we are puppets with perception, with awareness. And perhaps our awareness is the first step to our liberation.
  —*Stanley Milgram*

Having pondered the international development system, we now heed
the advice of the King of Pop and turn our attention to ourselves. More specifically, in this second part of the book, we are concerned with the way that
development workers fit in and contribute to the international development
system.

On inspection, we find that the boundaries between the system and the
self, what we think of as external and what we think of as internal, are extremely fuzzy. We are, after all, products of our culture, shaped and influenced
by social and economic considerations. And we are rarely the first to have

thought the thoughts that we think or to make the assumptions that we make. Most of these are inherited or borrowed from those before or around us.

There is also a collective element to this relationship between self and system. For example, hiring processes prefer people with certain characteristics and backgrounds over those without. As we enter into and adapt to organizational cultures, the sum result of our individual actions is a mass with the inertia either to resist change or, less frequently, to tip us into change.

As individuals, we each contribute to this larger whole even as we are shaped and held by it. It is through examining this relationship between the self and the larger whole that we can locate the opportunities to work effectively and gradually develop strategies that increase our range of choices.

People's work roles and their connections to the area they are working in influence the way that they are perceived and treated by others. As work roles and connections change over the course of time, so does one's own understanding and sense of commitment to one's work.

People differ in how they understand and adjust to the roles they take up and the relationships and assumptions that come with them. Historical power differences and more modern markings of status can cast some people into positions of relatively high power and marginalize others. The ways these dynamics happen and the consequences of these dynamics merit careful attention from anyone who is sincere in wanting to do good, honest work. The themes of relational power, reflective learning, and the need to clarify one's own motivations are thus key themes that run throughout part 2:

- In chapter 5, we look at who works in international development and why. We also examine the high-status roles often assigned to development professionals based on their designation as experts.
- Chapter 6 further considers the relationship between individual workers and the development system. In the first half of the chapter, we contrast the initial expectations that development workers commonly have with their experiences. The second half looks at the particular challenges that international development workers face in balancing their work lives with their personal lives.
- Finally, chapter 7 is devoted to the issue of work effectiveness. Assuming that development workers want to work effectively within the development system, flawed as it is, what are some of the strategies and resources they can draw on to do so?

5

Facing Ourselves

Dave Johnson is a dual Australian/Canadian citizen who came to Kenya in 1996. He'd initially come to Kenya for a short visit. When he landed in Nairobi, Dave had just finished a master's degree in environmental studies. Almost on a whim, he put in some job applications and ended up getting a job for a non-profit organization that worked with refugees. He spent over fourteen years there, moving up until he was country director. Along the way he got married to a Kenyan, had a child, and began to think of Kenya as home.

His organization had some regulations that had always struck Dave as unfair. One in particular was a hiring policy: senior positions were closed to Kenyan nationals—you could hold the position only if you were an expat. Dave had also benefited from this same policy as he rose through the ranks himself. As he stayed on longer than other expats, and as Kenyans were barred from higher positions, he became a prime candidate for promotion. But with time, Dave's views evolved as the issues became more personal to him. As he explains,

> I feel much more invested in trying to develop Kenya. My in-laws just got electricity two years ago, they're rural farmers, some of the motivation is now much more personal, it's not "rural Africa needs help," it's like, no, my father-in-law does! So that hypothetical "rural African" becomes much more meaningful.

His organization's headquarters were based in New York and kept the decision making quite centralized so that even as the country director, Dave could not change the policy without their consent:

> I was fighting with people in New York about nationalizing positions, and I lost. I don't know what was motivating that. I believe there

were issues of, if not racism, at least a very strong bias about people from the developing world—they couldn't possibly have such good skills in Africa, and "there's a reason why we have decision-making power and these people do not." . . . The person in that position was retaining a lot of decision-making power, I thought they needed to delegate more.

I think for me one of the changes was that once I married and had a child who was at least by definition half African, there were some things I might have accepted before; I have to say, "Wait a minute, you'd have to rule out your own daughter from that position" . . . and I might have to explain to her one day, why did I do that? There are structures in our societies that I don't necessarily need to contribute to as I have in the past. . . . I accepted that for a long time, and I benefited from those structures as I moved up the system. . . . But eventually I had to face and question those policies.

Dave's views and willingness to act on the issue evolved both as he got to know Kenyans better and became more convinced that Kenyans did indeed have the capacity to fill positions denied to them and as he felt more personally invested in the country.

When we work in international development, we become part of the international development system. The same influences that we encountered in the previous chapters also make their mark on the development workforce. Politics, funding, and prevalent ideas each shape who enters development, what kind of position they're likely to hold, who pays them and under what conditions, and their own thinking about international development, what it is, why and how they can contribute to it, and what they hope to achieve.

Two aspects of our identities are relevant to our work. First, there are the external descriptors of us: when and where we were born; our nationality, ethnicity, and religion; the languages we speak; the schools we attended; and the passports we hold. As individuals we may like to think this is all beside the point, especially if we subscribe to the view that we are all global citizens. But the world doesn't treat us all equally as global citizens. Our externally defined identities shape the opportunities that are open to us, and so some people are more likely to choose paths that take them into international development work. And once inside, people will have different experiences and opportunities, based not only on how they conduct themselves but also on how they are judged and treated.

The second aspect, which most of us hope to be the more important of the two, is what we bring in terms of our characters: our ideas, energy, and motivation. For some reason or another, we chose to work in development. Those reasons will get tested against experience; they will change or evolve with time. And whoever we thought we were, whatever we thought we believed, before we started working in development, these will surely change with the fire of experience.

This chapter is about the interplay between what we are, demographically and psychologically, and the larger international development system. In the first half, we look at how people enter development work: what motivates people to join, and then how they are selectively given entry through hiring practices and educational requirements. The second half of the chapter looks at what happens once people are in and specifically the role of "expert" that development workers are typically cast into. This second half is concerned with the way that international development tends to exalt formal, technical knowledge over informal, contextual knowledge and the implications of this, in terms of positional power, the re-creation of hierarchies, and work effectiveness.

Who We Are: The People Working in International Development

Those who work in international development animate it with their characters, ideas, energy, and motives. Whatever international development is, it is after all a collection of people working together in certain ways, based on their understanding of how things are and what should be done. While money fuels the system, the workers are its very body.

So then, who is international development? What factors distinguish those who work in it from those who don't? We'll consider two ways of answering this question. The first is to look at what, in terms of character, psyche, or motive, differentiates development workers from bankers, shopkeepers, politicians, computer programmers, or any other profession. The second is to look at common criteria that international development agencies apply when hiring and promoting people. This tells us something about the people they select and who is excluded, as well as what the system itself values and rewards in its workers.

Why We Join: Personal Motivation

As funding to international development has generally increased, the numbers of people coming into international development have also increased. Those who take postings working in development internationally number easily in the hundreds of thousands.[1] Their motivations for joining, naturally enough, vary.

The answer to "who works in development" depends on what part of the international development system we look at. Many national governments receiving aid are staffed with people who must engage with and report to donors or who run projects that receive special donor funding outside of normal government channels. These people are essentially civil servants who become part of the aid system by default. International NGOs are staffed primarily by citizens of the countries they operate in, and national NGOs are aid recipients too. So most people working within the international development system are nationals of the country in which they are working, and many of them are actually working for national institutions. Of those, a small percentage will eventually end up taking overseas postings and shift over to become expat workers abroad. In poorer countries it is often just economic good sense to get into international development work because development agencies are the best employers in terms of pay and benefits.

People originating from countries that give aid rather than receive it tend to have a different trajectory into international development. Sometimes they have some direct link to international development or to the notion of working internationally; for example, a parent who worked as a diplomat. Sometimes they or their parents are immigrants, and they feel a cultural or emotional connection to the country they came from and see international development as a way of giving back, or traveling back, or simply making good use of their linguistic and cultural knowledge. And some Westerners who get into international development have none of these connections, but they are interested in traveling or else they got exposed to the idea of development through university or the advertising for a volunteer program.

"Missionaries, mercenaries, and misfits" is the half-joking, half-serious popular classification of those who work internationally and especially in humanitarian or "hardship" situations. Some anthropologists argue that most international development workers, especially Westerners, are characterized by a particular kind of "liberal bourgeoisie" mind-set that is, in many ways, a legacy of historical colonial relations.[2] While many individuals working in international development might take exception to that, others might fear it to be true.

While some people drift into development work incidentally, increasing numbers of people deliberately choose to study international development and pursue it as a profession. According to their professors, students taking international development as their major tend to be idealistic and globally minded. In many programs, they tend to be academic high achievers. In Canadian universities at least, more women than men are enrolled in international development courses. In Western countries, students are typically a mix of national and international students, although the presence or absence of international scholarships can make a big difference to who is present and who is absent. Young students with little or no experience of international development often have a fairly abstract and ideal view of it. One professor, who has also worked as a development practitioner, says of her students,

> I think they are as naive as I was, at the beginning. So in the first class, I always ask them to write down or talk about why they want to do development, and all of them want to change others or to bring them something. And I think through this experience, they see alternatives too—about what is this development, what does it mean, what am I going to do? To ask questions, that's important, not to hold the truth all the time but to ask questions.

In some countries, students' programs of study are determined by marks rather than by students' choice, and in countries where job opportunities are limited, opportunity is always a factor in shaping what a student chooses to go into. If good-quality employment options are to be had through international development agencies, students will pursue the opportunity. Still, for most students who study development, it is fair to say that they are motivated and moved by the inequities, poverty, and suffering that they see, whether in person or through the media, and that they want to put their energy toward remedying these.

For many people, the choice to go into international development is motivated by a mix of lifestyle aspirations—we want to travel, to have adventure and different experiences, combined with the sense that we can make a positive difference; we can be a positive force for change in the world and relieve some of the suffering brought about by poverty. That initial impulse, especially for those from the West, is often a rather romantic and abstract one. Sheilagh Henry recalls her first childhood ideas about wanting to work overseas:

> When I was in grade eight, my teacher did that assignment—where will you be in twenty-five years? And I wrote that I was living beside the Nile, a navigable river—because that's how my friends and family were going to visit me, and I had an adobe hut, and a cat—

and close enough to the town that I'd have a lot of friends there, and close to the people to help them, and close to the river so my family would come and visit.

Clearly, our own sense of identity and motivation is linked with our ideas about the world more broadly. Why is there poverty and suffering in the world? What are its causes, and what are the solutions? What role might we play in bringing about a solution? Is there an attached moral obligation, or a motive of enlightened self-interest, that should drive us, or our countries, into action? Our ideas are influenced by our own experiences and observations or by things we have read, heard, seen, or been told about.

For many people from a comfortable economic background, the personal motive, or justification, to engage in international development is at least in part an ethical one. Coming from a situation of relative plenty, and knowing that there are other people living in relative scarcity and suffering because of it, one arguably has a moral imperative to do something.[3] Or, more mildly, it seems like a more meaningful occupation than making a rich business owner richer through one's efforts.

Some people recall specific high-profile events as points at which they became conscious of the immensity of human suffering and that fueled their desire to play some role in alleviating it. These include epic disasters such as the Nigerian-Biafran War of 1967–71 or the Ethiopian famine of 1984. For others, they are influenced by their schooling. Karolina Olofsson, who was working for Integrity Watch Afghanistan when we spoke, was attending high school when she decided to pursue her career path:

> I remember it very clearly when I decided I wanted to go into this line of work. It was my first year of high school. . . . There was this professor and he assigned us a conflict, to research, analyze, and understand. I chose Burma, not knowing much about it, and I felt there was such a huge injustice. Just because one or several individuals, mostly men, want to have something to make them feel better, they abuse their power and resources and ignore the grievances of the entire population. Because of that greed, entire masses suffered, and I remember thinking that's it, that's what I want to do, that's what I want to fight against.

Other people are immigrants or second-generation Americans, Canadians, or Europeans who decide they want to contribute to their parents' country of origin. One young development worker I spoke with was adopted and grew up in Sweden. She knew her birth family lived in a dangerous slum in Colombia and suffered because of it. This personal connection motivated her to get involved in international development.

Personal motivations can be even more direct in the form of a personal experience or direct observation of poverty or war. Bai Mankay Sankoh, from Sierra Leone, decided to study economic development after seeing the disastrous effects of poor economic and political leadership in his own country. He eventually joined the World Food Programme. John Gathuya grew up in rural Kenya and says he saw both the need for effective development projects and the problems that arose when development workers failed to listen to local people. So he also got involved in development and today works for an international development agency in Kenya.

Many development workers are motivated in part by religious or humanitarian doctrines exhorting us to be of service to humanity. People I spoke with cited Christian, Jewish, Buddhist, Muslim, and Baha'i teachings, as well as nonsectarian humanitarian principles, as sources of insight and inspiration.

Whatever the specific experiences or values that motivate people to work in development, however abstract or grounded they may be, they share a common characteristic. Those who make a deliberate choice to work in international development feel a sense of responsibility to stimulate social change.

Filters to International Development Work: Hiring and the Dual Labor Market

While your desire to work in international development may seem a personal, individual matter, realizing this desire usually requires persuading someone to hire you or to fund your work in some way. The labor market operates on the assumption that not all candidates are equal. So who tends to be favored when international development organizations are looking for workers?

Hiring practices within international development mirror practices in the broader job market. Formal selection criteria include a heavy emphasis on educational qualifications and relevant work experience. As with other employment, the people doing the hiring often have strong informal preferences for people they feel most comfortable with. These include people whom they or their contacts know or who are similar to them in mind-set, education, or other ways that reassure them their hires are likely to be dependable.

One particularity of international development is the dual labor market—the distinction within international agencies between national and international positions. The conditions of employment are different depending on whether one is hired as a national or an international, with the remuneration typically much higher for internationals. International staff may also receive other perks such as housing and travel allowance. This is justified by the fact that the average national wage is often much lower than the average international professional wage. In fact, national wages in the development sector are often far above the national average wage. This is sometimes seen to have a negative and distorting effect on the local economy, especially in areas where many aid agencies operate. It can also influence national workers to leave socially valuable but poorly remunerated positions in the government and private sector to compete for fairly menial jobs in development agencies when the conditions of employment are relatively attractive. For example, I have a Ugandan friend who left his teaching career to become a driver for a large international NGO, which pays much better.

The different employment conditions for international and national staff, who may otherwise have similar capacities and responsibilities, often results in tension. One way of resolving this tension is to justify the higher remuneration of internationals by emphasizing the relative importance of their jobs, which then creates hierarchies between the national staff and the international staff. Speaking of her experience as an Iranian working for UNICEF in Iran after the Bam earthquake, Sogol Zand recalls,

> There were a lot of clashes, big clashes between the internationals and locals. All of us were very educated there. You didn't see any difference. But usually, when the internationals arrived, first they'd say, "All right, now we're going to make things different here."

This is a difficult dynamic that is hard to get away from. Development workers have to face the uncomfortable realities of global inequalities within their own workplaces, with two different sorts of economies stitched together along a jagged, ugly seam.

Most jobs in international development require a master's degree, and national jobs typically require an undergraduate degree. These requirements are relatively recent and reflect broader trends in the job market. Whether they always enhance the overall quality of work is debatable. What these requirements do is up the stakes for people to invest in their own education before they're able to work in international development. This tendency for "educational inflation" is as true for people from, and working in, developing countries as it is for people from the West. Although scholarships can even things out a little, this means that most people who gain the formal credentials necessary to compete for development jobs are from relatively well-off families. Many people get into international development by first volunteering. When volunteers are required to cover living and travel expenses, this further raises the financial costs of entering development as a career.

The most powerful aid institutions often prefer to hire from Ivy League schools. This can have the ironic effect of re-creating class hierarchies within organizations that claim to be committed to fighting poverty. Of the United Nations, Michael Soussan says it "is not a place where people start in the mailroom and end up in management. Myriad rules are there to prevent support staff from moving to higher levels of professional responsibility. We're not talking about a glass ceiling here. More like reinforced concrete with armoured plates."[4]

Although far from universal, the trend is that development workers tend to come from the comfortable middle class, irrespective of their country of origin. Those who don't come from the middle class often comment on this fact about themselves because they recognize themselves as a minority within the cadres of international development workers. Tom Vincent, who grew up in Texas, explains the link between his own background and his choice to work in development:

> I grew up not in the world's greatest neighborhoods, and it was my background to see how difficult it is to cope with poverty, to cope when bad things happen to you, and no one reaches out to you. I always wanted to make up for that. . . . I'm not the usual sort of person who gets into this, and I used to think, and still do, that there are lots of kids in the places like where I grew up who would make great development workers. But you're not encouraged to think like that—you're not encouraged to get graduate degrees; people's expectations of you are low.

The idea that development work is a profession that carries some marker of status, that it's a "noble occupation" for those who can rise up to it, seems to be on the increase. Fifteen or twenty years ago, many people working in international development fell into it or dabbled in it; they thought of it not as a fixed career path but as something that they would do for a few years before returning to work in their home country. But increasingly, those drawn to international development see it as a career possibility from the outset—something that can be chosen and studied for and pursued. The trend appears to be global.

GB Bandara, who went to university in India some years ago, found himself back then "a bit of an oddball" when he chose to work for a development NGO. But now, he observes,

> The development industry is becoming its own sector, a good career choice. People going to top universities in India are consciously taking the choice of coming into community development or development—and I'm sure the same is true in the West. So it's becoming, I think, a career choice for many people. I don't know if it was before like that, but it is a big change I see with young people.

In Uganda, the first program in development studies began at Makerere University ten years ago. Now all universities in Uganda offer development studies, and Makerere has recently introduced a policy that all undergraduate students should take one course in development studies.[5] Throughout the world, new graduate-level professional programs in international development have opened up in recent years.

While this trend toward professionalization creates potential to improve development practice, it also exaggerates existing tendencies to filter people, so that those who work in development are more likely to be relatively privileged.[6] An American development professional, working as a senior political expert in East Africa, worries about this trend. She says,

> There's a degree of clientelism involved in it. . . . I think many development professionals view themselves as the "haves" and the recipients of development as the "have-nots." . . . It's a bit of an "I'm better than you" mentality. . . . It's true that the professional, if they're any good, should bring skills that their clients need, but we should also see that the client also has stuff to bring to the table.

Given the idealism that draws many to work in international development, it's ironic that the filters into the international development workforce can reinforce social and economic hierarchies that they hoped to oppose. Likewise, once people become development professionals, they inhabit the awkward space between the "haves" and the "have-nots."

International development is founded on the transfer of resources from rich countries to poor countries. This is driven in part by the vastly unequal distribution of resources between countries. The role of development practitioners is essentially that of a bridge or a broker between two worlds: the world of having, and the world of not having. They must balance the expectations of those who give with the expectations and interests of those who are judged to be in need and so receive. And this means that they are often people caught between worlds. They are caught in the politics between worlds: the ideas, the interests, the culture, the values—all of it.

As brokers, development workers face constant contradiction because not all interest groups have equal power to negotiate what they want. There may be instances where interests and views align and there is no inherent conflict between them, but these are quite rare. And development workers themselves may often be more aligned with one group than another.

It is entirely possible to be a middle- or upper-class person committed to issues of an international nature or to fighting poverty. In fact, there are many such people who have a deep and genuine dedication. But these people will often face an inherent conflict of interest in their work because the international development system often accords them more authority than people who might have a greater understanding of the situation. If they are really conscientious and committed, they must constantly be aware of this and try to transfer or extend their authority to those best suited to act. On the other side, people who do not have as much social or political standing may find that, despite being motivated and able to act as agents of change, the development system may marginalize them from doing so.

Insiders and Outsiders: Knowledge and Power

Ideas about knowledge define the role of the development worker. These ideas are embedded in the power structures. Indeed, it is the more powerful people and countries that are able to say what knowledge is important and even, as in the case of the international financial institutions, prescribe policy as a condition of receiving aid. In this section, we review the justification for expert technical knowledge and its limitations in application to real-world development issues. Despite calls for more participatory "bottom-up" approaches to the way we value, share, and apply knowledge, international development practice has been extremely robust in maintaining its knowledge hierarchies. We end the section by looking at psychological explanations of how development workers tend to do this.

Technical Expertise: Justifying the Need for Outside Help
What justifies the need for outsiders from other countries, or other communities, to intervene in development in the first place? One of the biggest

justifications is the knowledge that they bring. As we saw in chapter 2, this stems all the way back to Truman's "Four Point" speech in 1949, when he stated that America's greatest gift to the world, more so than funding, was the great technical knowledge of her people. The transfer-of-technology and technological know-how has been one of the foundational and most enduring ideas in international development.

Sometimes outsiders bring in particular technical expertise, facilitation and training skills, or ideas from other places. People working in international development may be water engineers, human rights lawyers, political scientists, anthropologists, social workers, doctors, economists, educational experts, or agronomists, for example. A key question that cuts across all these areas is how much the expertise gained under one set of assumptions or in one culture may be applicable in another one. Technical knowledge can certainly be useful in varying contexts. There is an obvious benefit to bringing a doctor to an area that does not have any medical care, for example. On the other hand, there seems to be a certain arrogance embedded in the assumption that external, often Western, knowledge is more advanced than the knowledge of the people who are to receive this lauded advice. And from a more Machiavellian perspective, technical advice can provide an easy pretext for pushing the interests of the country providing the advice. Expert economic advice about opening markets and reducing trade barriers can seem particularly suspicious in this regard.

Insider-Outsider Tension

People working in development are professional interveners. Most come in as outsiders to the communities that their work affects. They may be coming from another country. Even within the same country, they are often coming from another area and from a different class and lifestyle than the people they are aiming to serve through their work. The fact that outsiders have such a prominent and important role in international development and that accountability is often to the outside—to funders located away from the project area—lends international development some of its paradoxical character.

Those outside a community may neither understand it nor be truly invested in what happens to it. Despite all the rhetoric of learning from the beneficiaries that has become standard in the past few decades, it is still shockingly easy for development actors to routinely overlook beneficiaries' views or to manipulate them to fit what they would have done anyway. Astrid de Valon recounts,

> Sometimes when you enter your office in the morning, you really wonder—does everyone know who we are working for? We do not

work for a structure, for a head office, or to provide donors with reports. We need to keep beneficiaries at the center of our operations. I was really shocked that the Irish government evaluation on what impact their support through implementing partners has had in the reduction of poverty included 230 consultant days with travel, but not a single interview with the beneficiaries!

While the views of those who are supposed to benefit from development efforts are often overlooked, the knowledge of so-called experts is often greatly overstated. Mary Abukutsa recalls many international consultants coming into Kenya without any knowledge of the context. She explains, "There was one brought in as a tea expert, but he couldn't recognize the tea plant when we brought him there!"

Mary has noted some slight improvement in international development in this respect—less reliance on international "experts" and more reliance on nationals. This makes sense as national capacity in various technical areas increases and as donor attitudes become less paternalistic. But the change is often slower than we might presume, and there are still many development organizations that bar national staff from senior positions, as we saw with Dave's former employer at the start of this chapter.

How Useful Is Technical Expertise in Addressing Development Issues?

One problem international experts are likely to face is whether their expertise is able to address the issues that they encounter. Most people working in international development, whether national or international, and whatever their area of expertise, end up dealing much more with systems, people, and social change issues than with narrow technical issues. This is particularly true as they gain seniority and rise to more senior posts. For example, Claudia Hudspeth, chief of health and nutrition for UNICEF in Uganda at the time we spoke, explained,

> I think the issues are very, very simple, public-health-wise; it's not the "what." The what is so simple to design programmatically . . . it's the doing that's the challenge. . . . The what right now is safe water and access to care. It's not about complex tertiary care; it's about primary basic health. You can have such a big impact—that's why I went into health care. But now . . . I think we don't need to talk about what is needed to change children's lives, but it's about how. We don't spend a lot of time thinking about that. I think it

comes with experience, that it's not about the details of is it going to be this medicine or that medicine—it's actually getting the medicine there that matters.

In other words, Claudia, who has expertise in medicine and public health, finds that the issues related to improving health care in Uganda are challenging not at a technical level but rather at a social and policy level. It isn't about bringing in doctors; it's about creating a health system that can keep its doctors. Many of them leave in frustration, not just because of the potential for making more money elsewhere but also because the health system is so dysfunctional that they can't do their jobs. One Ugandan doctor who had moved to Australia explained to me the frustrations of working in Uganda. Hospitals often didn't have medicines because they were diverted to private clinics, and everything required a bribe. One time an accident victim came into the emergency ward in critical state. The doctor had to go herself to get blood for a transfusion, and the person working in the blood unit wouldn't give it to her without a bribe. She told him that without the blood the person would die. The technician was unmoved. He answered that people died every day and asked what it was worth to her. So it's not about the "what," it's about the "how."

However, as outsiders, what we usually lack is knowledge of the local context, which is so crucial for understanding how to start tackling the "how." Sometimes those coming into work don't know the local language, or they have limited knowledge of the history, culture, politics, customs, ecology, or local concerns and perspectives. International development tends to systematically undervalue all of this local knowledge and to overvalue formalized and generalized forms of knowledge, the sort that comes with a formal degree. Such accounting in favor of formal, general knowledge over informal, local knowledge is hard to justify in practice, because the latter is usually essential in solving development issues. It seems fairly obvious to say that solutions to poverty must be predicated on an understanding of the social, economic, political, and ecological contexts in which the poor live. And yet development workers often move between countries and continents to new positions because this knowledge isn't highly weighted in hiring practices.

The Movement to Value Local Knowledge

Robert Chambers has been one of the most cogent voices to argue for a reversal in the way we value knowledge in development.[7] This viewpoint began to gain mainstream currency in the late 1980s. He argued that the simplistic and abstracted knowledge of development experts is often not particularly relevant or useful when applied to the complex realities of the poor, whereas those living in poverty have rich insights into their own condition and needs. He called for development experts to "hand over the stick" and listen to poor people. Chambers's view of a development professional focuses on an ethos that includes a moral commitment to working together to fight poverty, the humility to listen and learn, and a series of techniques that are all process focused and seek to shift the balance of power and knowledge generation toward development beneficiaries. The idea of a professional's role in international development as being one of process rather than of content has had an enduring influence on many people.

The popularity of participatory development, adopted by such staid institutions as the World Bank, brought great excitement in the 1990s among many people who saw that international development could potentially be undergoing a transformation for the better, becoming more democratic and responsive to the needs of the poor. Chambers's call hit a chord with many sympathetic development workers, who were cautiously delighted at seeing its broader influence. And yet in the end a substantial transformation never materialized. The status quo largely continued undaunted.[8] Some of the reasons for this can be explained by the broader political, economic, and social factors described in chapter 3 and by the characteristics and tendencies of development institutions explored in chapter 4. But some of the reasons for the resilience of the development hierarchy are essentially psychological. Even though foreign development workers generally share a philosophical belief in the rightness of "bottom-up" development, they are conditioned to a system that functions differently and that in so doing favors them. It is hard to break out.

Subconscious Tendencies to Cling to Privilege

Despite our best intentions, we human beings are not well constituted to voluntarily give up power and privilege. We're also demonstrably bad at recognizing our own weaknesses and limitations. Jonathan Haidt reviews the evidence from psychological studies showing that people routinely overestimate their own skills and virtue. This tendency is so stubborn that he concludes, "Even when you grab people by the lapels, shake them and say, 'Listen to me! Most people have an inflated view of themselves. Be realistic!' they refuse, muttering to themselves, 'Well, other people may be biased, but I really am above average on leadership.'"[9] So when we find ourselves in positions of relative privilege, we tend to justify it to ourselves by assuming that we deserve it, that our skills are indeed more valuable, and that our limitations are indeed of minor issue.

Of equal importance, when we start working in international development, we learn subconsciously just as we learn consciously. And again, human beings are demonstrably, and sometimes terrifyingly, good at adapting themselves to assigned roles and social norms. The famous Stanford Prison Experiment showed how powerful social forces can be in shaping our behavior. After vigorously screening a group of male college students, the experimenters took in only those who were most psychologically normal and well adjusted. They randomly assigned them to two groups, prisoners and guards. They set up the basement of one of the buildings to be a "prison" and gave the guards uniforms and instructed them to keep order but not to use excessive force. The prisoners were likewise given prison uniforms and brought into the prison through a typical intake procedure. Although the experiment was due to run for two weeks, the experimenters had to end it after six days. Because the young men had so quickly and completely assumed their roles, many of the guards were engaging in such sadistic behavior that the group's well-being was judged to be at risk.[10]

International development interventions, since they involve power imbalances, knowledge gaps, and differences in perspectives, as well as a high degree of complexity, may cause us to be particularly prone to these powerful psychological forces of self-serving bias and social conformity. Much of this is difficult for us to come to terms with because it is largely subconscious and invisible to us. We are able to observe these tendencies in others but are often blind to them in ourselves. We tend to be especially blind to biases or privileges that benefit us. We may think of ourselves as very egalitarian, but we still may unconsciously use such privilege very easily. Likewise, we can be unaware of the extent to which others give us preferential treatment or ignore inappropriate behavior if we come from the "right" background. Development anthropologists have been particularly good at pointing this out to us. For example, Crewe and Harrison describe an instance in which a cheerful British development worker walks casually into the house of a community member to look at her stove.[11] The local people are visibly taken aback at this, although they do not complain, and he appears unaware he's done anything out of place. It certainly isn't a social norm to walk into a stranger's house uninvited in Britain. Did he really think it was appropriate behavior in this setting, or was he unconsciously making use of his privilege?

Another intriguing example of the strange behavior of expat development workers comes from another carefully observed case of foreign development workers in Madagascar.[12] In this instance, a young French woman was first thrust into the role of gender programmer, apparently for the sole reason she was a woman. The agency for which she works is concerned that some local women are involved in prostitution. It is decided that they need some sort of empowering alternative. The development worker has therefore decided to teach them how to cook some dishes, with the idea they could start a small restaurant or catering business. But, among other issues, the recipes are French and their ingredients are too expensive for the women to buy. The resulting dishes would probably not have much demand among customers, who again wouldn't be able to afford them anyway. Nonetheless, the project proceeds, and the local women treat the whole event as a party. They get to spend time together and cook and eat strange exotic food that they can't normally afford. They know it wouldn't be a viable business, and they don't waste much time thinking about it.

Why did the French development worker not see through some of the glaring flaws in her reasoning? How typical can this really be? When we consider the structural, social, and psychological forces at work, they all blinded the development worker to her own limitations and the limitations of her intervention. The removal of normal social cues and controls combined with ignorance and power is a recipe for behavior that would usually be considered unacceptable. These sorts of conditions are widespread in the development system, and they make the likelihood of embarrassingly bad development projects all the greater. And according to the psychological evidence, we're each much more at risk of making these errors than we'd like to believe.

Conclusion

Both our view of development and our place within the development system will change over time. The way the development system treats us will bring out different aspects of ourselves. If we want to maintain as much conscious control as possible, we need to be critically aware of both the system and ourselves. Otherwise, we risk being like the students in the Stanford Prison Experiment or like some of the seemingly unthinking development workers documented in various ethnographies—defined by our socially prescribed roles.

Many of us join international development because we genuinely want to contribute something positive. Perhaps we start off a little naive; perhaps we'd also like to travel and enjoy ourselves. But our intentions are, on the whole, good. If the intentions are solid enough, and if we're willing to be self-critical, then it needn't matter so much what our initial backgrounds are, because we can learn. We have to work around, and factor in, however, the way the system will treat us.

The globalizing world is full of inequalities, inequalities in lifestyle, incomes, access, and rights. When we enter international development, we come cheek by jowl with these. They become personal, because they become about us and our coworkers, us and the people around us, us and the people whose lives are directly or indirectly affected by our work. And so international development itself is full of inherent contradictions, claiming to be fighting poverty and exclusion while being exclusionary. In some sense, it can't help reflecting the order of the world it belongs to. But it often seems to re-create that order, the same order it claims it wants to change. And if we, as development workers, believe we are trying to change inequalities rather than maintain them, we have to play a very difficult balancing game. It's impossible to sidestep these contradictions altogether. But the key argument of this book is that it is possible to fruitfully work within these contradictions. This requires a careful balancing act and a lot of critical awareness. In the next two chapters, we look further at this process of adjusting and balancing.

Notes

1. DevEx, one of the largest online job databases for international development positions, claims to have over 375,000 individual members registered as of November 1, 2011. See http://www.devex.com/en/.

2. Barbara Heron, *Desire for Development: Whiteness, Gender, and the Helping Imperative* (Waterloo, ON: Wilfrid Laurier University Press, 2007), 27–41.

3. David Crocker, *International Development Ethics.* Paper presented at the Twentieth World Congress of Philosophy, Boston, MA, August 10–15, 1998.

4. Michael Soussan, *Backstabbing for Beginners: My Crash Course in International Diplomacy* (New York: Nation Books, 2008), 728–36.

5. Interview with Mwambutsya Ndebesa, Professor of history and development studies at Makerere University, on April 21, 2011.

6. Uma Kothari, "Authority and Expertise: The Professionalisation of International Development and the Ordering of Dissent," *Antipode* 37, no. 3 (2005).

7. Robert Chambers, *Challenging the Professions: Frontiers for Rural Development* (London: Intermediate Technology Development Group, 1993).

8. Bill Cooke and Uma Kothari, eds., *Participation: The New Tyranny?* (London: Zed Books, 2001).

9. Jonathan Haidt, *The Happiness Hypothesis: Finding Modern Truth in Ancient Wisdom* (New York: Basic Books, 2006), 71.

10. Philip Zimbardo, Christina Maslach, and Craig Hanley, "Reflections on the Stanford Prison Experiment: Genesis, Transformations, Consequences," in *Obedience to Authority: Current Perspectives on the Milgram Paradigm*, ed. Thomas Blass (London: Psychology Press, 2000).

11. Emma Crewe and Elizabeth Harrison, *Whose Development? An Ethnography of Aid* (London: Zed Books, 1999), 2–3.

12. Rita Verma, "Intercultural Encounters, Colonial Continuities and Contemporary Disconnects in Rural Aid: An Ethnography of Development Practitioners in Madagascar," in *Inside the Everyday Lives of Development Workers: The Challenges and Futures of Aidland*, ed. Anne-Meike Fechter and Heather Hindman (Sterling, VA: Kumarian Press, 2010).

6

Learning the System

Ajay[1] grew up in a remote rural village in a poor mountainous country. The village had no running water or electricity and was far from any roads. The mathematics and English-language teachers, coming from outside, typically lasted only a few months until they fled back to the comforts of the city. Ajay saw his first car when he was sixteen years old and heading to the capital city for the first time in his life, going to pre-university studies. As one of the top students in his district and the best student in his rural school, he barely managed to gain entrance to the university, having to compete against much better prepared students in the city. Still, he succeeded and was one of a very few people from his village to obtain such an education.

At university, Ajay studied applied science with an agriculture and rural development focus. These were topics that seemed of direct relevance to the farmers of his village. But he found that there was a gap between the theories he learned and the needs of the people he'd grown up with. On the last day of his undergraduate exams, he recalls, a professor said to him, "Ajay, you're the best student in a hundred. We have taught you for four years, now this is your chance to ask us a question." Surprised, Ajay quickly cast his mind to the problems faced by people in his village and asked his professor the same question that they had been asking him when he went back home on his term breaks, a question that had never been touched on in any of his classes—"How can we protect our crops from being eaten by monkeys?" The professor could only suggest growing hot chili and ginger, crops that the monkeys wouldn't eat. But the villagers, living far from the markets, depended on growing their own rice, wheat, and corn to eat. If they had tried to follow the professor's advice, they would have starved.

When he finished his undergraduate studies, Ajay got a job as an agricultural extension officer for the national government. Much of the government's funding came from international donors such as the World Bank, and sometimes donors attached conditions to influence the work. Again, he found that there was a gap between his own ideas of how development should work and what the government demanded of him. He recalls,

> I had one idea that I'd be able to compare organic and inorganic vegetable farming in a small plot with farmers, and the farmers were also interested, but when I came back to the office and talked to my boss, he said, "You know, Ajay, this is not our job; our job is to promote new technologies—not to show that the old technology is good."

After some years in the government, Ajay won a scholarship to a master's program in Europe. He found the program to be rich and stimulating, particularly the exchange between the students, who came from many different low-income countries. He came back to his job anxious to share what he had learned and put it into practice. But he found this was very difficult to do. It seemed to him that the government system was interested in self-perpetuation and rewarding political connections, and little else: "If you want to make a difference, you need to change all those connections there—the political economy—and that is a huge task." He decided to again leave and pursue a PhD, this time in North America, continuing to research issues related to rural development and agricultural extension. This time he did not return and instead stayed in the West to teach the theory and practice of international development to a new generation of undergraduate students.

Reflecting on his experiences and his choices, Ajay says that staying in his own country, where he found himself unable to effect the change he wanted, was a case of "brain decay," while leaving his country was "brain drain." Now, he is seeking a way to "brain recycle" through his teaching and research. Some of the students he teaches, most of whom are Westerners, will go to his country, some to the same community he came from. He believes that, as outsiders, they have a better chance of leveraging change than he did:

> I'd rather stay in the region, but now I'm free, I can critique [the government] more openly, and if I'm able to continue my work in international development, I feel I can make more difference than if I was doing the same thing for the government. I have more freedom to explore, better resources. . . . We're trying to teach nineteen-year-old kids in the West how things happen in developing countries, and very few of them have the experience of developing

countries. I feel that I have the obligation to teach them, because they are coming to development from the top, and I came to it from the bottom. I'd be able to tell some stories and make a difference. You know, the life experience of the dominant international development worker and my life experience are completely different. And that way, through education, it comes back full circle. . . . These undergrads are very committed, and they could work as a critical mass to change how development is working.

If I take five of my students and lead them to my country and bring them to my previous bosses, they would listen to those five kids more than to me.

When I asked Ajay if he didn't feel frustrated by the fact that his much-less-well-qualified students would be taken as experts when he, who taught them, was discounted, he shrugged and said that is just the way it is. He sees it as part of the legacy of the colonial past. Having accepted this, Ajay has managed, according to his own understanding of the forces prevailing against him, to find a way to work within and influence the international development system. And as he says, the commitment of these students, as young and inexperienced as they may initially be, bodes well for what the future of development could be.

Most people coming into international development are in a position closer to Ajay's students, with the same historically conferred privileges that, if used wisely and conscientiously, could be a chance to effect change within international development so that it is more responsive to its target beneficiaries. We can't know if these efforts will be enough to change the system, and there is also the danger they may simply perpetuate it, despite their best intentions. As with Ajay, they must each test their assumptions and seek out a niche from which they can work in a way that fits with their own ideas, priorities, and strengths. This is a process of discovery and balancing that is particularly important during the early years of our careers, but it continues throughout our work lives.

The previous chapter looked at what motivates people to work in international development, how they get in, and the roles they adopt once they enter. In this chapter, we continue their journey by looking at two forms of adjustment that development workers all face. First, people have to face up to the mismatches between the way they thought international development would work and what they find. Second, they must balance among working effectively, making good career choices, and managing their personal and family lives.

Learning the System: Expectations Meet Experience

When we first enter international development, we also learn about the international development system, which many of us hoped or assumed would be much more rational, effective, and apolitical than we find it to be once we get up close.

Because learning about international development, whether through school or through firsthand experience, is often a process of revising assumptions downward, it can be frustrating, disillusioning, and disheartening for many people. Many professors who have taught international development note that their students come in with large expectations and then frequently undergo a crisis of confidence and become quite cynical. A senior university administrator explains,

> Many come in thinking that they want to change the world, they want to be part of that. . . . And after three years, I often hear them say, "I got my degree and I've learnt that I should stay home—development doesn't work." They hear all the failures, it seems really negative—they learn about how development can be bad. . . . And also they don't learn any practical skills—they don't learn anything other than why the world is screwed up. They think they're going to learn international development to learn how to make a difference, and instead they learn that those who went to make a difference made a bad difference, and they don't have any skills to make a difference anyway.

People's experiences when they go out to work are more varied, as international development tends to be more diverse in actuality. There are some people who don't really experience much frustration in their work and immediately find a role in which they feel satisfied. Perhaps they had more realistic expectations to start out with, or are blessed with a particularly supportive work environment, or are just oblivious to the limitations of their efforts.[2] But most people starting out in development are surprised or disappointed by the development system in at least a few ways. Four of the most common are as follows:

1. *Politics and development:* Realizing the extent to which international development is influenced by politics, which often overrides its stated goals, such as alleviating poverty;

2. *Aid institutions:* Realizing the various flaws of aid institutions, whether they be donors, NGOs, the UN, or contractors;

3. *Other people:* Becoming frustrated because people, whether donors, coworkers, partners, or beneficiaries, don't act the way we think they should; and

4. *Paper-pushing:* Finding themselves trapped in bureaucracies writing reports and going to meetings rather than working directly "out in the field" with the poor.

One issue that lies behind all of these concerns is complexity. Development work is often a lot more complicated than we imagined. We didn't imagine the chains of relationships, the tangle of mixed and competing philosophies, interests, and personalities. We tended to imagine that someone, somewhere knew what was going on and that the distance between cause and effect would be short and the path more or less self-evident. But that is rarely what we find. Let's look at each of these areas of surprise or disappointment and see what some of the common concerns are and what are some typical approaches for resolving them.

Politics and Development

We already saw in part 1 that politics shapes development work in broad ways. However, not everyone working in development gets his or her face pressed immediately against the political dimensions in his or her work. Junior posts are often more shielded from the politics of funding and institutional decision making. Those working for donors and the UN, or working directly with recipient governments, are usually more exposed to politics. Many people learn more about political influence in development when they study it than they do through their early career. Of course, stepping back not very far, it is possible to see political influence throughout development, especially through funding. But like everything in development, it is not uniform.

A senior official at a UN agency explains, "The international development worker is an ideologist, and there are factors that cause us to compromise. For the UN the factor is political consideration."

For most people, the influence of politics is not a great revelation, but people can feel disappointed in their particular agencies when they seem less principled and more politically influenced than they had hoped. And politics comes in cycles, so when the political winds shift within a particular country, it can change the whole development scene. One donor staff explains,

Right now I'd say most of the Western aid agencies are having a bit of difficulty because of changes in volume and politics—Norwegians, Dutch, even—because most people in ID are left of center, and most governments have gone in the other direction, and we have some difficulties—to implement policies we don't really agree with. Part of it is just accepting it's our job and this is how it works, but also when you're on the ground and implementing, you do have a lot of leeway in how a project is implemented. You can't alter the volumes of the funds, but you still have a lot of leeway in how the funds are directed on the ground.

When a particular institution or situation becomes so politicized so as to make work difficult or meaningless, some development workers may try to act as buffers and continue to uphold the "ideology" of apolitical development, others will choose to leave, others will drift along, and others may speak out.

One man I spoke with was working for Denmark's Ministry of Foreign Affairs in Eritrea when the government decided to pull its aid program from that country for reasons that were in large part politically driven. He strongly believed the government was making the wrong decision, and so he spoke out against it publicly:

I wrote letters to the minister, the press—I put my job right on the line, most organizations would have fired me—I never expected to work for the Danish Ministry of Foreign Affairs again. So I frankly thought I'd never work for this organization again—I'd put the dirt all over the papers. However, I did—because underneath the minister and so forth, there were some very well-intentioned people who could appreciate my sense of frustration, and when I checked whether it was worth applying for another job [in DANIDA], I was told that of course it was, in no uncertain terms.

Although he didn't stop Denmark from pulling out of Eritrea, he shared his opinions publicly and, luckily, continued with his career. This decision to speak out publicly on issues of aid and politics was motivated by a deeper personal commitment to the principles underlying his work. Likewise, many people working in development may choose to get involved in political issues as private citizens, based in part on what they learn through their work.

Anyone working in Afghanistan is likely to face the reality that while political influences have led to the availability of funding, they have also led to poor development decisions. One donor staff explained to me how multi-million-dollar projects were rapidly approved for Afghanistan that would never have been approved for another country, because of the great political pressure to spend. For most people, however they choose to respond to it, politics is ultimately a force to be worked within. As one person says of his experience working in Afghanistan and Pakistan,

> [These are countries] where development is shaped by the whole political system. To change that you have to change the whole god-damn political system in the globe. I don't know if you can have that as an ambition, although you can be critical.

Aid Institutions

We already saw in chapter 4 many of the limitations of aid institutions. They can be ineffective, inefficient, disorganized, and focused more on their own survival than on their stated mission. At their worst they can be hierarchical, hypocritical, and discriminatory in their practices, hijacked by political agendas or entirely corrupt. When development workers enter such organizations and face these flaws, they often feel very disappointed.

Jean-Luc Lemahieu, head of Mission for the UNODC in Afghanistan, explains that he has always been disappointed after he has joined an organization that he held in high esteem, because he ended up realizing that it was filled with human beings with all their weaknesses and foibles:

> It occurred to me, "The closer you stand to a big man the more you will see the dirt on his knees." . . . When joining the political Cabinet of the Minister of Cooperation and Development[3]—being invited to it was like becoming part of a holy place of enlightened political decision making. Yet once inside, you see the political mechanisms at work and the dirt of the game. One starts to realize that it is all humans set to work—nothing holy about it, humans with their strengths and shortcomings as individuals and as a team. Then I went to the UN, the imposing blue flag which I held in big esteem—a dream come true, becoming part of an entity where common people such as me should not have a place to start with. Yet again it was a rather disappointing experience. Most of my colleagues are as common as myself.

In Lemahieu's view, this realization is a simple process of maturation, of realizing how vulnerable and flawed we are as a species and how delicate and precious human cooperative action is. So in essence, it is about realizing our assumptions that someone somewhere knew what was going on and had all the answers were not true. Now, he says,

> My naïveté has vanished. I realize we're all humans, and within that realization I am amazed that we, as humankind, were able to get even a rocket landing on the moon. Yet it still scares me by moments that there's not one small room where there are the twelve super smartest people . . . who are making all the right decisions about humanity and correcting us, the mere humans. There isn't. We can easily destroy ourselves as a species; it's scary.

Of course, we can argue that we should indeed expect more from the international development system than it currently offers, that we need to hold it to a higher standard. Raising these issues and seeking to address them is important.

At an individual level, we are faced with the immediate question of what to do when we find a gap between our ideas and reality. At the very least, we need to adjust our ideas about the current situation, even if we stay steadfast to our ideas of how things could or should be. For most of us, this means revising our expectations downward and also being choosy about where to put our energies and which organizations to work with.

Other People

One surprise about people in development is just how much they matter—how much one person in a key position can influence the process, whether for good or for bad. A young development worker working on justice sector reform in Afghanistan explains,

> When you study international development, or even the legal system, in school—in theory it seems that it makes a lot more sense. It does make sense, but when you're in it, it seems a lot more chaotic. And also how much personality is involved, how much ego and personality is involved. That's the biggest surprise, how much a person's opinion can influence the process, whereas when I studied it in school, the focus was on the institution rather than the individual.

Other people have a habit of thinking differently than we do and wanting different things, often to our frustration. When individuals working in development seem less committed or less competent than we think they should be, this can be a source of disappointment and stress, as we will see in chapter 8.

It can also be frustrating when people don't need our help in exactly the way that we thought they would, or they feel differently about their needs and priorities than we thought they would. Elsa Powell, an American, faced this in Afghanistan. She was working as an advisor to an Afghan government ministry and had doubts about how effective she could be in the situation she was in:

> I felt like I was begging for a meeting with them. I thought, "This doesn't make any sense, they should be begging for a meeting with me—I'm the advisor." I've thought about it a lot, and I think it's because they don't have any stake in the game, there's zero incentive for partnership, and they don't want an advisor; they want someone to come in and do some work for them.

In this situation, no matter how hard Elsa worked to fulfill her role, the outcome was likely to be disappointing because many of the key people she was working with had different goals than she did. Fabienne Glauser, a program officer at CIDA, muses,

> I think the biggest thing [I learned] . . . for me as a development professional, we really have to manage our own expectations, because people do have the right to take it or leave it. Whether to use the tools available is ultimately the choice of the government and the people. . . . The role that I'd choose for myself in light of that is more that of a witness; I'd more like to bring tools and skills to bear that might support people in a country—they're going to do it their own way, and I think that is as it should be.

Fabienne is surely right, while Elsa's experience shows us that beyond managing our own expectations, we must understand the situation well enough to know what tools and skills might be relevant. In Kabul, I spoke with a senior advisor at a US consulting firm who has worked internationally as an organizational facilitator and organizer throughout his career. According to his analysis, frustrations about other people often come from a weak understanding of culture and motivation:

I see problems with some expats coming here [to Afghanistan], and their approach and frustration. . . . It's not a matter of developing or developed, but everyone has a culture—it's a matter of coming in and saying, what is the culture and where are the handles I can leverage?

I've been having big discussions here where people say, oh, Afghanistan is autocratic, and people don't learn and don't take initiative. My analysis is that like many places in the world, the relationship is key to doing work, and it's a hierarchical system. So if you want to get people to perform, don't do a performance appraisal system, because who's going to give a bad appraisal [when that will endanger the relationship]?

Once I was working in West Africa and Michigan simultaneously. The comparison was fascinating. In Michigan, the US culture values risk, so I had to rein them in. In Nigeria, working with West Africans, in many ways they were better educated people that I was working with there. They got what I wanted to do, they agreed with it, but it was like pushing on string, because taking initiatives and risk was not rewarded—you might offend your boss. So you had to push to get things moving. Each culture is unique, and it's got its unique ways of dealing with issues.

The need to understand others' motivations and perspectives applies to any unique situation or system. It is about understanding the incentives, priorities, and values of people within any given situation. Sometimes, though, we can feel we understand it to some degree, but we just disagree if we see people behaving selfishly, irresponsibly, corruptly, or outright criminally. And within cultures, there is plenty of room for varying opinions. More than any other factor, other people continually cause us to test our assumptions.

Paper-Pushing

Many of us get into development work because we like the idea of working with people in communities, but many of the positions in development organizations keep people behind desks and doing paperwork. John Gathuya imagined that working in development would put him back in the rural areas that he grew up in: "I thought international development would allow me to be on the ground—interacting with people, with the direct beneficiaries of international work. That's where the fun is . . . to see the impact, listen to people's stories, not to sit in the office and just interact with colleagues; it doesn't bring the real idea of development." Although John works for a major development agency, his career has been in administration and finance, and all of his work has been office based. Like John, Fabienne Glauser imagined she'd be working out in impoverished villages. Instead she holds a desk-based job with CIDA in Ottawa and rarely gets to visit the field. In both cases, they adapted their expectations and see real value in the roles that they play. While many people can appreciate that desk jobs may be a necessary part of aid work, and may have value, they find it harder to know what effect their work is having. One young UN staffer explains,

> When you're in the office a bit too long, motivation can really fall—
> if it's running around and doing contracts and payments, it feels a
> bit too detached. So my motivation sort of comes in waves, but at
> the end of the day, I still think that I'm proud to work for the UN,
> and what the UN stands for and tries to do.

Some people know they have no interest in working a desk job and so deliberately take positions where they'll spend time in the field, even if it means accepting less pay or avoiding promotions. On one level, this gives them more control and more satisfaction in their work. It also helps them to work below the radar as far as all the politics go.

But other people argue that by focusing only on the small and tangible, development efforts won't make a lasting difference. The next chapter considers this debate further. A senior UN official working on food issues explains how her views have evolved on this issue:

> As I assumed higher positions . . . that gave me insight into how
> the whole so-called development world works. I think it's naive to
> think we can make change only working with farmers—because it
> will only affect those farmers.

Adjusting

When I was a kid growing up in the United Kingdom, we used to come over to Canada for our summer holidays. The Canadian kids I played with would be fascinated by my accent. Sometimes they would ask me why I had an accent. When I tried to explain that they also had accents, albeit different from mine, they didn't believe me. The strangest thing was, although I normally couldn't hear my own accent either, after I had been in Canada for some time and got used to the way Canadians spoke, I could start hearing the British accent in my own voice. Similarly, for most of us, when we start working in international development, aspects of ourselves that were previously invisible will become clear when held up against new experiences and different ways of thinking. We may have held assumptions and ideas that seemed so obvious or universal that we weren't even aware we were holding them, until we find them contrasted against a reality that disproves them and others who think differently.

How we deal with the almost inevitable mismatches between our understanding and our experience is a major factor shaping our professional experiences within international development. In *The Reflective Practitioner*, Donald Schön argued that one's ability to experience and experiment with surprising outcomes in one's work is central to professional learning:

> The practitioner allows himself to experience surprise, puzzlement, or confusion in a situation which he finds uncertain or unique. He reflects on the phenomenon before him, and on the prior understandings which have been implicit in his behaviour. He carries out an experiment which serves to generate both a new understanding of the phenomenon and a change in the situation.[4]

While this can be true for those working in international development, they also face some likely complications in attempting to develop more accurate understanding. Expat workers especially are often dealing with newness on various levels—not just the specific development initiative but the whole cultural and social context in which it is taking place. Then development theories and the goals and markers by which success is defined and measured are also subject to frequent change, most often at the behest of the donors. And finally, many development workers, especially expats, tend to cycle through jobs and contexts every few years, so that context-specific understanding essentially gets lost. We'll be returning to these issues in the next chapter.

Besides learning the specifics of a particular work issue, our evolving understandings of how the development system operates influence our decisions about where we want to work, whom we want to work with, and under what conditions. Of course, our decisions about where to place ourselves in the system are not just based on our desire to be effective; we have to consider what opportunities we have and our broader career and personal aspirations. The next section is about this balance.

Evolving Goals: Balancing Work and Life

Whatever our motivations for wanting to work in international development, they must be accommodated among the other goals that we have for ourselves, such as being able to earn a living, to achieve social recognition and approval for our work, to be happy in our personal lives, and to fulfill familial obligations.

Sometimes these all fit together and complement each other well. Many people are drawn to international development in part because of the lifestyle it promises—the potential to travel, to experience challenges and even danger. Development work is often viewed as laudable and praiseworthy, and international professional posts are often well compensated.

And yet, as we've already seen, international development is full of contradictions that become more apparent as one becomes more acquainted with its workings. Its methods of accountability can create perverse incentives in which concern about the impact of one's work becomes an afterthought. And lifestyle aspirations change as people get older or go through different stages. What happens when one has had enough adventure? How can one balance the travel requirements of work with raising a healthy family? These questions become major preoccupations for many development workers. Even those who are most dedicated to ensuring their work is done well must still face and balance out these other, often competing, concerns.

This section considers some of the dilemmas and trade-offs that development workers face in balancing their desire to do good work with other needs and desires.

Career Goals

Despite their mission statements and lofty rhetoric, development institutions often don't reward the behavior that is most in keeping with these espoused goals. Both Ajay in this chapter and Dave in the previous chapter have faced this in their work. In fact, it might be difficult to find people who've been working in development for any length of time who haven't encountered this unfortunate truth at some point or another.

Wendy Quarry has an anecdote about the differences between rhetoric and actual expectations that development institutions place on their staff and partners. She knew a Mozambican government official who was carrying out a water project funded by the World Bank. The World Bank's terms of reference had specified a "demand-based" system in which the communities should both pay for and later manage their boreholes. Following these terms, the official was going through a consultative process with communities to set all this up. Doing such things well requires time, and he took a year. But the World Bank was not happy with him and put him under great pressure to hurry up. Wendy saw a World Bank officer and asked her why the bank was giving the man such a tough time when he was doing the job it had asked for. The woman replied, "Wendy, the Bank is a bank, and our job is to disperse funds."[5]

When the gaps between official rhetoric and norms of practice are so taken for granted that they can no longer be called into question, we can really wonder about the health and the legitimacy of the institution, as, indeed, many people have wondered publicly about the World Bank. It must be hard not to be a little cynical in the midst of such apparent hypocrisy. Wendy also recalls working at the bank some years ago and asking her own boss, who seemed more caught up in pleasing the people in Washington than anything else, why he did his work. He paused before answering, "For the poor, I guess."[6]

If our espoused purpose is at best an afterthought, then our real purpose must be our own career advancement within the system. And indeed large aid bureaucracies, particularly within the UN system, can sometimes appear to function more effectively as advocates for the advancement and well-being of their own staff than for the poor.

It would be entirely wrong and unfair to say that no one within the World Bank or the UN is genuinely committed to the espoused goals of their organizations—namely, to contribute to, as the World Bank puts it, "a world without poverty." To be effective, people, and the organizations that they belong to, need resources and power. And that means that they need to cultivate relationships with those who already have power, which means they have to play the game. Is one more likely to be effective within a big bureaucracy that is closely tied to the political status quo but has huge resources at hand and immense clout or outside such a bureaucracy, with much greater independence but fewer resources? These questions often come down to personal disposition as much as anything. But those who play the game too much may become caught up in it and forget what they started out to do.

Lifestyle

Many people are drawn to work in development because they want adventure and to travel the world. Still, for those traveling to other countries, the lifestyle of many expat development workers abroad can be a shock. I spoke with a social worker from Scotland who volunteered with VSO in Bangladesh. She recalls,

To be honest, I don't know if I knew much about what international development would be. . . . I was thinking it would be nice to go and do similar work in a different country, and get the experience of living in a different culture and learn about how they do social work in a different country, and share some of what I'd learnt. But I didn't know so much about international development and this machinery and how it all works. And it was a bit of a surprise to me, when I got to Bangladesh and saw all these organizations, and the expats working in them and the kind of lifestyle they had.

I was very much based in my organization there. . . . I was concentrated on getting my work done. But I'd go out in Dhaka; there was a part of Dhaka where all the expats lived. We'd go to the British Club because that's where you could get a drink. We'd get local transport because we were volunteers, with not much money. [The other expats] would be nervous about that; they'd get picked up by big cars. To me that was a big shock. I felt safe to walk, safe to go to the markets, to take rickshaws. But when I went to the rich expat areas, I felt the local people viewed me differently; there was more a feeling of "them and us," and you'd see the expats living in big houses with big walls and guards, whereas we lived in an ordinary flat amongst Bangladeshis. We were integrated in the local community, and we as volunteers were paid according to the local salary scale, so we did not get high salaries. I felt lucky because I got to live with normal people and not in a segregated part of the city.

A young American development worker had similar observations, especially of the USAID people she met during her first time in Mali:

My meeting with USAID, I walked away a bit sad about it. I housesat for the second in command there and had dinner with her. She was appalled that I'd take local transport, and at the neighborhood that I'd been living in. I learned that there's clear disconnect. She was a wonderful person, she had a whole career with the Foreign Service, but her distance from the people I worked with every day really didn't inspire me to work with the [US] government anytime soon.

While many people, both expat and national, can find this exclusivity alienating and upsetting, others enjoy the comfort and status of the international development lifestyle. And many people argue it is wholly appropriate that professionals live in comfort and are well compensated for the work they do, just as Western professionals might be in their own country. It's a debate with proponents on either side.

Those most strongly against the exclusive expat lifestyle see it as both a symbol and a perpetuation of the exclusivity and hollowness of mainstream development itself. Hector Vivero, a Mexican working for a development NGO in Afghanistan, suggests that the expat lifestyle is part of a broader process to create a local hunger for imported Western lifestyles while reinforcing the existing global order:

> You basically have an elite, which creates these sorts of role models that everyone aspires to, to promote the status quo. Kind of like the American Dream. They make you believe that everyone has a chance and can work hard and everyone can make it, but it's not true. I think [international development] is very successful in terms of having a Western elite—foreigners living in developing countries or countries in conflict. You and I, because we're foreigners, we're already considered experts, not that we are—but we're considered experts and superior, and then you add to that the fact that we live an elite lifestyle, compared to a lot of the population. It's a re-creation of what happened in India during colonial times; we're the role models of how they should be, and continue perpetuating the status quo.

Cedric Fedida disagrees. As an employee of an international entity within the international system, he thinks he is entitled to reasonable compensation for his work. He wonders why development workers seem subject to different standards than others:

> For a lot of people, some journalists, for example, who wrote about being shocked at parties in Kabul, we're not supposed to earn a decent living, and certainly not supposed to have fun and party like others in Europe. We're supposed to suffer, because we're in Afghanistan helping the poor Afghan people; we shouldn't have weekends. That's totally ridiculous. A lot of people have this image that if you work in aid and development, you have to be poor and take a vow—I don't agree with that. We also have to live a normal life. There's a big issue in general about money in this line

of work—who gets this salary, is it fair or not, or this guy earns too much for what he does, and the UN has nice offices, you hear that all the time, it's a theme. I think there is some truth to it but it's a bit overstated. At the end of the day, what really matters is whether or not people are good at what they do and if they really believe in it.

I think the misconception in Europe is that people don't consider it as a normal job. They wouldn't say that to people working in a cosmetics company in the West or to a banker—oh, your car's too nice, your working conditions are too nice. But we come from the same backgrounds, all of us could work in a corporate firm, no one would question our living conditions or what we earn. . . . I'm not talking about making a lot of money, just about having normal working conditions.

Both sides have some reason to them. The problem, similar to the problem of different employment conditions for national and international employees, seems to come down to the very nature of globalization and the way international development highlights and continues existing inequalities, at the same time it claims to be redressing them. In a globalized system, which national norms prevail?

Individuals working in development cannot step away from the fact that inequalities exist, but they all form their own ideas about where to draw the line, what they feel they are entitled to, and what they feel is excessive and unjust. The way they are compensated also affects their relationships to people within the countries where they work. Those working as volunteers typically feel much closer to local people, while UN and donor staff find themselves more likely to associate only with other expats and perhaps the national elites. One senior UN staff in Uganda explains,

Here, when I get out of my office, my sanctuary is with people I have things in common with—so it's mostly been expats. The other day I went and had drinks with the director general of the Ministry, and we're really good friends, and we had a good chat, but there are things you don't say—like you don't say that much about your personal life.

As careers develop, lifestyles change and so do the types of relationships that expats have with local people and with the places they live. Having families often changes people's lifestyle priorities, as we consider in the following section.

Family Life

For many people working in international development outside of their home country, balancing a family with their career is a particular challenge. Many who continue to work overseas choose to stay in one place longer. Mark Adams, who is British, works as the deputy director of Oxfam Uganda. He and his wife, who is also British, have lived in Uganda for nine years and have raised their two children there. But in the long term, as Mark explains,

> What happens in the future is very problematic really. A lot of it's really around the kids—we like this country very much, but at the end of the day, we're not citizens, we don't have any particular rights here, so we'll probably head back to the UK. The key point is around the girls' education—when they're getting close to university. The girls are eight and seven right now. To enter university as a UK resident, you have to be three years resident prior.
>
> A big concern is what we'd do back in the UK. My wife is a nurse and studied international public health to master's level . . . but if she was to go back to the NHS, she'd go back to her grade when she left around twenty years ago. They wouldn't recognize what she'd done since; she was health coordinator for GOAL in Sudan, that's where we met, and also worked for Merlin in Rwanda, GOAL here in Uganda, so she's had some good experience, but people have always said our experience isn't really recognized in the UK. In fact that was one of my reasons for moving to Oxfam from an Irish NGO—it also has a base and visibility in the UK, so I believe it will help me with the move back to the UK.

People with families are usually more concerned about financial security and personal safety and stability than single people are. On one hand, this means they may feel less able to say no to income opportunities even if they disagree with organizational policies. But on the other hand, people with families often seek longer term placements and have a different kind of relationship to the places they live. The overriding concern for most people with children is education. Mark Bidder spent over ten years living and working in Ethiopia. As he explains it,

> It became a deliberate choice, because the longer you stay the more fascinating it is, and the more you learn. My unit was used by other parts of the UN as a source of information and guidance, so in the

end it came quite hard to leave—I felt I had almost become an Ethiopian citizen. I felt like I either had to agree to stay for the rest of my life or move here [to Nairobi]—and it was partly a family decision; my kids needed better schools.

Sometimes people are required by their organizations to move. Donor agencies and the UN typically repost people on a regular basis. Within the UN system, some postings are typically to "nonfamily duty stations" where political instability and insecurity mean that families cannot come. And in any case, not everyone is willing or able to uproot his or her spouse and children every few years. So some UN staff spend years without living with their families, visiting them only during leaves. One long-term UN worker reflects on some of the shifts and trade-offs in her career:

Initially there was this wish to be an international development worker and to help. It was so exciting to go to places like Rome and El Salvador. Then I had my two children, and I was so busy I couldn't think about my career—that was a twenty-four-hour job. Now I'm getting into a different level of international cooperation, where I can address these political components of international development, which is very exciting, meeting ministers and deputy ministers. That's one part of the story; the other part is that I've been out of [my native country] so long and been out of my area of expertise for so long that I'd find it very difficult to find a job back there. Yes, I could work for FAO or something like that . . . but it's the same field, still international, so it's golden handcuffs. I have worked in several countries that have been nonfamily duty stations, and I have missed seeing my children growing up. I see them and my partner in my home country every six weeks.

People who enter international development as "national staff" in aid recipient countries face similarly tough choices. If they are able to get into the highly competitive international system by taking a position out of their home country, they will be treated as expats and get much higher salaries and greater opportunities for professional advancement. But they will have to leave behind their family and friends. One route into the system is to go to places such as Afghanistan with a high demand for skilled expatriate staff. It sometimes seems like a Faustian bargain, pitting personal commitments against professional advancement.

Conclusion

For anyone working in international development, learning how the development system works, the processes of revising one's understanding and balancing goals and priorities, continue throughout one's work life. But it is in the first years of work that it is most important to seek out experiences specifically for the purpose of testing your assumptions and finding the roles that seem to best suit you.

One danger in this process of exploration, however, is that some people never seem to leave it. As they flit from one short-term assignment to another, their understanding of each situation remains at best superficial. Another danger is that of getting stuck with a particular skill set and career path that becomes more and more difficult to leave with time. One career development worker explains,

> The longer you work in the international area, the better qualified you are to work internationally; however, it also disqualifies you from working locally. Whenever I went back to Australia and perused the wanted ads, they'd say, "knowledge of local industry required." . . . But that's what you don't have. . . . People do get trapped; I know several people who got trapped.

Once the choice to work within international development is no longer really a choice, the balance between work and life, and the sense of commitment to working well, can become more difficult. People in such situations are at greater danger of losing motivation and so losing their critical edge. Managing to avoid this trap can be difficult, but some people make sure that they maintain skills and networks that are still relevant for their home countries, or return home periodically to work, or are sure about the commitments they are making and are able to live with the consequences. Returning to work for head offices is a fairly typical solution, especially for those who want their family to be more settled.

Whatever situation we find ourselves in, and whatever path we choose to pursue, we can adapt by cultivating the conscious reflection and inquisitive attitude that Donald Schön talks about. By engaging in this reflective learning on our experiences, we can begin to make peace with the inconsistencies and vagaries of the development system while clarifying and continuing to pursue our own goals. The wisdom of those with decades of experience within the international development system is that they've been able to soften their expectations and accept the way the world is. That doesn't necessarily mean that they've compromised their principles. Rather they are not expending unnecessary energy by fretting about what they cannot change but have instead learned how to focus on what they can. It is by understanding the system and refining our own understandings that we can begin to learn how to be effective within it, which is the theme of the next chapter.

Notes

1. Name has been changed for anonymity.

2. These are all possibilities that we'll explore more in the third part of this book.

3. Within the European Union.

4. Donald A. Schön, *The Reflective Practitioner: How Professionals Think in Action* (New York: Basic Books, 1984), 68.

5. Personal communication with Wendy Quarry. Also recounted in Ricardo Ramirez and Wendy Quarry, *Communication for Another Development* (London: Zed Books, 2008), 105.

6. Ibid., 39.

7

Learning to Be Effective

Hema Vyas recalls the moment she realized that no one necessarily had the answers about how to address poverty. She was in Gujarat, working on her master's degree at the time:

> I remember sitting in a little rickshaw [with a staff member from the Self Employed Women's Association (SEWA)], we were going to SEWA Bank, and there were people literally sitting on the street, they didn't have anything. And we were chatting, and I said, "You know, our work is aimed at people who have homes and who are living hand to mouth, but how do we help these people on the street?" And she looked at me and said, "You're asking me?!" and I didn't realize—I thought she'd have an idea, but the real complexity of what do you do, nobody knows what to do, and it's so sad. There isn't this solution that you work together to create; you just work, and you don't know.

Starting to tackle what at first glance appears an obvious problem or immediate need can often lead both individuals and organizations to an awareness of broader structural constraints. Kibera in Nairobi is famous as the largest slum in Africa, and the conditions for residents are terrible. Life expectancy in the slums hovers at around forty to forty-five years, due largely to high infant mortality.[1] Nairobi also hosts many donors and UN agencies, and some of them have sought to improve conditions there. A staffer at UN-HABITAT explained to me why some of these interventions had been disastrous for the residents. The donors had not quite factored in that most of the Kibera's residents rent their homes. Most of Kibera is owned by rich landlords—exactly who is unknown and almost unknowable because it is middlemen who collect rent from the residents. Rumors abound that the ultimate landlords are in fact rich politicians.

The rent system in Kibera is very sensitive to the market, and despite their low purchasing power, the large population makes the rent market a lucrative prospect for investors. For example, a woman trader coming from an outside community will need to pay transport costs to reach Nairobi. She can buy herself a bed in Kibera at a rate that is slightly cheaper than return transport to her home, saving herself a bit of money. When transport costs rise, landlords raise the nightly cost of the bed, making sure that it is still just cheap enough to remain a better alternative to the return fare. When donors invested in slum upgrade projects, they immediately increased the value of the housing in the neighborhoods they had invested in, rents went up, and some residents could no longer afford to live there and had to leave. The benefits accrued to these shadowy landlords. Under these circumstances, it seems that only structural and political change can really help improve the living situation of people in Kibera, and no one is quite sure how to do that.

These sorts of issues can be daunting. Development issues that may seem straightforward at first rarely are. They quickly get tied into power dynamics and varying perspectives and different ways of doing things. So most of the time, the only real way to know what will work is to try it out, see what happens, and keep experimenting. Analyzing why things are the way they are, weighing other options and solutions, deciding which ones are better, and then trying to pursue them—this is a winding and unpredictable path.

Donald Schön found that professionals in a wide variety of fields build up tacit knowledge of practice through years of experience.[2] This includes knowledge of all the intangibles that are rarely taught but that matter so much in the "real world"—organizational politics, resource limitations, and the influence of various personalities. All of these things certainly feature large in the experience of development workers.

It's through deliberately and consciously engaging in learning that professionals can test assumptions and cultivate a more refined and valid expertise. When experience doesn't match expectation, the development worker must rethink her ideas of how things work. It is through this cycle of experiencing, adjusting understanding, acting based on the revised understanding, and learning anew from the resulting experience that understanding is continually refined and expertise develops. As we saw in chapter 5, people quickly learn and adapt unconsciously, adopting roles and implicit norms that may even conflict with their stated goals and values. Conscious reflection is fundamental to correcting that.

The first part of this chapter looks at strategic trade-offs in deciding whether to put one's energy into small but tangible projects or into larger, but often amorphous, efforts at broader policy and structural change. The second part focuses on tendencies within development organizations that pose a risk to effective practice and on resources that can mitigate these tendencies and improve one's odds of working effectively.

Strategy: Where to Put Your Efforts?

Given the complexity of development problems, one question that many people struggle with is, "Where should I focus my efforts?" There are two schools of thought on this. One argues that it is better to focus on specific goals at the local level, where you can see the effects of your efforts. The other argues that it is better to focus on broader strategic changes, to advocate for policies, and to build up systems and capacity at a higher level—perhaps national or regional.

There are arguments for and against each approach. People often base their career decisions, to some degree, on which approach they subscribe to.

Small-Scale Development

When I was interviewing people for this book, I thought that most people who had been working in development for some time would be proudest of their largest and most far-reaching accomplishments. But I was wrong. When I asked, many people fondly recalled small projects near the beginning of their careers in which they had a leading role. They felt proud because they knew exactly what their impact was. It might have been small, but they could see it, and they knew it had affected people. Sometimes they had kept in touch with people or found out that what they had done had some lasting impact, and this was even more satisfying.

Some people make a deliberate effort to choose positions and situations where they are able to see the impact of their work and avoid large aid bureaucracies. Sometimes it is because they feel such bureaucracies are ineffective, but often it is simply because they don't find working within them personally rewarding. Dirk Ullerich is head-of-project for Welthungerhilfe, a German NGO implementing a range of livelihood and environmental activities in Karamoja, Uganda. He explains,

> I think what makes the charm of this kind of work is that you see directly the effects of what you're doing. . . . Here, these sorts of things, you're given a task but you're quite free to implement it

in the way that you think is the best one, so you try and you see right away the impact coming out of it—you see whether there's a benefit for the target group immediately. And if it is not, then you still have possibilities to adjust, you're involved in the work with the population and the planning. . . . This is, in my opinion, really unique.

Dirk has found that at the more localized level, things are still personal enough that he can directly see and understand the impact of what he is doing. Other than reporting requirements, he's outside of most of the bureaucratic aspects of larger agencies, and he is directly involved in implementing projects.

Dai Peters did her PhD research in Madagascar. She spent two years living in a tent and knew everyone in the four villages she worked in. She's had a few experiences where she's worked on projects and known every person she was working with personally, considering them all friends. She's continued to stay close to the field, working mainly for NGOs, but she most valued those deep personal links where she could have a very rich sense of how what she is trying to do is likely to play into each person's life.

This is essentially community development, done internationally or supported by international agencies. Its ethos is that by staying close to people, it can build on their strengths and focus on their priorities. For a lot of people in development, it has appeal both philosophically and as a lifestyle. It is what many people think of when they envision development, as we saw in the previous chapter.

But one of the main arguments against this local approach, also the argument against overreliance on NGOs, is that it fails to add up to substantial change at a broader level. This sort of intensive local engagement is usually limited to some areas where NGOs are active, while other areas may be neglected. It is uncoordinated, and it fails to address larger systemic issues. If the national government is not providing any health services and medicine, or proper education, or proper roads, community projects may not really compensate that, especially once the NGOs stop running. After years of development work, Dai wonders,

Well, am I really accomplishing things? I am, within the project, we are accomplishing things. But it's the overall development—maybe we're accomplishing things but the overall war is lost—you've won the battle but lost the war. Does this really contribute to the development of Africa in general?

Many development workers share similar doubts, doubts about what one can hope to really change given how complicated and entangled all the problems seem to be. People often take solace in the idea that it is through the training and knowledge sharing they exchange with their colleagues, especially national counterparts, that they may leave a legacy. A former coordinator of the United Nations Volunteers program reflects,

> The more you're in a country and learn about its history and the impact of colonialism and the West, it's complex. You wonder, "Should I be here at all?" I think that it is better to do something than nothing. But the way I feel I need to engage is on a more personal level. The times I did see an impact is when I was working with individuals, with the volunteers. You think—OK, there's an impact, that's sustainable, because they'll stay in the country and go off and do whatever. I think it's on that level that you'll be able to improve some individuals' lives and understandings, and that's about it.

Working at a "Higher Level"

The second approach is to work at a higher level and, rather than address problems directly, to work with and through broader systems, whether it be the state or the market or perhaps civil society, so that they can address the problems. This is the philosophy behind the Paris Declaration on Aid Effectiveness, which recommits donors to the notion that nations should have more control over setting their national development priorities and agendas and that aid should be channeled through the state so that state structures are strengthened.

The most obvious problem with this approach, as we saw in chapter 3, is widespread state corruption. It is also much harder to see the impact of one's work and to adjust when the issues and the systems are so big. Even the aid bureaucracies can become so mazelike that it is difficult for those within to know what effect their work is having, if indeed it is having any at all.

As people move further into the development system, the feedback they get becomes more indirect, and they may never know what the final outcome of their efforts was. They can only hope that by continuing to fulfill their role within their bureaucracy, they are therefore contributing to development. But as we've already seen, the development system's patchy performance shouldn't lead anyone to take it on faith. In any case, for most people, being a cog in the system is not very gratifying. Still, some people believe they have found points within the system from which they can tackle strategic issues.

One senior advisor at a UN agency had, earlier in his career, worked for an NGO. He explains his motive for moving to the UN:

> NGOs are much more connected to the people and the real problems, but they're also small—that's the problem. If they build a clinic, it's very good for the people in that area but doesn't really change the health situation in the country.

Within the UN system, he's been able to engage governments and shift policy processes:

> I've really been lucky enough that I can say that yes, I've been part of processes that have changed societies. And of course, it's important to know that there are results in what you're doing, positive results—but it's very difficult to measure results in processes. And it's a danger—many countries that give money want results, and it's easier when you can measure them. But the number of clinics isn't really important, but how are these clinics helping the society— so you should rather measure the health of the people in the area where the clinic was built—but you need to wait ten years. So results-based management, it's very interesting and very difficult. I was also part of projects and processes that didn't work because elements were missing. You know what's normally missing? Political commitment. So you're involved in something where everyone is committing time and money and hope and effort, and then there's no commitment from those making decisions, or they have other interests, maybe corruption or other interests that aren't visible. Then you get really kind of, well, you get sad. So it's important, as an individual, that you put yourself in environments where those you work with have more or less the same goal.

The Middle Path

The arguments for and against both the "local" strategy and the "high-level" strategy are pretty convincing. In practice, there is plenty of room for middle ground, since attempts to do straightforward things at a local level often run into systemic problems. We've already seen this in the example of donor attempts at improving the Kibera slums.

Many of the most effective development approaches have taken this middle ground, trying to achieve something fairly clear and well defined, encountering obstacles, and then taking adaptive action to address them. Up-hoff, Esman, and Krishna give a typical example:

> Plan Puebla, based in Mexico, was initially conceived as an agri-cultural extension project, but field implementation quickly ran up against constraints that had to be dealt with before the new technol-ogy could become a viable option to poorer farmers. Banks had to be persuaded to change their lending procedures and to advance credit to farmers' groups without insisting on individual guarantees. Before that could happen, farmers had to be organized into soli-darity groups. Coordination had to be arranged among disparate government agencies that dealt separately with input supply, trans-portation and warehousing, crop insurance, and grain pricing.[3]

One of the reasons that Plan Puebla worked is because the staff had the flexibility and time to work through these issues. If they'd been bound to an inflexible agreement from the outset, they couldn't have done it. Being on schedule and being successful are two different things.

One classic attempt at the middle path is to start small with initial pilot projects in a few places, check that things work, adjust systems, and then scale up. This strategy has had mixed success, perhaps because it often gets hijacked by development's more managerial tendencies. Sometimes the pilot projects become demonstration projects, ends in themselves and means of showing that something has been done. Robert Chambers calls these "shining islands of salvation."[4] It's often hard to scale them up because they're very expensive. Often there isn't enough flexibility and adaptability in the scaling-up process to make sure that what works in one place will still work elsewhere. Sometimes there just isn't enough time. Funding cycles are usually two or three years; de-velopment takes its own time.

At a personal level, another, perhaps more radical and powerful, ap-proach to the middle path is to commit to something over the long term and see it through. We saw already how Dave's (see chapter 5) increasing sense of belonging to Kenya changed his own professional priorities and choices. Kaia Ambrose also talks about this same quality among people she has admired:

> I met my thesis advisor in Ecuador while I was working and study-ing there. He lives on a farm outside of Quito; he's deeply commit-ted to practicing in his own life what he preaches in his professional life, around social learning and integrated agriculture and health.

A lot of our friends and colleagues in Ecuador are very active in policy change and advocacy—their "professions" as "development agents" are seamless with what they truly believe in as individuals and bringing change to their country—or in the case of expats, a country they now call home—and to the region. They are not external agents swooping down with advice about how things should be done. There is deep-rooted dedication and passion.

These are the sorts of decisions and commitments that can take many years to reach full fruition, but it can be very gratifying when they do. Sally Humphries's work is a good example of this.

Sally Humphries is a professor of sociology and director of the International Development Studies program at the University of Guelph in Canada. She is also a member of the Foundation for Participatory Research With Honduran Farmers (FIPAH). Sally began her career in international development as a Rockefeller Foundation social science fellow in agriculture at the International Center for Tropical Agriculture (CIAT), where she worked from 1991 to 1994. CIAT, which is headquartered in Colombia, sent her off to work with farmers in Honduras on participatory research in marginal agricultural areas. Sally maintained contact with the Hondurans she hired to help her with the work there, and together they formed FIPAH, of which she remains a member today. Sally found that leaving CIAT and joining the university gave her the flexibility to maintain a close connection with the people she had started working with in Honduras. Had she stayed with CIAT, its preference for basic rather than applied research and the high overhead costs associated with the institution would have made it much more difficult to work with farmer groups over the long term. As it is, the Honduran NGO has developed and furthered its work, and Sally has helped the NGO by acting as a link between it and its primary funder, the Unitarian Service Committee of Canada. Also, as a university professor, she has been able to support them through academic research projects, linking graduate students looking for research topics to some of their research needs.

One of the things that Sally came to learn and believe in through her experience was the importance of long-term sustained development efforts. As she recalls, she didn't always have this understanding:

I remember when I first came to Guelph, they gave me some start-up research funds, and I thought, "I'll do an impact assessment." Well the program had only started a year ago—there hadn't been any impact! So I'm a big believer now that development support has to be long term, although governments typically only want to support short-term work, and you can't achieve sustainable results in the short term. I'm much more realistic than when I started out.

The other thing that happened for Sally over time is that she developed a strong commitment to the group of people in Honduras:

> I suppose that what happened is that I've become part of a community of people in Honduras, and it's a lifelong relationship, and I'm just not going to give it up for some opportunistic reason. I'm willing to take on some other work—but nothing that would affect my commitment to the group in Honduras. I feel a tremendous commitment to these people, more than to further my career as a professor. . . . We haven't solved all the problems, so why would I switch? I have a role to play, so why would I just abandon it to further my own career? I won't. And it's not just altruism; it's what I want to do. It gives me personal satisfaction; I just wouldn't want to do anything else.

Although Sally chose to focus her efforts largely on one initiative in one location, this has also begun to have a much broader influence as the work in participatory plant breeding has been recognized internationally, particularly by CIAT and other international agricultural organizations, including the International Maize and Wheat Improvement Center (CIMMYT) and the Food and Agriculture Organization (FAO). Even the Honduran government, after many years, has begun testing seed varieties bred by the farmer groups with the goal of releasing them nationally. Because these seeds were bred in marginal highland areas under the conditions that poor farmers actually face, they are well adapted to those areas and are much more appropriate for the highlands than the varieties bred in lowland agricultural experiment centers under very different conditions. The wider breeding and distribution of these seeds means that more poor farmers will be able to plant them, and when they do, they will get higher yields of their crops. The Honduran government has been painfully slow to recognize the value of these farmer-bred varieties, but it is finally starting to give them the attention they deserve. It is often these political issues, as Sally notes, that take so much time and patience.

The long-term nature of the project, the stability of funding, and Sally's own continuous involvement have all helped both her as an individual and the project as a whole to continually learn and adjust. Sally's position at a university has meant both she and graduate students have been able to conduct formal studies on various aspects of the project. Building up long-term relationships and trust means that she is in a relatively sound position to understand the nuances of the organization and the context it is working within.

Working Effectively: Risks and Resources

Choosing one's employer is a key decision that will shape the way in which one is able to work. In Sally's case, working at a university gave her both sufficient institutional support and sufficient freedom to continue her work association with FIPAH.

Back in chapter 4, we looked at what it was like to work for different kinds of development institutions: donors, the UN, NGOs, and aid contractors. Across all these are common traits shaped by shared thinking and commitments, funding cycles, and reporting requirements. And within each of these, there is great variation.

Ideally, we'd like to seek out and work for organizations that provide really supportive, proactive work environments, where our individual efforts are guided by, and add cumulatively to, the collective wisdom and efforts of those before us. And such organizations, or teams or departments within larger organizations, do exist. They are the pockets of sanity in a system that contains some serious endemic impediments to effective work.

Within organizations, there is often room to negotiate one's role. The ability to negotiate work terms and the work environment usually increases with seniority. Ricardo Ramirez has one anecdote about someone he knew who took on a position as country representative for an aid agency but only on the condition that he would not spend any money for the first year, because he wanted time to learn the country. The agency agreed to the terms.[5] However, even junior employees often have some leeway to negotiate their roles, especially when they are working for smaller organizations or have sympathetic bosses.

Realistically, no work environment is likely to be perfectly conducive to effective work. Three major risks that often get embedded in the culture and practice of development organizations are a failure to listen to the people they are supposed to be serving, a fixation with accountability, and institutional forgetfulness. We'll consider each of these work perils in a bit more detail. As external risks, they hamper the activity of reflective practitioners, who must work around rather than with their institution. When these risks are commonplace in a work environment, the even greater risk is that individual practitioners are more likely to unconsciously adapt and adopt practices that include these same weaknesses.

On the other hand, development workers can seek out and find resources, whether within their own organization or through their own approach to work, that could extend beyond their immediate employer and could span various positions. Three key resources that most development workers can draw on if they choose to are time, relationships, and existing research.

These three resources can be used not only to be more effective in one's own work but also to challenge organizational practices that hamper good development work. Those who report having been able to challenge and change practices within their own organizations usually recall that it took time, the building of trust, and a concerted effort on their part to yield results.

Since all of these risks and resources have the potential to shape one's work practice and work effectiveness, let's now consider each in turn.

Risk 1: Not Listening to People

At the extreme, when international development agencies don't listen or learn and come to a situation with preprogrammed functions rather than appropriate responses, the results can be heartbreaking. Marina Fakhouri has seen tragic examples of mismatched development priorities in life-or-death situations:

> [You have] a UN agency showing up in the south of Angola, building this pretty school where there were no teachers trained and three out of five children died before the age of five. They could have had a perfectly good immunization program, but instead they built a school, which wouldn't be used. It was culturally wrong and had problems with the ventilation too. If they'd just asked what the population wanted, they would have said, "Save our children first so they can go to school" or "We have no possibility for agriculture because everything is mined." And the mortality rate was so high because there were no antenatal services and the malaria rates were out of control. There were children dying in masses because they were given deworming tablets, and they were suffocating from the worms coming out their throats. Then you have a major donor coming and saying, "OK, let's empower women!"

Asking the people whom you are trying to assist what they need seems obvious, but it still isn't the starting point of a lot of development programs. And if success is defined as meeting organizational objectives, then responding

to the masses of dying children is not a priority, but rather women's empowerment, or whatever issue the donor is keen about, is a priority because it has
already been agreed on and put in the strategic plan.

Anders Fange, the former head of the Swedish Committee for Afghanistan, agrees that many donor priorities are made on an a priori basis for political or ideological reasons:

> You read the Swedish strategy for development for Afghanistan—
> the Swedes are of course suckers for human rights, women's rights,
> education, and so on, and then you take the strategy for a country
> like Tanzania—there are a few changes, but you can see that it is
> otherwise more or less the same . . . so, it's not like this—that they
> are coming in here, they are sitting down with, say, research orga-
> nizations, some trustworthy politicians, some other development
> people from other countries, and they actually sit for a month or
> two and try to chisel out a strategy. They're all coming in and doing
> their own thing.

Human rights, women's rights, education, and many of the development
aims that donors claim commitment to are often laudable. But when they are
being pushed from the outside, they may overshadow more immediately relevant and pressing local issues. The only way to know what these issues are is
to ask people. This seems so basic, so transparently obvious, that it hardly bears
stating. And yet, it still doesn't reflect the way most mainstream development
is done today. An NGO worker who has run into the same issue explains,

> I just had an experience where one of our country offices wanted to
> focus a large program on nutrition, based on the very good work
> they already do; in approaching the donor they were told, "No, nu-
> trition is not a priority for us in this country." Priorities are changed
> from one year to the next, regardless of the effort and resources put
> in. Implementers are expected to change their direction and focus
> at a whim.

How can donors whose stated objective is to support development make
apparently arbitrary decisions to exclude some pressing issues and to prioritize
others? This returns us to the question posed in chapter 2 about who development answers to. As we saw there, development organizations, and especially
donors, often respond to political imperatives and to the imperative of their

own existence. Downward accountability is weak. This filters through the formal mechanisms for reporting, accounting, monitoring, and evaluating, which provide feedback to the development system and so are its main formal mechanisms for learning and adjusting.

Risk 2: The Accountability Fixation

Donors should demand accountability from those whom they give or loan money to. After all, an awful lot of aid money has been outright stolen, and much of it has been spent incompetently and ineffectively. For example, billions of dollars of cash have been reportedly flown out of Afghanistan in the period from 2001, much of it essentially stolen aid money.[6] Looking at this and many other recent examples, including the Anglo-Leasing scandal in Kenya described in chapter 3, we can say that donors should be doing more to prevent the misuse of funds that were supposed to be spent in the public interest. But accountability is usually done by agreeing beforehand on exactly how the money should be spent and then checking that it has been spent as planned. This doesn't leave a lot of room for learning. As Dave Johnson notes, "We do need to learn from mistakes, and that is lost with heavy accountability, but that's hard to measure—did you learn from your screwup, or did you just screw up?"

Detailed reporting can also eat up a lot of time for grantees. Different donors have different reporting requirements, and some are more onerous than others. USAID and the World Bank are notorious as donors that require a lot in terms of documentation and have a tendency to micromanage. The Nordic and Scandinavian donors are broadly seen as more flexible and easier to work with. While it is wise for any organization receiving funds to diversify its sources, complying with multiple donor demands takes considerable time and paperwork.

It's also not clear, in the end, how much value all this reporting has. Researchers in South Africa and Uganda found that the reporting requirements that donors and international NGOs placed on local NGOs diverted organizational energy away from fieldwork.[7] Reporting formats often fail to capture what is happening on the ground. Because the donors lack contextual knowledge, it is difficult for NGOs to accurately communicate what is happening in their projects. They have little incentive to do so anyway, since in their attempt, they risk being misunderstood or micromanaged by the donor.

Those within the UN face internal accountability requirements from their auditors. Many find these so stringent that they threaten effective operations. Jean-Luc Lemahieu, heading the UNODC mission in Afghanistan, says,

At the moment my greatest frustration is that the bureaucracy can do what the Taliban was not able to do—to halt my operations. So we need to decide what we want—delivery or a high score from the audit company? A high score from the auditors doesn't necessarily bring food to those in need. . . . Accountability and transparency have their own undeniable merits, but we can bring in so many checks and balances that after a while we are paralyzed.

A UN procurement specialist working in Somalia agrees:

There's a huge gap between headquarters and the field. Those who have never left HQ have absolutely no idea about what we do. They sit in a little box and bombard us with information requests for their reports, they don't actually think we're trying to deliver, and they have checkboxes, and you have to fill the checkboxes, and we find it very hard in procurement. . . . In Somalia if we try to explain the context we're working in, with few qualified contractors, etc., if you try to explain it to the HQ and get a waiver, they say, no, you have to do these things. We say we've tried but we can't. . . . They're unwilling to take the blinkers off and say, OK, yeah, this should be an issue. . . . You can't get higher risk than Somalia.

Many donors require aid recipients to submit their programs to evaluation by third parties. Done well, these external evaluations can be extremely useful in helping the organization understand both the nuances and the consequences of its work and so improve its effectiveness. But those involved in monitoring and evaluation work say that such types of evaluation are still very rare. Like reporting, evaluations are mainly used to check accountability and compliance with preset goals. Kaia Ambrose, who has focused much of her work in development on evaluation, explains,

The conversation and practice around "appropriate" monitoring and evaluation approaches have been really heating up and gaining momentum over the past several years. Most donors and implementing organizations are focused on proving their impact through a very clear and precise demonstration of attribution. There's another group of individuals and some organizations who recognize that the work we do occurs in very complex realities and that paying attention to emerging issues, trends, and surprises, combined with the need and ability to be adaptive, necessitates a very different philosophy and set of tools for monitoring and evaluation. I still think this group is the "deviants," though—not the popular kids in class. When it comes down to it in practice, my experience is that most people are uncomfortable with complexity and change; they want neat boxes, simple solutions, and seemingly cause-and-effect operations so that impact can be proven "easily."

With a more linear, fixed approach to formal evaluation, the opportunity it offers for substantive learning is greatly reduced. The fixation on accountability and showing results can also lead to short-term thinking. When there is pressure to meet targets, it is natural to focus on what is easiest. Those coming into a new country for two years tend to establish working relationships with the same people whom their predecessors did, and those people often end up as powerful brokers and gatekeepers. Projects seeking to make tangible changes in people's incomes and well-being may tend to focus on those who are already organized and relatively easy to work with. Sometimes several donors may end up taking credit for the same work—the same boreholes drilled. In one extreme example, someone told me of a project in the Congo being evaluated by the FAO. The group had not managed to reach its targets and asked farmers participating in a similar project run by a different organization to post signs in their demonstration plots crediting the FAO for the work while the evaluators were there.

Many people working in development worry that the focus on short-term results has undermined many development efforts. One person I spoke with had worked on agricultural development initiatives for many years within various NGOs. Some of these were aimed at stimulating and improving the chain of production so that farmers had more income opportunities, but she is quite skeptical of their track record:

> To make it look like it works, you give people machines and then you can report to the donors, whether that will make it all work is questionable. [But] you can say we tried and got something going. . . . We got this many groups and this and that, but don't mention that as soon as you leave, the whole thing collapses, because there's no more subsidy. And the donors don't want to know, they file it—we did this, we did that. Donors, just like us, it's a career thing that makes them look good too, and just like us, they want to file the report and make themselves look so good—this and this

and this; it serves the purpose for all the people whose career has been enhanced by all of this—like all of us.

Risk 3: Forgetfulness

Perhaps one reason why the development system can continue for so many years with these bad habits is that it tends to have a short memory. In the country office of a donor, even two years can be a long time, and people can start to forget what they have done. One long-term development worker who recently joined a USAID country office said,

> My boss, who has been here for two years, has admitted that he's only been to the field twice. . . . They were all delighted that I joined them because they said I've plugged them into the local net-work—and so it's nice to be able to maybe facilitate USAID funds being more useful. One thing this separation has done is that AID has no institutional memory of the institutions of government—they keep saying there needs to be a study of farmers' organizations and cooperatives, and I keep saying there's been so much done . . . there's been so many documents.

Jim Shute encountered a similar institutional resistance to learning and remembering when working on a consultancy for CIDA in the mid-1980s:

> Canada decided it would be part of a newly designed model rural training scheme in Sri Lanka, but CIDA had no background mate-rial on the area in question. So our team went to Sri Lanka and did a creditable job, I think, of talking to male and female farmers and a variety of helpful local and expatriate informants, both urban and rural. In the process we accumulated a wealth of documentation from private sources, government agencies, the FAO, and other do-nors, even some documents given to us in confidence. We shipped this rich archival resource on rural Sri Lanka back to CIDA's head-quarters in Hull.
>
> Well, that project didn't get going for various reasons, largely political, and so two years later CIDA asked me if I would go back to Sri Lanka and redesign the whole thing. So I went back to CIDA and asked, "Can I see that material we deposited with you two years ago?" "What material?" responded the new project officer. "All that material that we sent back two years ago." And it turns

out they either couldn't locate it or hadn't kept it; I never found out which.

In any case, following fieldwork I recommended against the project because of the threat posed to the proposed training site by the growing civil hostilities in that part of Sri Lanka. CIDA, however, proceeded with it, and in months it had been blown up on account of the civil war, as I had warned.

Others have noticed that aid bureaucrats often don't bother to visit the field. It wouldn't be so difficult, but they just don't do it. One person recalls being shocked by this when she did her master's degree in Limpopo Province, in South Africa:

> It was my first time being exposed to the politics of development and feeling cynical about it. The head office was in Pretoria, I was in a former homeland in Limpopo, and I chose to stay there in the village for five months. . . . But [the organization I was working with] had an agenda, and they didn't bother coming to the village. They'd pick me up from the edge of the village, take me to dinner, and say, "So tell us about village life; what you're learning is fascinating." And I'd be like, "You've been here for seven years, why don't you go?"

Development workers must almost certainly encounter at least one of these three risky tendencies embedded within many development institutions: not listening, an overly narrow fixation on accountability, and institutional forgetfulness. They are all frustrating yet persistent. Luckily, we as individuals can access three types of resources that can help us to mitigate the dangers that these risk factors pose to our work.

Resource 1: Time

Alastair Taylor, from the United Kingdom, recalls some advice he got as he was starting out in agricultural development work. Someone advised him

> not to worry about the short-term stuff—if you're committed and you want to do something with agriculture, you can't do much in one year or two years. You're talking about growing crops, knowing the seasons, changing attitudes and, at times, even perceptions. It's not like sticking up a building where you do it and everyone is

happy. So he said, if they want you for four years, go for four years! It's not so long, will go by quickly, and if it's not for you, then you can go on to whatever's next in your life.

This is advice that Alastair took on. He stayed in his first post in northern Uganda for six years. He's been working in international development for over twenty years now. All of his jobs have been for multiple years. All have been in Uganda, focusing on agriculture and increasingly on organic agriculture and livelihood development. He can look back at what he has done and see the contributions that he has made. For example, he helped to establish the National Organic Agricultural Movement of Uganda (NOGAMU), which remains active and vibrant today.

Although this all seems simple and basic, time is the magic ingredient that many development workers skimp out on. Becoming too specialized in one area or sometimes even on one topic is sometimes seen as bad for one's career. Aid agencies often have two- or three-year postings. For some types of work, and especially for emergency relief, short-term postings are warranted. But for long-term development, they often mean that people come in with a steep learning curve, and by the time they've started to develop a level of understanding beyond the surface level, they're moving on.

Resource 2: Relationships

Time is so valuable because it helps us to build up contextual understanding and to adjust our actions accordingly. But one person, or even one organization, is rarely in a position to have a complete understanding of a situation or complete access to the points of leverage to change it. And so relationships are key. For younger workers, this often includes finding mentors and role models who embody the kinds of principles and approaches that they want to emulate. For any development project or program, it is about finding allies with complementary strengths and knowledge and investing in processes that allow stakeholders to voice and exchange views, learn from each other, and make decisions.

One example of this leveraging of relationships comes from the early experiences of the Swedish Committee for Afghanistan (SCA). At that time, in the 1980s, they had plenty of funding and latitude about what to do with it. They were based out of Peshawar in Pakistan, without any relations with the Soviet-supported Afghan government, which was in civil war against Western-supported mujahedeen commanders. Their mission during these early years was to run humanitarian projects in villages in Afghanistan.[8] Anders Fange, who headed the SCA from 1982, when it started, until 1990, explains how they used local knowledge bases to check with whom they were working:

It was actually pretty simple, because what we did was we established clinics. That's what we started with, and then later we started schools. And the methods we used were pretty simple. There were the commanders at the time, and it was a cross-border operation.

We were setting up a system at the time to check them, and to give an example, we were setting up an office in Peshawar, and there was a rumor that there was an organization that was assisting cross-border, so then people came to us, often a commander or the representative of a commander, and they wanted to have a clinic. Then there were pretty intensive, profound interviews with them; they had to introduce health staff themselves—we didn't do that, they had to—doctors and paramedics and so on.

We did two checks on them. One was technical, on the staff—some people who called themselves doctors, in the worst case they'd taken a three-day International Committee of the Red Cross (ICRC) training, so we had to check what their level of health knowledge was. And one was what we called political checking. We could get a guy who said, "My name is Abdul Malik and I'm from this area, fighting jihad." And we'd ask him, "What is the size of area you're controlling, what party are you aligned with, how many people are you controlling?" And then we'd send checkers—police and so on, who were refugees but were used to doing these kinds of checks—and we employed them. You went out in the refugee camp, because in the camp you had people from that district, and you looked for mujahedeen who were out for their rest break and were from the district and asked them too. And usually it was seven or so sources that you checked about this Abdul Malik—and maybe they'd say, it's true he's from here, but he's been living in Peshawar for five years and he and his brothers are running a pharmacy, and he's out to get medicine to sell it. Or maybe, they'd say, it's true—but he doesn't have five hundred mujahedeen, only fifty—then there's an opening. And that is how we'd do it. There was more loss than if we could do it under more orderly conditions. But we got a pretty good reputation for keeping away the bad guys, the pretty corrupt people. You'd call them the good and bad Muslims; that's what the Afghans called them. So we sought out the good Muslims, while staying away from those who were corrupt and sucking the blood of their own people.

Different situations and different goals call for different sorts of relationships and alliances. But if there are ways of working with people and verifying motives and identities in the midst of a complex and bloody war, then there are ways of doing so in almost any situation.

Resource 3: Existing Research

Over the years, there have been many studies conducted, reports and theses written, and theories developed on international development issues, approaches, and the areas where such work has been done. Some would even argue there are too many. When the *ujamaa* approach of Tanzania under President Julius Nyerere was popularly seen as a potential role model for rural development, it was so overrun with foreign researchers that at some points, some villages had more researchers than residents.[9] And yet one of the ironies of international development is how little we make use of all of this, how we can feel like we're just starting out despite all of this great amassing.

Some people like Jim Shute make it their work to collect and share this kind of documentation, trying to remediate what they see as a systemwide problem. The information is out there, and not so hard to find, for those who make it their work to find it.

Pockets of Sanity

Individuals working in development clearly can't count on a wide culture of support in learning how to be effective in their work. The development system is more likely to place obstacles in their path: onerous reporting requirements that take up too much time, the need to show results in an unrealistic time period, the need to chase funds and respond to donor priorities, and limited space and time to reflect on and learn from what is actually happening. Some organizations may require or encourage them to move on a regular rotation, meaning that they'll be back to square one with their understanding of a particular situation.

So if individuals are really committed to doing good development work, it has to be a personal commitment; the onus is on them. They will have to work around and within the obstacles.

The development system as a whole tends to lean toward simplicity, short-termism, and political expedience. That doesn't look likely to change radically anytime soon. But within it there are many institutions and people who act as voices of reason, who learn and remember and focus their efforts on what they understand good development to be. And these people talk to each other and share ideas, and so there is a fair body of knowledge on what works and what doesn't work. Some of it is perhaps common sense, and some of it is less common. People like Jim Shute, Kaia Ambrose, Sally Humphries, and many others act as counterbalances within the system.

When such individuals have been around long enough and have enough seniority, some manage to put organizational emphasis on monitoring and evaluation systems that will help them and their colleagues learn. We'll meet some of these people in chapters 9 and 10. Some NGOs do well at this too, and some donors do try to be flexible and allow space for learning and adaptive management. Working against the prevailing trends in international development is often a matter of individual professional conviction and tenacity. But with like-minded allies and sustained efforts, these individual efforts can join and grow to increase the precious pockets of sanity.

Notes

1. From an anonymous interview with an aid worker. Existing documented estimates on life expectancy in Kibera vary but place it at between thirty and forty-seven years of age.

2. Donald A. Schön, *The Reflective Practitioner: How Professionals Think in Action* (New York: Basic Books, 1984).

3. N. Uphoff, M. Esman, and A. Krishna, *Reasons for Success: Learning From Instructive Experiences in Rural Development* (West Hartford, CT: Kumarian Press, 1998), 116.

4. Robert Chambers, *Challenging the Professions: Frontiers for Rural Development* (London: Intermediate Technology Development Group, 1993), 115.

5. This incident is also described in Ricardo Ramirez and Wendy Quarry, *Communication for Another Development* (London: Zed Books, 2008), 118.

6. Susan Cornwell, "Angry US House Lawmaker Cuts Aid to Afghanistan," *Reuters*, June 28, 2010.

7. Tina Wallace, Lisa Bornstein, and Jennifer Chapman, *The Aid Chain: Coercion and Commitment in Development NGOs* (Bourton-on-Dunsmore: Practical Action, 2007).

8. By the 1990s, SCA's work was focused on longer term development.

9. Graham Hancock, *The Lords of Poverty: The Power, Prestige, and Corruption of the International Aid Business* (New York: Atlantic Monthly Press, 1989), 114.

Part 3

Different Ways to Engage

For what it's worth: it's never too late or, in my case, too early to be whoever you want to be. There's no time limit, stop whenever you want. You can change or stay the same, there are no rules to this thing. We can make the best or the worst of it. I hope you make the best of it. And I hope you see things that startle you. I hope you feel things you never felt before. I hope you meet people with a different point of view. I hope you live a life you're proud of. If you find that you're not, I hope you have the strength to start all over again.

—*F. Scott Fitzgerald*

We've now reached part 3 of the book, which is where things really get interesting. We've finished looking at the international development system writ large, its main institutions, and what it is like to work there. We've looked at some of the key issues that development practitioners face in their work and the types of decisions they must make over their careers. We've looked at some of the inequities and dysfunctions common within the international development system that threaten to usurp or pervert good intentions if they are not tempered with careful, honest reflection and genuine commitment.

So given all this, what are the different ways that practitioners can approach their work? And of these approaches, which appear most likely to be successful, in terms of both the quality of their work and their own well-being?

This part of the book answers both of these questions by drawing heavily on the interviews with the development practitioners described in chapter 1.

The ways that development workers engage in their work differs depending on circumstance, personality, and their particular understanding and commitments at a given time. It is certainly not uncommon for people to try out different approaches and to refine their approach, as we saw in the previous chapters. Perhaps during a particularly rough patch, they become unmotivated and behave more passively than they normally would. Perhaps because of an inspirational mentor or a particularly worthy opportunity, they become supercharged and particularly passionate and committed to what they are doing, with great result.

Two dimensions that underlie the full range of possible approaches to development work are criticality and engagement. Criticality is closely related to reflectivity, which I've already argued is key to being an effective development practitioner. In fact, we can say that reflectivity is a particular form of criticality. It is possible to be critical of the development system or of a particular development agency without considering the way that relates to one's own position. Reflective criticality includes oneself as a worthy object of critical thought, all the more so because it is much easier to change oneself in response to a critical insight than it is to reform, for example, the governance of the United Nations.

Engagement is the degree to which one is committed to one's work and practically involved in it. So again, it is very closely related to motivation. Engagement can best be thought of as motivation in action, a happy situation where one is doing what one wants to do.

Reflective criticality and engagement are the two crucial ingredients for effective development work. Without being actively engaged or committed to our work, we are prone to drift through the aid system. If we are critically inclined, then in the absence of engagement, we become cynical. Or else, if we lack both critical thought and engagement, we become passively aligned to the status quo of the development system, and in conforming to it, we tend to reinforce it.

There are two main approaches that contain both criticality and engagement in high measure. The first one I have termed, albeit not very imaginatively, "critical active engagement," and the second is "negotiation." They differ mainly in the type of engagement, as well as the degree. Active engagement is like signing up to a team with a philosophy that is compatible with one's own and then working toward the team's goal. Negotiation is more like using existing resources to achieve one's own goal and perhaps even starting a new team for that purpose. These more ambitious goals often demand a deep and enduring passion to realize and hence an exceptionally high level of engagement.

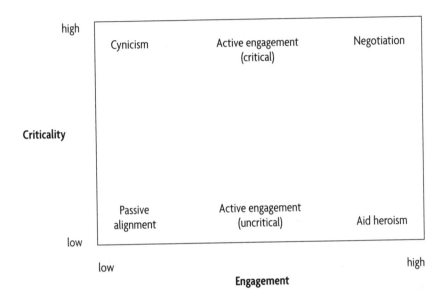

Figure 1

Both critical active engagement and negotiation have their more problematic counterparts, when engagement is high but criticality is low. I have termed these "uncritical active engagement" and "aid heroism."

Figure 1 visually summarizes where these six approaches (cynicism, passive alignment, critical active engagement, uncritical active engagement, negotiation, and aid heroism) fit in terms of the two dimensions of criticality and engagement.

Over the course of careers, we develop habits. Our understandings tend to crystallize into something ever more fixed. Most people tend to fall into a groove where the commitments and decisions and approaches that they have used before are the ones that shape their opportunities and that they continue to use. This is further stabilized by personality. Some people seem naturally disposed to find opportunities where others tend to see defeat. Some people retain a sharply critical edge to their thinking, whereas others have moved into a comfortably blunt acceptance of the way things are. Hence, it is often possible to characterize people themselves as fitting into one of these approaches on a stable, if not necessarily permanent, basis, so that the approach becomes a persona.

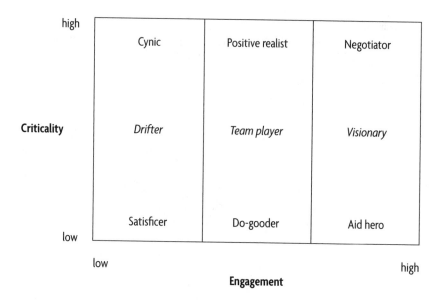

Figure 2

Figure 2 gives names to the personas associated with each of the six approaches. We can usefully categorize these personas into three categories, based purely on the degree of engagement. Those with the lowest degree of engagement are the drifters. Those with higher engagement are the team players, and those with the highest are the visionaries. Each of these personas has two different faces, depending on the degree of criticality. Drifters can be satisficers or cynics. Team players can be do-gooders or positive realists. And visionaries come as either aid heroes or negotiators. Satisficers, do-gooders, and aid heroes are all content to assume the best of the system or to actively create stories that frame their efforts in the best light. Cynics, positive realists, and negotiators are all critically aware of system limits and of their own limits within the system, although they vary in the degree to which they feel a responsibility to act.

People rarely fall permanently or perfectly into one persona. For one thing, a person's approach and the outcome of his or her work also depend in part on the situation. A person might excel in one situation but burn out entirely in another. On the other hand, although situations influence work and outcome, this isn't deterministic: a situation that one person faces passively, another may actively engage with or may be so frustrated with that he or she is prompted to leave development work altogether. By thinking about these different approaches, the different situations that evoke them, and the different insights they tend to prompt, we can become more conscious and deliberate in our own practices.

Most of us will have tendencies that resonate more or less with a particular persona. Taken with reservation, these personas can be useful ideas but should never be seen as immutable truths. It can be helpful to think of the approaches we might adopt or personas that we might take on as we navigate our way through international development. Some of them serve as warnings—if we feel ourselves identifying with elements of these too much, we must be careful. Others serve as inspirations—as what we can aspire to be in our work lives, of the kinds of peers and mentors we can seek out.

Each of these personas is considered in more detail in the following three chapters. Chapter 8 covers the drifters in both incarnations, chapter 9 explores the team players, and chapter 10 describes what it means to be a visionary. In each chapter, we consider the circumstances and the mind-set and choices that tend to foster such an approach, as well as the consequences of each approach. We do this by drawing in some detail on the stories of those interviewed for the book, whose experiences in some way or another exemplify an aspect of these approaches.

Chapter 11 is devoted to considering why and how people leave the international development system to pursue work that is sometimes related or sometimes completely different. Those who choose to opt out of the development system are all over the spectrum in terms of both engagement and criticality. Once people leave the international development system, many find other ways of staying engaged in similar work.

8

The Drifters

In the first part of this book, we saw some of the forces and structures that shape the international development system. Drifters are those who are carried along by the currents of this system as it flows through time and space. They are largely passive. Cynics are passive because they have come to the conclusion that they can't take effective action in the system. Satisficers are just uncritical about international development or their roles in it.

I assume that if you are reading this book, you care about development work and want to do your own work well. Probably, then, only extremely challenging circumstances could provoke a persistent sense of helplessness and passivity within you. Development workers do sometimes encounter such circumstances in which it seems that one's best efforts will never make any meaningful difference. Those who find themselves in these situations can feel levels of stress, distress, and exhaustion that are hard to bear for prolonged periods. This chapter considers some of the factors that lead to burnout and turn people into cynics. It also touches more briefly on the satisficers—those who are not so much cynical as disengaged, happy to believe that their limited efforts fit some larger function that someone else is responsible for.

When cynicism and indifference are widespread, they have knock-on effects on institutional culture within development agencies and beyond. We look at this phenomenon in the section titled "The Contagion of Indifference." Finally, the chapter ends by considering some of the moral dilemmas that people have faced in their work. These dilemmas raise questions about what we can and should try to change and what we should accept.

Burning Out and Distraught Cynicism

Peters Nyawanda is a Kenyan who went to work in Sri Lanka for several years, starting in 2003. In 2005, in the midst of the civil war, he joined a small NGO that used nonviolent means to protect civilians trapped in the conflict. The staff used their presence and their positive relationships with local communities to create neutral spaces to resolve conflicts and follow up on particular issues within the conflict, such as the recruitment of child soldiers. He spent a year working for the NGO and recalls,

> This job was the most intense job I'd ever done, in terms of time demanded, the traveling, and the stresses that come from dealing with so many difficult actors, and being able to absorb the traumas, the emotions of the different families. People would come and tell you, my boy was just shot, or they blew up our family's house. There were a lot of emotions to deal with . . . so you find that most of the people who joined never worked beyond six months—one year was a long time—and their moods, their reactions, the way of thinking—all of it was kind of affected. The way we were working, I didn't think you could do it for a long time. There was support for the staff, but it was out of the country, and it was just support over the phone, which I didn't find very useful. But there was a lot of support for your colleagues in the organization; we'd cry together, laugh about it, but it was really stressful.
>
> We were also a target—we were attacked three times. . . . [One time] some Sinhalese came and surrounded our vehicle and started to accuse us of supporting the Tamils and being spies. They started hitting and breaking our vehicle, and we were surrounded by these soldiers with grenades and pistols. They didn't speak English. We tried to remain calm, we thought the soldiers would help us, but they didn't—they encouraged them. Then one old man we knew intervened and stopped them, after about an hour. Another day a grenade was thrown into our compound, injuring one person and killing our dog. The Norwegian peace monitors were actually attacked, and they called us in, because we had very good relations with the communities; that was our support, our protection. So these were not really very nice experiences.

Peters's experiences are ones that most of us would find very stressful and difficult to deal with. Burnout is one possible result from such experiences—a psychological state that people reach when they find themselves unable to cope with prolonged stress. According to Maslach and Schaufeli, two psychologists who pioneered research on the topic, job burnout has three main characteristics: exhaustion, cynicism, and inefficacy.[1] We risk burnout when we are faced with a situation in which we feel responsible to act, but it seems impossible to do so effectively, such as being a custodian of peace in the midst of war. Peters in fact recalls that his work did manage to help some families keep their young boys from being taken as soldiers and to help warring communities resolve their differences peaceably. But this was always in the context of a much larger, messier conflict.

When we think of workers burning out in the context of international development, we tend to think of those who work in sites of conflict or disaster, exposed to great human suffering. And many development workers do find themselves in such situations, especially those who take positions on the humanitarian side of the spectrum. The trend in international development is that more people are working in such "complex humanitarian emergencies" not just as relief workers but also on longer term development projects. Both Afghanistan and Iraq, for example, have had long-term development projects in the face of continued insecurity and instability.

A small but growing body of academic literature on burnout in humanitarian workers suggests that it is a widespread problem and that most aid institutions have very limited support in place to help workers cope. For example, one study in Darfur found that just over a third of workers could be classified as burned out or at high risk of burnout. National staff were at greater risk of burnout than expatriates, which was not surprising as many were also displaced victims of war.[2]

Undoubtedly, some situations place us at greater risk of unmanageable stress and burnout. Such situations can also test people's faith in humanity and in themselves. Development workers often find themselves faced with conflict, insecurity, and the reality of human suffering. Unfortunately, such experiences are frequently coupled with experiences of human incompetence, greed, and cruelty. It is this juxtaposition that people often find most difficult. Sometimes these human weaknesses are evident within their own organizations, and this is for many people the most troubling of all.

Marina Fakhouri, who has worked in various humanitarian emergencies for a variety of NGOs, argues that it is the weakness and incompetence of organizations and workmates that cause the most stress for people dealing with tough situations. She speaks based on research she conducted on the topic, as well as her own firsthand experience:

> Burnout in particular is often systemic. You know before you start in this work that you'll be faced with hardship, the security situation

is dubious, but I think what you're not aware of is that you're going to have colleagues who are going to have a different motivation level than you, that they often join for the wrong reasons, that the admin may not be that effective or supportive, and that sometimes you're surrounded by people who are just blatantly incompetent, and I think that's what often causes the burnout. I've spoken to a lot of field-workers. And that's what I've confirmed in my own experience. For me, my daily stresses are often related to issues with colleagues and the organization I'm working for.

Likewise, someone working for the UN Assistance Mission in Afghanistan says that for him,

by far, the UN has been really the most frustrating. People think, you're going to come to Afghanistan, it's going to be really stressful—but honestly, Afghanistan itself hasn't given me stress at all. Every stress I face is directly a product of working for the UN. I feel there's zero support from the Mission. I'm constantly late for meetings because of car trouble.

Even Peters, contrasting his time in Sri Lanka with later experiences in Afghanistan, recalls the latter as more difficult. Although he was never attacked or in the midst of immediate conflict in Afghanistan, he found the cultural and linguistic gap between himself and the Afghan people more difficult, and the security restrictions more constraining:

I think Afghanistan, culturally, it's very different; it's one of the most difficult places, especially socially. The security restrictions were far worse than anything we had in Sri Lanka; even when it got so bad there, we could still walk in town. The work [in Afghanistan], we were working—basically we were doing direct implementation ourselves, and we had a language challenge; most of our field staff barely spoke English, so it was difficult to engage in meaningful conversation that would help you really understand what they're doing in the field, because you have a lot of restrictions on where you can go, how long you can stay in the field. The other challenge was where you have to work with the government; communication with the government was fairly difficult. Actually, knowing when you have a commitment from a staff of the government—a firm commitment—would be very difficult. They may say it, but then they change; you don't know why they change—if they didn't mean it or they've gotten communication from higher authorities.

Ultimately, Peters found these structural constraints on his own effectiveness more frustrating and difficult than anything he had encountered in Sri Lanka. Communications problems and political shifts within the government meant that much of his work effort was wasted. As Marina observed, we expect war situations to be difficult, we expect that being a witness to others' suffering will be hard, but structural incompetence is much harder for many people to accept. Those who feel a keen sense of responsibility and then feel they are unable to be effective are often those at greatest risk of burnout.

People face cynicism and despair when they feel like what they are doing is unlikely to ever make a difference. Perhaps they are trying to work with a government that appears hopelessly weak and corrupt, or they are trying to advocate for change on an issue for years and years without any sign of breakthrough or without any way of judging their effectiveness. In such situations, we try to weigh the possibilities that our efforts might lead to worthwhile change and decide whether to continue. It's sometimes hard to tell. Sometimes, especially when people are feeling stressed and burned out, it is really difficult for them to have that bigger perspective. Something could be challenging but still worth doing. Or maybe we're just throwing ourselves against a brick wall.

When I think back to my own time working in Afghanistan, the times I got most discouraged were when I could see the effects of war and poverty and yet the leaders seemed more interested in helping themselves than helping the country. If I'd been involved with a health program or education program with stable funding and I could see the progress there, the political situation would still have bothered me, but it wouldn't have been so personal. But I was working for a research organization, and my job was to develop strategies to influence policy through the research we produced. And yet it often seemed that evidence, or even simple reason, was not the sort of thing that policymakers were worried about. In the summer of 2010, during a particularly trying time, I wrote to friends about a high-level planning meeting between donors and senior government officials:

What really bugged me was the giant abyss lurching between what participants, especially government representatives, promised and planned, and . . . well, and reality. And the fact that they didn't seem particularly bothered about it. Many of the donors appeared to be a sad combination of frantic and resigned, while the most senior government leaders acted irritatingly smug. "This doesn't seem very realistic," the donor representatives would say. . . . "It seems in these plans like there is no war in Afghanistan?" And the lead ministers would say things like, "It's good to be ambitious." And then the US, in the person of Ambassador Eikenbury, would promise some more funding, and the ministers would be happy, and the meeting was adjourned.

I found myself struggling to find the motivation to do my best work during this time. Much of my energy was spent on being dismayed. That experience has left me with a strong admiration for those people who tough it out even when the odds are stacked, not with a grim fatalism but with an intelligence that doesn't see everything as fixed in place. It does require some political savvy. And probably a pretty good support group of like-minded people.

Working Through Burnout

For people who feel responsible for their work, and who feel the need to be responsible, neither the exhaustion nor the cynicism that results from burnout are states that they can maintain. For expat aid workers, taking time out from the source of stress is relatively easy, or if necessary, they move on to another posting. For national staff, this can often be a little more difficult. But as long as people can find time to relax and reflect, they are usually able to work through their burnout. And insofar as being cynical represents feeling serious doubt about the effectiveness of one's efforts, or the efforts of which one is a part, it can be instructive. It can provide pause for reflection as to its cause and its solution. Such reflection may prompt some people to change their role or work location or even to leave development altogether. However, most development workers cope in part by adjusting their expectations around what they and the institutions they work for can do. As we saw in the previous chapter, most development workers find they have to adjust at least some of their initial expectations about their work, especially early in their careers. Burnout, however, tends to result from the most intense and emotionally potent forms of mismatched expectations.

Anna[3] began her career in international development but then became involved in humanitarian work, much of it through the UN. Recalling her initial expectations, she says,

I was highly idealistic, I guess, when I first started. That has changed. If I look back at it, honestly my main driver was my quest for adventure or exotic places I'd never heard of and wanted to explore and learn about . . . but it was sugarcoated by a lot of wanting to change the world and make it a better place.

It's changed—I think reality hits you in the face as soon as you land.

In Anna's case, one harsh reality was realizing how little she, and the UN, could do in the face of political violence in one of the first countries she was posted to. She recalls,

People—some weren't even known activists, some were just simple farmers who'd gotten frustrated and said something against [the ruling party], and then their house was burnt down. So some came to the UN, and then you sit there as a bureaucrat and tell them you can't do anything, and that was heartbreaking.

In fact, however, Anna did do something. She convinced her boss that they should document the abuses, so that at least it was possible that at some point in the future, action might be taken. This seemed to her the best possible action she could take under the circumstances. But, as she says, it was of little comfort to the victims. And so she learned to scale down her expectations:

It's more like an honest partnership now—I want to look at myself in the mirror and feel I've earned my salary honestly, but I don't want to have unrealistic expectations of what I can do or what the system can do. If I feel I've done my best, and what is right, that's what I want.

Like now, my responsibility, what people can hold me accountable to, is to support authorities and their development partners in the countries where we work, to increase their preparedness for emergencies, and help them respond to emergencies. If I do that well, then I've helped a little bit, and if I look back at some of the situations where I've worked, I think we can honestly say that we did help . . . but that hasn't changed the bad guys from doing bad things, unfortunately.

Anna reduced her expectations of what was possible, but she still finds value in her work and feels that her decisions make a difference. Some people don't manage to do this. They feel so disillusioned by the limits of what is possible that they do not find much satisfaction in their work. The burnout persists as bitterness, expectations so reduced that they feel trapped, caught up in the system without being able to change it or act in it in any useful way. If this attitude pervades mood and thinking unchecked, and if the individuals so affected do not choose to leave development, they are likely to become the cynics that many development workers have encountered and feared to become. We fear it because on our bad days, we know those feelings and thoughts well. But when we settle into it, we give up our own agency and become passive puppets of a system we doubt. The next part of the chapter considers the consequences of doing this.

Drifting

Burnout can lead to cynicism and passivity. But while people who burn out began with a deep sense of responsibility that they then find themselves unable to act on, others who come into development just never cared that much in the first place about the purpose of their work. They see their job just as a way of making a living. Of these unengaged people, some, the cynics, tend to be critical of the system and to work on the assumption that their work won't really make a difference. Others, the satisficers, assume that their work somehow fits into a larger whole in some helpful way but don't concern themselves very much with inquiring into how. That's someone else's job. There's a continuum between these two camps, and many people fit somewhere in between. We now look in a bit more detail at the cynics and satisficers in turn.

Cynics

Cynicism is a very common characteristic of and justification for the passivity of the aid drifter. Cynicism naturally deflects and denies personal responsibility. By expecting little from human beings en masse and from human social systems in general, cynicism implies that the actions of one person to effect broader change are doomed to failure. This attitude is self-defeating, but it is also, at the same time, self-protecting. When one is unable to effect change, one is excused from culpability. And by lowering expectations, one can protect oneself from disappointment.

People working in international development are often working on complex issues in difficult environments. Mostly, they have only incomplete information about the issues they are dealing with. They understand only certain perspectives. They may not be fully aware of the context. Sometimes they don't know all the languages of the people affected by the programs or policies they are working on, much less the intricacies of their daily lives and their thoughts and aspirations. They may become frustrated, not because of insights about the limitations of the system but rather because their understanding is limited. Sometimes people are tempted to externalize their frustrations and blame those things that they do not fully understand or cling to quite shallow explanations of why and how something is a problem. In such cases, cynicism becomes a lazy theory of why things don't work. Things don't work because the people here are corrupt or lazy or incompetent. A young development worker in Afghanistan noted this about some of his expat colleagues:

> The natural reaction when you come to a developing context, and you're not comfortable with the context and your job, you put this discomfort on the elbows of the locals—you complain about their capacity. I had a colleague like this—he was a bit overwhelmed by the job and so was putting the burden on the notion the locals were bad. That was what you don't want to give, that's not what you should communicate at all. . . . When you're not able to keep your frustration to yourself anymore, you should leave. Afghans already have enough—they know they're in a country that's had war for thirty years, that it's a frustrating context; the history of the people is frustrating, so you shouldn't add to this your own frustration. What you add to this is your dynamism. That's the day I will leave, when I can't keep my frustration to myself, I have to leave, for their good and my good. That's not good development.

Cynical attitudes tend to oversimplify because they take negative observations and treat them as general rules. Some environments can be incredibly tough. One person recalls of his time in Djibouti:

> I stayed in Djibouti for almost a year—far too long, Djibouti's a horrible place to live. It's very hot, and working with the authorities is a pain in the ass—extremely corrupt and incompetent at everything, apart from cheating and chewing khat—they're completely high in the afternoon. It's a nightmare working there—people are so corrupted, it is hard to do anything sustainable, clean; on top of that, you saw abuse. I was glad not to stay too long—this is one of those places, if you stay too long, you lose your motivation, your competence.

However difficult a place is, a cynical attitude rarely makes it easier. Expats who band together and share experiences in foreign places are often in great danger of turning their frustrations into general rules about the way people are or the way things operate. These generalizations can obscure rather than reveal reality and opportunities for positive engagement and change.

Satisficers

Big aid bureaucracies have plenty of people on staff who don't feel a strong personal commitment to their work and tend to put in the minimum amount of effort that they feel it requires. As a staff member at one donor comments,

> The greatest challenge is dealing with those who aren't really passionate about the work and aren't willing to put in the time to really research the project or issue at hand. Reading an article in *The Economist* doesn't make you an expert, it's more complex—a lot of people are 9-to-5 bureaucrats, and that doesn't cut it in the aid world, where it is so complex. But too many bureaucrats, they won't put in that effort.

Within small NGOs, more people are passionate. But in some smaller NGOs, and especially those operating in "hardship" situations, there are also relatively few checks on people who are inept and inappropriate. As one humanitarian worker notes,

> Some of these people are tax evaders or want-to-be dictators—you can do that in a humanitarian mission, wave your sword and treat people like shit. [It's because of] a lack of accountability—there's a lot more leeway given here.

Motivation matters, clearly. Those who come into development with a vague and weak desire to "do good," the assumption that the system largely works, and a disinclination to bother themselves too much by being critical or trying to follow up on the effects of their work can find themselves a comfortable spot in the aid bureaucracy. They may realize it doesn't work quite as they thought it would, but they won't think too hard about it, or they may just accept that the circumstances won't allow them to do the good they had hoped to do, and they leave it at that. A development worker in Afghanistan says,

I'm disappointed with a lot of what I see, not just with international development but also with the government—I don't think it has the capacity to receive a lot of that help. The structures, the people—they just don't exist. And if an advisor comes here and tries to help, first they get disappointed, and then they say, well, I'm making a big salary. . . . There is lots of corruption, where people just spend money on really expensive trips. And I see the donors who just make trips, they just want to make high officials happy, put them in five-star hotels, and no one even questions, "What is the outcome of your trip?"

Some people have drifted into development and stayed. Others came deliberately but then tire of development and find it is difficult to get out of aid work. They become trapped in the system, progressively less invested in the outcomes of their own work. The gradual decay of resolve and passion is a particular risk for people who are working in large aid bureaucracies or in situations where they are otherwise removed in time or place from the consequences of their work.

The Contagion of Indifference

Institutional Drift

In the best of all possible scenarios, aid drifters are largely neutral and benign. They are not the most passionate people, many may be quietly doubtful or open cynics, but they do their jobs, and as long as their leaders have a vision and the organizations they work in are fairly well structured, and the work is of a routine nature and not too demanding, all is well.

However, in most instances, development work is complex and messy. There are always competing interests seeking to set agendas and capture resources. When development workers only concern themselves with what is immediately in front of them, when they focus on narrowly achieving the objectives set by a specific project, as measured by predesigned indicators, their work is at greater risk of having effects other than those intended. And when development work is ineffective or wasteful or corrupted, this simply proves the cynics right, becoming a self-fulfilling prophecy.

When organizations are filled with enough people who are disinterested or cynical about the outcomes of their work, the mood shifts and the organizational culture becomes collectively concerned with other things—often with increasing the comfort and perks of working conditions. One longtime development worker observed such a trend at the African Development Bank (ADB), where he worked from 1986 to 1991. This was a time period where performance was poor and corruption was a visible problem:

> There were a lot of different nationalities put in to improve the standard, at the same time the ADB put in some young African professionals, who'd been shown to work well in their own governments. . . . They were very good and stood up and made critical comments about these projects they'd been assigned to. . . . You could see them being very put on by senior people who were there for thirty years, and you could see them thinking, "This is a good position with better money than I'd ever get at home," and you could see them thinking it through and thinking, "If we stay quiet, we'll be up there in five years"—so all the enthusiasm and ability got knocked out of them. Some of those people left immediately and got other jobs in the private sector, and the ones who stayed—I'm not saying they're no good, but they could have been better.

While this was a case of effective young professionals being weakened, others have noted that weak organizations often have nepotistic or politically motivated hiring practices or just fail to attract strong talent, again leading to higher levels of institutional incompetence.

Cynicism can become so pervasive within groups involved in international development that it becomes part of the fabric, part of the underlying ethos. When it spreads like this, it can become a self-fulfilling prophesy, eroding trust to the point that beneficial collective action through formal development intervention becomes very difficult.

Broader Misgivings

When aid agencies become stocked with enough drifters and are compromised by various personal and political interests, others notice. For example, people working in development in Nairobi often commented on institutional problems they had encountered with the UN. One young development professional in Nairobi was particularly upset with what she had seen of the UN there:

> Money is allocated for political reasons; people in charge don't always know what they're doing and are massively incompetent. . . .

I saw a lot of bad development practice in terms of preaching, not listening to people on the ground, paying people to come to things, not working with the people that might be best to work with because politically you're not supposed to—all sorts of HR and accounting disasters, poor organizational management. The UN was a massive letdown. UNDP—I've never had a single positive experience with them, and I'm horrified by what I've seen—a complete lack of accountability in spending money, a lack of effort in homework for figuring out what they should and shouldn't be doing. I hold them responsible for the practice of high per diems and consultancy fees. When you walk into a country like Kenya and pay $2,000 per day for a local consultant—how is a local organization supposed to hold on to talented people? What are you going to do to the country? Even an [international] organization like mine can't hold on to the best people because the UN pays them too much, and so local organizations can't compete for sure.

And I've had meetings where the head of the democracy program doesn't know anything about the country where they're working. And I've seen millions of dollars spent with nothing to show. . . . I'll give UNDP the credit for creating more jobs within the country, but is that it?

If such negative impressions of the UN or other development agencies are widespread in the places where they operate, how does this affect the relationship between agencies and the populations they are supposed to be working for?

Given the imbalances of power and resources that characterize most development interventions, combined with aspects that clearly represent political or economic self-interest of donors, many groups are prone to feel excluded and disadvantaged by development and can become distrustful and cynical about it. Oskar Semweya-Musoke is a Ugandan school principal who also hosts a weekly public affairs show on the radio. He says,

Like many, I'm quite cynical about international development and aid and donors. You know, it's very debatable how much of it is really about the intention to help, rather than for the development of the donor country. . . . Take the example of USAID and the British one, DFID. In DFID, now I do know some senior people who are Ugandans, but they're the minority, and they're not senior enough. And in USAID, I don't know if there are any, and if you just go by the salary package, I wonder how much of the money is going back.

Such distrust can often extend to the target beneficiaries of specific development projects. When clued-out development workers show up, don't understand the language or culture, and don't take the time to understand the situation, local people have little reason to expect they're going to benefit from their presence. Speaking of the Karamojong people in northwest Uganda, one unusually well-informed development worker says,[4]

> If you listen to people here, pastoralists don't trust the agenda so much—they've learnt over the years that the agendas that are designed to do something with them are generally not so much in their interests, so there's a lot of mistrust. . . . I don't think that many people here really think that what is going on will improve their lives. . . . And after seeing so many people come and go implementing their projects with huge budgets . . . in the end, life is still hard. To master life here, you still have to be skillful in the way your father or mother has been telling you—it's still about going out with goats, getting firewood. Do the people coming here even know the different kinds of grasses that grow here and their importance? Most of them don't have a clue.

The skepticism expressed by the pastoralists reflects their concerns over the likely impact that outside interveners will have over their way of life—a way of life that outsiders often appear to neither understand nor respect. It also reflects a long history in which outside intervention, whether by colonial powers or by the postcolonial government, has been largely negative for the Karamojong and their land. Such doubt means that the Karamojong are likely to limit their involvement and investment in externally instigated development efforts, using them only for immediate and tangible benefits.

If supposed beneficiaries are skeptical of the agendas of the development agents who come to help them, so too are some of those who are hired to work on development programs in their own countries. It is hard to work effectively when trust is low. And when people don't trust a system, they may feel more justified in seeking to fulfill their own personal interests at its expense, further contributing to widespread distrust and cynicism. Local coordinators of Uganda's National Agricultural Advisory Service (NAADS), a program intended to provide training and technical support to smallholder farmers, found such distrust could often cripple their work. Farmer groups would dissolve when members assumed that their leaders, who were volunteers, were getting money while they were being left out. These rumors were untrue, but many groups fell apart when members refused to meet unless they were paid. Those groups in which members trusted each other and were able to access and share some resources were often able to pursue activities that benefited all the members. But because so many people were cynical, such groups were a minority.

In resource-scarce environments, international development and humanitarian relief programs are sources of largesse that can attract the wrong kind of interest. Scandals become commonplace. In Uganda, top government officials siphoned millions off the Global Fund to Fight AIDS, Tuberculosis and Malaria.[5] Although a few officials were prosecuted, the biggest fish stayed free. Ugandans still refer to this as evidence that there is no real accountability for aid funds. As one person told me, "It was a real mess, and Uganda was almost off the Global Fund, but now we're back, and no one knows which fundamental changes have been made." Another Ugandan commented, "We keep wondering if the donors really know what's going on, and yet we're sure they do. . . . Like the Global Fund . . . it keeps being an apparition in our society."

In Uganda, corrupt politicians have often manipulated widespread public distrust to accuse local civil servants of corruption if such civil servants resist their efforts to access and misuse public funds. This was a widespread problem in the NAADS program. Some NAADS staff were corrupt, but others were clean but accused of corruption by corrupt politicians and put under a great deal of pressure. Rumors abounded, and it was very difficult for farmers to separate truth from lies and to know whom to trust.

Development workers trying to navigate such environments are at risk of becoming cynical themselves and even paranoid. The solution has to be time invested in understanding the context and building trust. That takes a genuine commitment too, and a real belief in the purpose of their work, or else it just isn't worth it. In the most difficult situations, you can never be 100 percent sure about the motives of anyone. I spent several years studying the operation of Uganda's NAADS. As I got to know how it worked, I learned what incredible political pressures many of the field coordinators faced just to do their job. They were often bribed, threatened, and cajoled into diverting resources and decision-making power to various local power holders. Some of those coordinators were consummate diplomats, pursuing their work under difficult circumstances while balancing the egos of politicians, understanding the nature and limits of their powers, and working it all like some kind of dance. At the same time, they faced great distrust and skepticism from many of the farmers, who often had inflated expectations of what the program could give them and often believed the coordinators were stealing money even when they were not. I had great admiration for those coordinators. I suppose I wouldn't be able to stand in judgment of those who buckled, as I don't know how well I would do myself in such a situation.

Moral Dilemmas: When to Act?

Burnout results when one feels one ought to act but cannot. Aid drifters are ones who have given up on feeling that imperative to act, or who never had it. Almost all people who enter development go through some process of reducing their expectations of what they can achieve, as they come to understand how the system constrains them. Still, those working within international development are often faced with the question of what to do in the face of flaws and injustices. When should they act, when can they act, when is it wise to act? Maintaining this capacity for discernment and the strength to act accordingly is one key element that separates aid drifters from the critically engaged workers whom we encounter in the next chapter.

One of the most challenging moral dilemmas I was told about was in Afghanistan. Because the story is recent and to protect the identities of those involved, I have used pseudonyms and left out or changed some key details.

I heard this story from a few people, but I tell it here from the perspective of someone who found herself in the midst of it. Julie[6] is a well-educated but fairly inexperienced expat development worker who got a position coordinating a program to provide social services to marginalized people in rural Afghanistan. The program had already been running for about four years when Julie arrived. It was serving 50,000 individuals in remote communities where the existing government services did not yet reach. The program wasn't flawless—there were some problems with the quality of services because of the resource challenges at the community level. But still, it provided services to people who otherwise would have nothing, people who had never had these services before. Community members, especially young women and girls, used and appreciated the services. In many communities, all people eligible for the services used them. Chances seemed good that the quality would improve with time. Over the longer term, the idea was that the program would be handed over to the government and integrated into existing government systems.

Just after Julie arrived to her new position, the program was under review and due to be extended. The NGO running the program had already been promised by the funder, USAID, that it was to be continued. But something went wrong. USAID denied the extension and instead demanded that the NGO transfer the program to the Afghan government over a three-month period. Julie knew that this premature transfer would have disastrous consequences. Government staff did not understand the program or yet have the necessary systems in place to run it. The time period was too short to hand over existing staff and institutions to government control. Instead, everyone who had been involved with the project would lose his or her job, and everything that was built up would be lost. The government would gain the responsibility but would not be able to deliver any services to these same remote communities for many years. By that time, they would be again starting from scratch, and all the people who had built the program would be long gone.

The problems had started when USAID auditors decided that the program was flawed. Some of the points the auditors raised showed that they had either not received or not understood the information they had been sent because that information already clearly addressed the auditors' concerns. When Julie and her colleagues prepared information responding to auditors' concerns and explaining why they needed the program to be extended, she got the impression that their USAID project officer had not passed the information on. He seemed incompetent. Julie said, "That guy is a scandal. He actually used to work for one of our partners, and they said that, well, there's a reason that this guy is no longer working for us. I'm sure that there are good people working in AID, but we haven't met them."

Julie and her colleagues were never sure why USAID had made such an abrupt decision. It appeared to be part of a policy shift to channel more USAID funding to the Afghan government. In itself, such a policy might be justified and worthwhile. But in this case, the way it was being carried out was clearly disastrous:

> We're dumping 50,000 [people] on the ministry, but they're not ready for it at all. . . . This is what we said in the request for the extension—that we need another year to hand over to the ministry and build their capacity in a responsible way. These are . . . in very remote, hard to reach communities—that's the whole point of these services, to put them in very hard to reach, small remote places where there isn't going to be a government equivalent, or at least not any time soon. And they talk of a transition phase—this is ironic; to me a transition involves a time element. And now when they talk about a transition, it's a couple of months, but that's not

nearly enough to get that kind of system up and running. We're supposed to be providing technical support, but the people we're supposed to be providing technical support to haven't been hired yet—they're just a dot on the org chart. USAID dropped the ball, and so did the ministry to some extent. There's no reason for USAID not to understand; when the project ends, it's gone, the people are gone, the systems are gone—it's gone. You can't just say three or six months down the line, "Oh, that was a mistake, let's start over." There's a lot of capacity that's just lost.

Julie's bosses in the NGO chose to respond in a very cautious manner. This may have been because they had other large projects also funded by USAID. In any case, they did contact USAID to object to the decision but only by letter to a midlevel official in Kabul. Julie wasn't sure that USAID people in Washington even knew about the decision. There had been some internal talk that her NGO headquarters in the United States should directly contact senior USAID staff in Washington and alert them to what was happening since it seemed so clearly wrong. Again more cautious people within the NGO decided this was an inappropriate breach of protocol. But the small actions they'd taken were clearly inadequate to change the tide of what was happening:

> I'm not in the position to make those decisions, and maybe I'm naive or not sufficiently aware of what could be the wider consequences of getting people to be aware of it; it's very frustrating, it's like watching a train wreck which is going to happen. You see those trains? They're going to crash, but let's not call 911 because they might be upset. This is not a difficult story—it's so clear this is wrong. . . . Now these communities feel abandoned—by us, by their government. And the communities have invested a lot in this . . . now we're going to pull the plug. They have every right to feel betrayed, I think.

Julie said she had lost sleep over this project. But she felt like she could not overstep the clear directive set by her boss. Her boss felt unable or unwilling to speak out further. Some people within the NGO felt what was happening was wrong but were unable to gain a broader consensus that they felt they needed to speak out. Some people within USAID were concerned about the decision but also didn't know what to do about it. And the project, several months later, closed. So many people involved in the project felt that what was happening was wrong, and yet no one was willing or able to change the course of events. As with so much of international development, they moved on in their work lives relatively untouched by the consequences. It was the people in the communities who had to live with it, and they had no recourse at all.

Julie was in a difficult position, as she was new to the organization and quite new to development work in general. As her project was shut down, Julie decided to stay in Afghanistan and get another job. "I want to stay—that's a recommendation, isn't it? It's a triumph of optimism over experience!" After all, she was still establishing herself in her career, and Afghanistan has many opportunities for those looking for experience. She will have questions and ideas that she carries on with her from her first taste of "real development." I don't know how these will shape her future professional identity and practice, but they will, somehow.

When I heard Julie's story, I wondered what I would have done in her position. What would we be willing to risk our careers over, to inconvenience ourselves over? On what issues do we take personal responsibility, and on what issues do we concede that although we feel bad, there is nothing that we can, or are willing to, do? I don't really think there are any clear or right answers. But sometimes thinking through these issues before we face them is helpful.

Ricardo Ramirez and Wendy Quarry argue that it is much easier to speak out when one is further established in one's career, with greater financial security and perhaps without the pressing financial responsibilities of a young family. They point out that often people choose to speak out, if at all, only after having worked for many years within the establishment and having established their own credentials.[7] William Easterly and Paul Collier are both examples of people who have worked within the development mainstream and, with well-established careers and impressive credentials, have provided public critiques of the aid system.

Our own sense of career security is one factor that is likely to weigh in on our decisions, but it is not the only one. Our sense of responsibility is tied to our sense of commitment. Those of us who know we can easily walk away tend to find it easier to shrug our shoulders and wash our hands when faced with situations that we feel are wrong.

Many of us face difficult situations of various sorts that force us to choose our battles. Julie felt she was unlikely to be effective if she had tried to break organizational norms and break the decision-making hierarchy. Perhaps if she had taken the risk, she could have changed the way the program was shut down. But it seems unlikely. The judgment about when to accept what we see as beyond our control and when to act is not an easy one. The status quo is a powerful current. We are all drifters sometimes.

Conclusion

There is an artful balance between accepting what we cannot change as a reality that we must work within and critically engaging it. Those who burn out have lost that balance because they expected more of themselves than they could give, trying to shift the orbit of the earth by jumping up and down on it. The only sane action is to reduce one's expectations of oneself. And most of us do. Some of us, however, take it too far. We begin to believe that our actions don't really matter, and by doing so, we absolve ourselves of responsibility.

Some cynics have become cynics because it can be heart wrenching to see all the flaws in the development system and yet not be able to change it. Others are cynics because it is intellectually convenient for them. Cynicism in small doses can be a reality check, but in large doses it can be poisonous. Marina Fakhouri explains,

> On my good days, I believe there are a lot of committed people out there, and there are needs, and these needs are being addressed. On my more cynical days, I worry about the agendas for doing it, the durability of it, and whether we're really helping in certain instances or whether we're creating a different type of dependency, dependency with no sustainability, and that's my main concern.

It is ironic that those who are disengaged and lack commitment are a major source of stress for those who do care. And such stress, when it becomes overwhelming, can lead to burnout and cynicism, which can cause people to disengage. And so, like swimmers caught in an undertow, those who cared deeply find themselves and their beliefs turned upside down.

Still, it is far too trite to say that effective development work requires a positive, "can-do" attitude. Development workers often do face very real structural constraints or disincentives that would make doing the right thing, from the view of effectiveness, career suicide. One of the biggest dilemmas that many of us face is deciding what is beyond our ability to influence, or just not worth fighting, and when we should stand up. It is about judging how much agency and influence we really do have and how we can best use it. Most of us work through this, although never in any definitive way. It's an ongoing struggle, and one in which the struggle itself is a good sign, as it shows that we are still trying.

Notes

1. Christina Maslach and Wilmar B. Schaufeli, "Historical and Conceptual Development of Burnout: Recent Developments in Theory and Research," in *Professional Burnout: Recent Developments in Theory and Research*, ed. Christina Maslach and Tadeusz Marek, *Series in Applied Psychology: Social Issues and Questions* (Philadelphia: Taylor & Francis, 1993).

2. Saif Ali Musa and Abdalla A. R. M. Hamid, "Psychological Problems Among Aid Workers Operating in Darfur," *Social Behavior and Personality* 36, no. 3 (2008).

3. Name changed for anonymity.

4. This person had a background as an anthropologist and had extensively studied the lifestyles of pastoralists within the region.

5. "Uganda Shaken by Fund Scandal," *Washington Times*, June 15, 2006.

6. "Julie" is a pseudonym. Likewise, specific details of the program are not given or are changed to provide anonymity to those involved.

7. Ricardo Ramirez and Wendy Quarry, *Communication for Another Development* (London: Zed Books, 2008).

9

The Team Players

Those choosing to work in international development have no assurance that their own purpose and motivation will align with and be supported by their workplace and the broader development system. In the previous chapters, we've seen many of the obstacles and challenges that can lead development workers to the edges of despondency and despair. And yet, many people do still manage to align their energies with the broader situation. How do they do it? This chapter considers some experiences of those who have felt that they've by and large managed to find a supportive organizational environment and to work effectively in development. The secret to their apparent success lies in a combination of pragmatic optimism, careful decision making, hard work, and a little bit of good luck.

Aligning one's own ideas and aims with one's work situation depends foremost on knowing what one's aims are. For most of us, this is not as straightforward as it initially seems, because our ideas about how things work, what is possible, and even what is important change with experience. What we value most in our work is also quite a personal thing. For some people, the most important aspect is the relationships with fellow workers or with beneficiaries. Others are motivated by humanist or spiritual ideals and want a workplace that reflects that. For some it is about the method or process. For others, it is a particular issue that they are passionate about, such as health care, child protection, or women's empowerment. As one's own ideas and ideals of the world change with time, so too can one's relationship with work be renegotiated. And as one's work situation changes, so too do opportunities to pursue work that one finds motivating and energizing. All of this is to say that active engagement is always dynamic. It is also, to a large degree, serendipitous and opportunistic. The ideas of "fortuitous accidents" and organic, nonlinear career paths recur frequently among those who feel that they have happily found their niche in international development and are able to do effective work.

All of this makes sense, because being effective in development work fundamentally requires learning and adapting to the particularities of a situation—the needs and opportunities it brings. And this isn't something that can be preplanned, or even properly understood, without moving through the experience in its own time.

Effective adaptation requires critical reflection. Without questioning the likely effect of one's actions and the limits of one's knowledge and without seeking feedback, one remains held back by the necessarily simplistic ideas that one started out with. These are the do-gooders, the people who assume they know more than they do, who assume their efforts are benign even when the consequences may be unwelcome. When a development worker isn't really critical or is insulated from effective feedback, she is living in a myth. It could be a happy and self-aggrandizing myth—she could be a hero in her own mind, saving the world. This might align with the perceptions of distant publics and the public relations materials of development agencies. But it is unlikely to align much with reality, and so it isn't going to help guide her in effective development work. And if she's reasonably thoughtful and committed, she is due to get disillusioned soon enough.

Effective alignment is critical alignment. Those who find this, the positive realists, possess a degree of professional maturity combined with a degree of serendipity, insofar as finding work situations that allow for, or even nurture, effective work. Without this serendipity, many of us find ourselves working in what Ricardo Ramirez and Wendy Quarry term "the grey zone." This is the space where capricious bureaucracies can block or undo our careful efforts because of a policy change or a leader with other ideas. It is the space where although we might manage to win some of our battles, we can't win them all. We're not certain we'll get the support essential to see our efforts through and make the necessary adjustments. We have to measure up the odds and try to make things work. It can often be frustrating and disappointing.

This chapter further explores all these ideas. First we look at uncritical engagement and the world of the do-gooders. Then we turn to positive realists. We look at the stories of four people who have found active alignment in their work while maintaining critical awareness, at least for chunks of their careers. There are some common threads that run through all four of these accounts. Finally, we briefly touch on the challenges of working in the grey zone.

Uncritical Engagement: The Do-gooders

Gilbert Rist, in *The History of Development*, argues that international development tells a simple and seductive myth about how development intervention can save the world.[1] The myth can be at best only an idealistic approximation of reality. At worst it can be a pretext to interfere in unwanted and damaging ways.

The development myth is most seductive from a distance. As we get closer to any situation, the myth breaks apart as we see the complexities that belie it. And yet, although it breaks down for so many of us, it still persists as an idea at large, an idea with power. One reason, as we saw in chapter 2, is that the biggest funders of international development are Western taxpayers. Far enough away from places where development is done, they tend to understand the situation in simpler, generalized ways. In explaining development work and seeking help, agencies explain their work in ways that are understandable within this general framework. Often, these explanations tend to reinforce the validity of development as myth.

A classic example of this is child sponsorship. The simplicity and directness of child sponsorship appeals to many people. For only a dollar a day, the Western public is told, you can change a child's life, promise her (or him) a future that she wouldn't otherwise have. You can ensure access to clean drinking water, basic health care, and education. You can get regular updates on how she is doing, see her grow, see the way your money is helping her. Child sponsorship has been one of the most successful and enduring ways of raising public money for development. But almost all the promotional material around child sponsorship is at best misleading. And although it is an excellent model for fund-raising, child sponsorship is a terrible way to approach development. The overheads for providing support to one child at a time are high, and it makes much more sense to invest money in improving things at the community level—building a school or securing a clean source of drinking water. But because sponsors like the idea that they are having a significant effect in the life of one child, this is the way their donations are presented. Even worse, several exposés of child sponsorship schemes have shown that often very little money reaches the sponsored children. For example, Michael Maren quotes reports and internal memos within Save the Children in 1994 that found between 0 percent and 60 percent of sponsorship dollars were reaching children in its sponsorship programs within the United States.[2] He quotes an internal memo from the then-president of Save the Children, Charles McCormack: "As communities often receive a small portion of the sponsor's contributed dollar, they are obviously going to ask questions about where the money goes. All the explaining in the world would not make this question go away or our own strategy look good in an investigative report."[3] Promising the impossible isn't a good foundation for transparency.

From a distance, child sponsorship makes intuitive sense. Closer up, however, as we see the overhead costs involved in administering systems, the politics in selecting some children and excluding others, the folly of dividing small amounts of money rather than pooling them for larger community priorities, the room for abuse and distrust as external resources are directed into a poor community, and the danger of undermining parents and existing community support systems, we can see the problems with child sponsorship. But some of those are difficult to explain and communicate in short, simple ways. And then there is the danger of merely alienating the sponsors so that they stop giving altogether. It is much easier to sell the message that they can make a difference simply and directly, for a small amount of money.

Much of development works like this. What seems simple and intuitive at first appraisal often has consequences that are wildly different than expected. Food aid can lead to food dependence or even help to prolong deadly conflict. Poorly managed medical intervention can spread drug-resistant strains of deadly diseases such as tuberculosis and malaria. Interventions to "build capacity" can drive up wages and undermine the private and public sectors. Without considering existing social, economic, and political systems and how they work, many development interventions can fail or be disastrous. And yet all of this is often hard to predict or measure.

We might expect that international development as a sector has matured to the point that even if it has a hard time explaining these complexities to the public, it is internally aware of them and has developed effective strategies to navigate them. But this often isn't true. Blythe McKay observes,

> I get worried, just looking at a lot [of what happens]—like a lot of people at work, how uncritical they are about the work that they do. For example, there was a guy who was talking about the next Einstein Initiative, he's South African, he did this presentation . . . and he was talking about creating math schools in Africa to attract the best and brightest math students—these are new structures being built, a lot of the teachers come from around the world, and the majority of students end up not working in Africa. But he didn't talk about that; he just talked about the positive aspects. And I thought, OK, but why does it have to be new, why doesn't

he work with existing universities that are struggling? But most of the people thought he was amazing, they didn't have any of these questions, they weren't even thinking about it.

Why aren't people in international development more critical? Pierre,[4] a young French development worker in Afghanistan, thinks that it's a combination of politics and public ignorance. We act in order to feel good, and we don't really want to question it:

> We have to educate people that sending money doesn't necessarily help. I must tell my mum not to send money anymore! Originally it's just like this—you feel better when you give something to people—you feel better by giving, but you must always be very conscious of the impact of your gift.

Pierre's observations are driven by what he's seen in Afghanistan. He thinks that the casual intervention of development agencies is undermining development. For example, in the microfinance sector, where Pierre is working, one donor-funded project is spending large amounts of money irresponsibly. From Pierre's perspective, the project's saving grace is that it is so incompetent that the loans don't seem to be reaching anyone. Another distortion that affects Pierre's organization is that some development agencies pay such large salaries to national staff that they drive wages artificially higher. He has learned to hire people from the private sector and some NGOs but not those who have worked for USAID-funded projects:

> As soon as someone's working in a USAID project for a while, they're not ready to work the way we want them to work, with a lot of pressure and stress. The worst by far in this context are American contractors, who are really a disaster, a disaster for human resource development in this country. We have people we pay $400 [a month] for their work, and the day after they leave, they can get a job doing nothing for $1,500 for USAID.[5]

Pierre worries that over the long term, this kind of intervention is likely to weaken the resilience and resources that Afghans already have:

> My personal opinion on this, especially in a country like Afghanistan, there is money wasted, and when you see Afghans, how much—how

dynamic they are, they really got used to doing things by themselves. It has been a very tough thirty years in this country, you can't imagine, so people are used to adapting to the situation and surviving.

Without thinking about structural and systemic issues, international development efforts are not likely to add up to much over the long term. Sustainability in this sense of an enduring improvement is a major preoccupation of many people whom I spoke with. Pierre says, "What is exciting is that there is so much to improve in this field. But the question is, how? How do we analyze it, and how do we think about it?"

The cynics of the previous chapter may be aware of such systemic issues but don't feel responsible to address them. The do-gooders are actively engaged in their work and proud of it, but they just don't tend to look at issues critically and systemically. For example, I knew people in Afghanistan working for USAID-funded projects who felt that they were building professional capacity in the country by taking young, inexperienced Afghans and giving them big salaries and training. Older Afghans who were educated in the 1970s and worked in professional capacities were passed over because they didn't have English or computer skills. The cost of living went up in Kabul, and many people couldn't afford rent. Once the aid money stops flowing to Afghanistan, there'll be no one to pay the big salaries, just a lot of young people with high expectations. In November 2011, the World Bank released a report warning that Afghanistan's aid-dependent economy is in dire danger as donors pull out militarily and reduce funds.[6]

The expats who come to Afghanistan and work on a USAID capacity-building program for a year or two may never fully face the consequences of what they are doing, or as they realize, they will feel helpless to do much about it. These people don't feel a deep commitment to what happens in Afghanistan; they are explorers, aid adventurers on safari. They will gain career experience for their résumé, make some money, have some adventures, and then move on.

At the beginning of one's work life, it is wise to explore and try out various paths, seeking out new experience, while questioning everything. It is also wise to move on from this phase to a stage where you are clearer, and so more committed, in where you put your energies and can build up the necessary skills, understandings, and relationships to be effective. Unfortunately, some people never do this but rather remain as perpetual explorers. This often involves literal movement, from post to post and country to country. But more important, it is a psychological restlessness, a sense that the right solution is the latest one only to quickly discard it and move on to the latest. While early exploration is usually a time of intense learning, perpetual exploration becomes a way to continue adventuring while avoiding critical reflection and uncomfortable truths.

In 2001, Edward Clay observed British diplomats in Kenya during their three years in country as they became more acquainted with the realities of a corrupt political system that they couldn't fix: "In the first year, there was great enthusiasm: 'We must increase aid.' In the second year, revision set in. In the third year they all seemed to go bonkers, so disillusioned they couldn't speak or think rationally. I thought they'd all gone mad."[7] Of course, most don't go mad; they go on to their next posting and do their best to forget all about the last one. Likewise, by moving around before deeper understanding and possible disillusionment can set in, development workers can manage to hold on to some of their initial assumptions and illusions.

By and large, expats working abroad in development tend to come and go in one- to three-year cycles, just like the diplomats. In "hardship posts" such as Afghanistan, the turnover is even greater. As such, they are much more likely to face the risk of getting trapped in a perpetually superficial understanding of the aid dynamics within a particular place than are national development workers, who tend to have a much better contextual understanding. Even to the degree that expat workers do understand the dynamics, they have a relatively brief time to act on this understanding and follow through adequately on the results. Speaking of the expats in Nairobi, Dave Johnson observes,

> There are still a lot of one- and two-year contractors about, but when you get to the country directors and senior people within USAID, there are a lot more of those who have often married locally or internationally. In my organization, three of us were long term, with sixty expats, so that's one to twenty.

Of course, being in a place for a long time or engaging in one thing for a long time doesn't necessarily equate to effectiveness, and neither is the converse true. Not all those who move are perpetual explorers. Many have finished their role in a particular place and are moving on to the next in due course. Still, continual roaming is one of the most obvious markers of the restlessness of development as a profession. David Mosse describes development as "future positive," continually on the edge of the next big solution that will do what has not yet been done, without thinking too long or too hard about the past.[8] Sometimes it seems like the whole industry is in a perpetual exploration phase, and it encourages us to be too. It encourages us to justify our work by being less reflective, not more, by staying on the surface, going through the same introductory learning phase in a new place, throwing away the old theory and applying the latest, getting to the stage where we're starting to get a bit fed up, and then running on to the next interesting new thing.

We saw in part 2 of this book that widespread development practices and accountability mechanisms can actually stifle critical reflection. With little or no institutional support, many development workers find the issues and the complexity raised through a critical awareness of systems and interactions to be overwhelming. This partially explains why we within international development are not always as critical as we might be. It is difficult. It is uncomfortable. It can even be depressing. And then we don't get rewarded for it much by our institutions. For many expats, the people at home don't understand what we're doing and tend to see things in simple terms anyway. And for the sake of reporting, we have to overstate success and certainty. Still, Pierre and Blythe are two people who appear to be critically engaged in their work and yet fairly optimistic about their experiences, despite larger critiques of development systems. Their ongoing career decisions will determine how effective their critical insights will be in their own work.

Although critical awareness can make people uncomfortable at times, those who genuinely care about their work and who are willing to ask difficult questions are usually able to find the room to act. And this is what I mean by critical engagement. Critical engagement entails an attempt to work within the system and a general feeling that one can work effectively within the system, while also questioning and attempting to improve it. Those who are critically engaged recognize that there will always be limits to how much they can hope to improve the system. The strongest critics of international development may argue that anyone who is critically engaged with international development must eventually reject it entirely because it is systemically flawed and beyond reform. Those who are critically engaged and working within development are those who feel that despite its limitations, they can still work within international development to good effect. They are generally more cautious in talking about the overall outcomes of international development, but they do not feel that all of its outcomes are intrinsically and necessarily negative.

Critical Engagement: The Positive Realists

People who best exemplify the approach of critical engagement are those who have had positive experiences with international development that convince them that it is possible to do good development work. Often they describe themselves as lucky with their experiences. Their luck seems to be due in part to the decisions they have made and the mentors and role models they have encountered on their way. The theme of creating luck is one we encounter throughout this and the next chapter. A Canadian graduate student who has worked and researched on international development issues for ten years explains how her views on international development have changed through her experiences:

> When I started my master's and took courses in international development, I became very pessimistic about it. Not so much about the will, I think it's mainly goodwill, well intentioned. But I felt that participatory methods—they're not able to overcome the more top-down approaches to development. When they were used, they also imposed a top-down idea; this time it was that people had to participate.
>
> Then I realized, over time, really working with project facilitators in Honduras, and later with people in Malawi who use a similar approach, that it's not so much whether a project is participatory in its methods or approach but in its facilitation. So I learned, the facilitators in Honduras, and then also in Malawi, were truly compassionate both about the people they worked with as well as accommodating all the project requirements in various ways. So it was less about the project tools and really about the facilitators, who could really make or break the project. And so I have a renewed sense of optimism about the project and the field, which is quite lovely. . . . Because I think that there are people out there who really care about what they're doing, and it doesn't matter about the methods and the tools. I think it's because I've been really fortunate to have experience with these two projects, both led by Canadian researchers, who are really passionate about collaborating, and then facilitated by local practitioners and facilitators, who are absolutely committed to ensuring that programs are truly participatory, truly responsive, even to individual needs. And both of the programs are also long term, also unusual—they've managed to sustain funding for ten years. Both of those are unusual in development, but they've influenced the way I feel about the development field.

Both of these projects were long term and had been subject to rigorous evaluations that showed positive impacts for the farmers who were beneficiaries, including improvements in crop yields, food security, and household nutrition.

The best way to understand active alignment is through considering the experiences of people who feel they've managed to effectively channel their energies in their work and who feel optimistic about the changes they've been a part of. Many people working in international development fit within this category. We'll consider the stories of four people: Jonathan Bartolozzi, Blythe McKay, Fatou Leigh, and Simon Madraru Amajuru.

Staying Close to the Ground: Jonathan Bartolozzi

Jonathan Bartolozzi grew up in Italy and the United Kingdom. When Jonathan was still in high school, his dad got a job in Brazil. Jonathan credits the time he spent there for motivating him to work in international development:

> It probably all started when I lived in Brazil, because I got the feeling, what's going on here? There're a lot of poor people. And the inequality really got to me; it was in my mind for a long time, and when I studied in university, I realized there was something special about developing countries—an energy there, a desire for change . . . people working hard to improve the lots of their lives. That was attractive to me.

Jonathan went to university and decided to study international relations with a development focus. He always knew he was interested in people and the grassroots side of things. He chose to study household-level development efforts, and he made sure that he got field experience early on. He was worried that too many entry-level positions in international development were desk jobs in head offices that would keep him far from where he wanted to be. So he decided to go and volunteer in a small town in Kyrgyzstan. He stayed there for three years:

> I'd mainly lived in large cities, and living in a small town in a developing country gave me a lot of insight into community dynamics and a lot of the problems that people faced. I was the "volunteer in town"—so anything from helping with a car manual to helping organize a training to proposal writing for local NGOs. I was also teaching a lot in one of the schools—there was a new school established, and the head of the school wanted me to help them with making the school better. And also, I hadn't any plan to teach, but eventually I started teaching, teaching, teaching and ended up

really liking it—so that took up most of my morning hours. In the afternoons, I'd go off and do the other things. And the relationships I created were great, and more than anything, it was experience, right? Experience, understanding, and learning.

I worked with local NGOs, and I saw how international NGOs were coming into our town and working, and seeing the kinds of effects those programs were having, and also the fact that the local government was trying to deal with this, and be part of the process, as were the local NGOs.

Learning the language and getting to know the dynamics gave Jonathan ideas that he's brought forward with him to Badakhshān, Afghanistan, where he was working as the province manager for Mission East (a Danish relief and development NGO). In Kyrgyzstan, he observed how the international NGOs interacted with the local community. Often they were based in town and would establish links with the usual suspects, the same local officials every time. Those community gatekeepers got to choose what the international NGOs knew and how they perceived the community. Jonathan didn't think that they were getting the whole picture. He also learned how much impact specific individuals could have. In his community, there were some local women who were taking their own steps to improve community life:

[There was] one woman who ran a little quasi orphanage, totally out of her good heart, you know, and sometimes she'd get support from outside organizations. She was herself an inspiration. And a woman who ran the information center, another local NGO that worked with veterans' rights and retirees. So it really did emphasize how important individuals can be in the process, and if the road is paved for them to achieve their goals and what they've had in vision, even better. But if those individuals weren't there, no matter how hard you tried, seems like it wouldn't work.

In his work in Afghanistan, Jonathan has continued to maintain strong local contacts, learned the language, and paid attention to people and relationships. He achieved fluency in Dari within about six months, whereas most expats in Afghanistan never reach a working proficiency in the language. Working in Badakhshān, in the northeast of the country, he feels he has his dream job despite the overall political climate in Afghanistan:

When you first arrive, you're bombarded by lots of different things, but definitely after 2009, you definitely got the feeling that everything [in development] was completely politicized and connected to the military objectives, and that is definitely a completely different reality. It bothered me, because that's not how it should be in humanitarian and development work. But I managed to stay away from it over these last two years. . . . I've found a great place for myself in the Afghan context—in a small NGO with non-USAID-funded roots, and to have the freedom to choose, the flexibility to change based on what you've learned, and not have to deal with the bureaucracy.

Jonathan knew what he wanted from the outset. Then he gave himself the chance to experiment and experience development dynamics from a local community view. His experiences have reinforced that his approach is worth cultivating and that it's possible to find the space to do worthwhile work:

I think I've been very lucky; there are few people who complain as little as me and are as happy as me. There are a lot of people who wanted to do good work. There's this idea of second best—that you'll never be able to work for your ideal, you have to accept working for the second best—but the way a lot of people here work, they're working on fifth or sixth best, because there are so many limitations. I think people who are outside get a feeling that it's all a mess and nothing good is being done. Being on the ground, you see there's a lot of good being done. There's a lot of crap too, but a lot of good, and organizations and staff who are careful to implement work well, and they care.

A Passion for Community Radio: Blythe McKay

Blythe McKay, from Canada, whom we met earlier in this chapter, is someone who loves her job. She works as the manager of the Resources for Broadcasters Program at Farm Radio International, an NGO based in Ottawa, Canada, and is working mainly with rural radio stations across Africa. She's been there since 2005. Farm Radio International provides support to rural radio stations to develop and share content. For example, one project that Blythe is proud of involved participatory radio campaigns on agriculture-related topics. Participating radio stations would start by carrying out focus groups with listeners from key communities within their broadcast areas. Once they heard what people's priorities were, they would base the radio programs on that. In Malawi, for example, some farmers had been experimenting with a new approach to intercropping and others were interested in learning more about it. The programs were developed and aired over several months. They included follow-up with farmers within the audience about whether they were trying the agricultural innovation that was shared, why, and what their experiences with it had been. Follow-up research on the number of farmers taking up the intervention as a result of being involved in the active listening communities was really promising. Even in "passive listening" communities where the station wasn't actively involving farmers, one in five people who listened to the program tried the innovation they had heard about.

As with many people in development, Blythe found her way along through a series of lucky accidents. She had originally hoped to become a vet, but when her marks weren't good enough in her first year of undergrad, she looked around at other options. She ended up doing an exchange year in Sweden, which she recalls "basically transformed me." Her courses there, focused on organic agriculture and rural development, introduced her to the idea that academic work could be practical and also sold her on the value of participatory development processes. She pursued a master's degree in rural extension studies from the University of Guelph. Even before she began her master's, one of her professors included her in a rural radio and agricultural research project. Through this work she learned about a Ghanaian community radio station, Simli Radio, working closely with farmers. She was impressed by the station director's energy and dedication and decided she would like to work with them. She did her master's research on community radio in Ghana. She then continued pursuing work with community radio through an internship at IDRC in Ottawa and then began working for Farm Radio International. She has maintained links with community radio stations and individuals working with them that span back as far as 2001.

Looking back at her initial expectations of development, Blythe recalls,

[In my master's program] I remember there's a lot of critical introduction of development and how it's not succeeded. I remember joking, oh, I'm probably going to go to Ghana and there's not going to be a community radio station, and almost expecting the worst and hoping I'd be pleasantly surprised.

I was thinking the majority [of development projects] wouldn't be great, but from what I'd seen from Sweden and the approaches I'd been exposed to, I thought OK, there's a right way and a wrong way, and a lot of people are doing it the wrong way. But there are good ways to do it, where you involve the community, and also it's a matter of scale—where smaller, more community-driven projects were more likely to succeed.

Blythe's recollection of her experience is filled with inspirational professors and supervisors who have mentored her, advised her, and helped her to expand her ideas of what is possible. She's also in turn inspired others and spoken to classes studying international development about her work. Lynne Mitchell, director of Guelph's Centre for International Programs, says that students were really excited to hear someone talk about an example of development work that was positive and successful, after hearing many stories of failure. As Blythe notes, the niche she has found herself in is a bit unique: "Because I'm working with radio stations, they're not development projects. They can contribute to development, but they're also set up and meant to be an ongoing part of the area, and they broadcast for perpetuity." For Blythe, ongoing collaborations, relationships, and common goals that outlast specific projects are key to her work and are where she derives the greatest meaning and pleasure. Although Farm Radio International works through projects, Blythe has come to see them as a smaller part of a longer term engagement.

Strengthening Government Systems: Fatou Leigh
Fatou Leigh is an economic advisor for the United Nations Development Programme (UNDP) stationed in Kenya. When we spoke, she was still relatively new to the role, having joined UNDP for two years. Before that, she worked in her native country of the Gambia. First, she worked directly in government, and then she spent seven years working for a project called "Capacity Building for Economic Management" (CBEMP) that was funded by the World Bank and the Gambian government. Fatou headed the project, which aimed to improve statistical systems, improve public resource management, and facilitate private sector development, in part through developing a legislative framework.

As Fatou recalls with pride, "I spent seven years of my life doing that, and it yielded some very good work." A big part of the task included reforming the Gambia Revenue Authority, implementing the Integrated Financial Management System (IFMIS), and bringing greater efficiency and transparency to government procurement processes. Clearly, this kind of work is technical but needs great political commitment. Fatou explains she and her team had to convince everyone involved that the new system was in their interest and bring them on board. The team accomplished this through a combination of training, cajoling, and patient back-and-forth diplomacy. Fortunately, she enjoyed the strong support of both the minister and the permanent secretary of the Ministry of Finance and Economic Affairs.

The World Bank funded Fatou and her team to visit other African countries that had attempted similar reforms. They traveled to Uganda and Tanzania, where implementation of these reforms had gone well. A consultant who had previously worked in Ghana and Malawi, where attempts at reform had been less successful, also joined the team. Fatou felt that the key difference lay in the degree of ownership that each country had over the systems put in place. Taking that lesson to heart, she and her team spent over nine months developing their own business processes that they felt would be most appropriate to the Gambia's small size and economy. They borrowed ideas from Tanzania and got Ugandans to help them with their implementation. They also used Gambian staff rather than foreign advisors. She recalls,

> The suppliers were very clear about the background of the people they needed—we didn't have those people in the government, but they were in the private sector. We advertised, and they didn't even apply, so we headhunted, and we had to offer them higher salaries, funded by the World Bank.

But this then raised another issue:

> How were they going to work with the local staff working on government salary? Again we negotiated with the World Bank, because they don't do top-ups, but we convinced them it was necessary for the success of the system, and there was a top-up on that. So there was a lot of training, sensitization, buy-in, and then the support from the World Bank.

As a result of all these careful thoughts and efforts, the new systems were developed, embedded in government, and the whole thing works. Fatou explains, "Now, the Gambia has other countries like Nigeria and Ghana coming over to understudy our systems." After Fatou had seen it through from beginning to end, she was ready for a change and a new challenge. She explains,

> I thought I'd make a bigger impact, being international, and I wanted to learn from other countries' experience, and international

means meeting people who have even more knowledge than you. You learn from that network, and you have the feeling you're reaching more and more people. I'm sure you recognize that process of self-validation—if you make it locally and go and make it internationally, you actually feel like, I'm pretty OK at contributing to the lives of the people, you get that internal satisfaction. And you're contributing, in a small way, to something big.

And so she decided to apply to the UN. In her role of economic advisor, she often works with the Kenyan government, and she has a good understanding of its perspective and the challenges that it faces. This can be an advantage, but it can also be a disadvantage. While she says she remains objective because she is a UN representative, other donors sometimes see her as too sympathetic toward the government. She agrees that donors need to be tough:

> There's this climate of impunity. Basically there's been this impunity where people take things like it's their own property and nothing happens. There are a few families who own 60 percent of Kenya yet there are IDPs [internally displaced people] from the 2008 postelection violence who are still not settled. On the positive side, the Kenya Anti-Corruption Commission has recently been gaining the confidence of the people with the arrest of high-level officials.

For Fatou to have succeeded in her work, I imagine that she must be extremely skilled at understanding and managing the interests of different people. She doesn't seem to have any illusions about the challenges facing development, including the various political interests of all the parties, especially recipient governments and Western donors. And yet she gets on with things and has succeeded in creating more effective and transparent government systems. Eventually, she hopes to return home to the Gambia and teach at the university.

Community Development in Rural Uganda: Simon Madraru Amajuru

Simon Madraru Amajuru has been working in rural development since the early 1990s. Simon hails from the West Nile region of Uganda. Almost all his work experience has been within Uganda, and much of it has been within the West Nile. He spent his early career as a cooperative officer within the government of Uganda. In 1994, he joined the Dutch-funded Community Action Programme (CAP), which supported the rebuilding of the West Nile following a period of conflict. The CAP was the Dutch response to a government request to support a broader program dealing with the whole of northern Uganda. Studying the issue, the Dutch decided that the government's program was too top-down, as funds were directed by the Office of the Prime Minister, rather than communities. The Dutch also wanted to focus more specifically on the West Nile, which was no longer in conflict, whereas the rest of the north was still in civil war. Simon began as a field officer, supporting grassroots community facilitators in their work. The facilitators consulted communities to determine priorities for projects. The largest priority for most communities was primary schools. Health and clean water, roads, and bridges were also common projects. Later on, the program introduced agricultural projects and small savings and loans schemes to help with the local economy. In 1997, Simon was promoted to district coordinator for Moyo (a district within the West Nile), and then from 1999 he became the overall project coordinator, until the program was phased out in 2000.

CAP had always been planned as a temporary project because it undertook many activities that fell under the remit of local government. At the time CAP began, the region was emerging from a conflict, and local government capacity was very weak. Over the span of the project, as government capacity improved, it took over responsibility for schools and other projects initiated through CAP, and the Dutch began to fund the government directly for this.

Simon recalls that as the CAP programs phased out, the staff and the donor realized that there were some elements the local government would not take on. Specifically, CAP contained components for women's empowerment, income-generating projects, and functional literacy training for women that wouldn't fall under government remit. To continue these, the CAP staff decided to start a civil society organization for the West Nile. Simon became the executive director of this organization, called Community Empowerment for Rural Development (CEFORD), and the Dutch agreed to fund it. Simon headed the organization for four years and managed to attract other donors as it grew.

Over this time period, things in the West Nile were changing. When CAP began, Ugandan refugees from the conflict who had fled to the Congo or the Sudan began to return. Many international organizations came to the West Nile to provide humanitarian assistance to these returnees. Then the West Nile in turn became a collection point for refugees from conflicts in the Congo and the Sudan, and international organizations stayed and focused on serving these refugee populations. But by 2000, many of these agencies started to phase out operations and refocus on the conflict that was ongoing in northern Uganda, just east of the West Nile region. As international organizations phased out, local NGOs set up and took on some of their activities, but they were weak and disorganized. Seeing this gap, Simon focused some of CEFORD's activities on institutional strengthening of the local organizations.

In 2004, Simon moved on from his position at CEFORD, although he has maintained involvement in a voluntary capacity as chair of the board of directors. He decided to focus his efforts on working in private business in transport and construction. He also runs a secondary school that he says is more a way of giving back to the community, as the fees are kept low and the quality of education is good. As his company employs one hundred people and the school employs an additional twenty people, Simon sees this private enterprise as a valid way of continuing to contribute to development. He also continues to consult on development issues in both Uganda and the Sudan, often advising small development organizations on institutional strengthening. As Simon notes, "[When] they get more organized, they're able to access resources locally and internationally, so people can benefit from their services."

Looking at these four experiences, we see some striking similarities cut across them; primarily the pragmatic optimism and the sense each person has about the importance and power of his or her choices. These individuals have each had experiences where other actors—whether the organizations they worked for, donors, bosses, or teachers along the way—have inspired them and created the space for them to do good work. They've each taken the time and energy to understand the situation they found themselves in and to respond to it appropriately, build and negotiate relationships, and bring others along with them. None of them seem in the least bit naive about international development. But they're far from cynical, because they know that they can be effective within their own sphere. As far as development work goes, they've managed to find the sweet spot.

The Grey Zone

Serendipity doesn't always come when called. We can be critically reflective and engaged but not find the right team to sign up with, the right vehicle to channel our efforts. The world is imperfect, bills need to be paid, we need to do something, and we have to decide whether the situation, imperfect as it is, is good enough. Nothing good will come out of us waiting for perfection. As one development worker muses,

You can get frustrated by people who sit looking for the perfect solution, while so many people are suffering and dying. You'll never find the perfect solution. Sometimes you have to say this is good enough, let's do this . . . because the world is not waiting.

So we're always trading off, balancing different needs, working in what Ramirez and Quarry call "the grey zone." Both have years of experience in communication for development, applying communication tools and processes in development projects. But they've both found it challenging to get the right sort of situation lined up. They know the elements necessary for their work to be effective, but having all those elements in place the way they would like is a rare luxury. This is particularly the case when dealing with large donors and development bureaucracies, but they are the ones with most of the money and work opportunities.

So often we find ourselves working in less-than-ideal circumstances, making compromises that we would rather not. The outcomes, unsurprisingly, are often disappointing. Ideally, one wants the freedom to walk away from a situation if it seems unlikely that it is going to allow for effective work. For example, one consultant who has done a lot of facilitation work told me about one of his most disappointing experiences. It was a workshop on fisheries management in Tanzania. He was asked to facilitate it and he did, but he found that the convener was very manipulative. Because of this, the workshop was a disaster and resulted in conflict rather than a useful outcome. In reflection, he feels like he could have assessed the situation beforehand and realized that he should have said no:

> I didn't—because I'd just finished this really great conference in Ethiopia that went really well, and that's why she asked me. But she didn't organize it properly, and even worse I didn't. I just said yes, I didn't sit down with her and get the background first. It was a big mistake—it was a blot on my CV, because it meant I'd colluded with a bad process, I hadn't taken care to ensure . . . there was time, if I'd done my work properly, I could have changed the design of the workshop, so that it had a better prospect of success. I let her call the shots; I didn't challenge her enough . . . whereas her failure was that she didn't listen.

People's ideas of how to align, how to be effective, and where to put their energies change over time too. Both Ricardo Ramirez and Wendy Quarry decided to join the boards of local NGOs as a result of reflecting on their own professional experiences. The people they admired most, whom they felt were most effective, were people who made these sorts of contributions. Many other people talk about trying to act as mentors and advisors to younger people coming in. And this support can make a huge difference to the experiences and opportunities of those they mentor. One young development professional explains,

> I've been incredibly lucky; I've had some amazing bosses and mentors who are very specific about professional development, not just that they will support you, but they'll ask what you want to learn and give you exposure to opportunities—and that makes you more sensitive to it. If you've gone through a good process, you're more prone to think through good processes; if you've gone through bad processes, you might think through bad processes. Unfortunately it's not across the board. It's not institutional—I sought it out and worked my butt off, and thinking through it, I've been lucky with the number of strong, impressive women I've been surrounded by, which I think as a woman starting out in the field, it helps.

Anders Fange, who spent years heading the Swedish Committee for Afghanistan (SCA) in Afghanistan before retiring in 2011, writes editorials and other pieces in various journals and speaks publicly on some of the broader political and social issues that he experiences but cannot address through his NGO work. Many people working in development find that they want to exercise their role as citizens and through their work. They want to pursue positive social change on multiple levels and spheres. This is one drawback to the temporary lifestyle of moving from country to country and contract to contract, and some people purposefully maintain links to their home country for this reason.

Conclusion

Positive realists are people who are critically engaged in their jobs and organizations. They are both optimistic and pragmatic. They aren't fatalistic about development outcomes, either positively or negatively, but they're aware it is something they can work through patiently. They also tend to put more emphasis on their own skills and decisions. Through a combination of careful discernment and good luck, they are able to select environments and cultivate relationships in which they share goals and can support and be supported in achieving them. They often seem to be good at reading other people and social situations and finding and building on common ground. They're often passionate about their work.

Critical engagement is necessary for effective work. The people we've met in this chapter tend to be very clear in expressing the current limitations of their work. They have ideas for improving it, but they're also aware they can't change everything. They also tend to express deep concerns about the broader development and political context, but they are doing what they can.

When people have really found their niche and matched their skills and motivations, they are passionate about their work and its potential. But when the fit isn't quite perfect, it is more of a "muddling through" the grey zone, where we can see some of the elements, but there are some obstacles to navigate, and we're less assured of impact.

Critical engagement is necessary. But how critical is critical enough? How do you balance being critical with being hopeful? In most cases, there is no clear vantage point to judge this. Sometimes it seems to come down to personality. For some people working in development, such criticality leads to an almost chronic crisis of confidence about what they're engaged in, and others seem to have found a certain peace with it all. Is the first lot neurotic? Is the second lot complacent? I think in both cases the answer is no. Without some degree of creative tension, there is probably something wrong. But when it reaches the point where a person can't work, there's a need to reframe the issues or perhaps to leave development work. It's always very personal and a really tough call. But as a rule of thumb, whenever things look too simple, too neat, too straightforward, we should probably be suspicious that we are not being critical enough.

Notes

1. Gilbert Rist, *The History of Development: From Western Origins to Global Faith*, 3rd ed. (London: Zed Books, 2009).

2. Michael Maren, *The Road to Hell: The Ravaging Effects of Foreign Aid and International Charity* (New York: Free Press, 2002).

3. Michael Maren, *Save the Children: A Different Kind of Child Abuse*, December 12, 1996, cited March 2, 2012, http://michaelmaren.com/1996/12/save-the-children-a-different-kind-of-child-abuse/.

4. Name changed for anonymity.

5. As a point of reference, a midrange salary for an Afghan civil servant was about $200 a month at this time. Tom Bowman, *In Afghanistan, the Civil Service "Surge" That Isn't* (Washington, DC: NPR, 2010).

6. Jon Boone and Jason Burke, "Afghanistan Faces $7bn Annual Budget Shortfall, World Bank Warns," *Guardian*, November 22, 2011.

7. Michela Wrong, *It's Our Turn to Eat: The Story of a Kenyan Whistle-Blower* (New York: Harper, 2009).

8. David Mosse, *Cultivating Development: An Ethnography of Aid Policy and Practice* (London: Pluto Press, 2004), 1.

10

The Visionaries

Some people have a very clear sense of what they want to accomplish. They make use of the resources and institutions around them as tools for this end, negotiating them to fit their needs, sometimes starting their own initiative or organization. People taking this approach are often inspiring visionaries and leaders who manage to accomplish great things over the course of their careers.

The difference between critical engagement and negotiation is often one of degree rather than kind. Those who are actively engaged also have clear goals, but these are more likely to have come from, or be shared by, the organizations they work in. Even so, they may need to negotiate some aspects of the situation to make it work effectively. For example, Fatou Leigh's work on financial reform in the Gambia was based very much on donors' ideas of reform and what had been tried in other African countries. She believed in the value of those reforms for her own country, and she negotiated for terms and conditions that would make them work. Active engagement can also provide the space for people to take leadership roles within institutions that in turn give them the platform to negotiate their own visions of priorities and approaches. As they gain experience, they are likely to feel more confident in taking up such roles.

At their best, the visionaries often challenge and change the development status quo. In the course of pursuing their vision, they must shift and navigate institutions and convince others of the value of their project. For example, Muhammad Yunus, who pioneered Grameen Bank and the microcredit movement, began as a university professor doing his own outreach projects. As he sought resources to expand his venture, he interacted with the development status quo, but he was also critical of much of it.[1] Despite his criticism of the World Bank, his efforts convinced the bank of the value of microcredit, and it began to support and promote it widely. Yunus operated on his own terms, and yet because of his work, microcredit became a major staple of international development. Yunus led, and the development establishment, eventually, followed.

There is, however, an alter ego to the negotiator. Also a visionary, the aid hero is one whose own visions may block his or her ability to see and respond to reality. With its various distortions and blind spots, the international development system can sometimes provide a welcoming home for these would-be saviors.

This chapter first considers the character of aid heroes, why they exist, and what we can learn from them. It then elucidates the nature of negotiation through the stories of two people who have done well at this. Finally, it discusses the factors, both in attitude and in situation, that seem to characterize this approach.

Aid Heroes

When I was a little kid, one of my favorite TV characters was Super Grover on *Sesame Street*. Sporting a silver helmet and a red cape, Super Grover would fly through the air and seek out people in need so he could help them. Inevitably, after a painful crash landing, he'd get confused or sidetracked and completely misunderstand the situation. Meanwhile, the kids he'd come to help would figure things out on their own and solve the problem. Super Grover, clueless to what had actually happened, would proudly take the credit for saving the day before flying "up up and away" in search of someone else to help.

Like Super Grover, visionaries who are not critically self-aware are likely to be more successful at self-promotion than at solving actual problems. We've already seen in the previous chapters that international development as it is popularly understood in the West often has a mythical quality that tends to favor the lone creative Westerner with allegedly superior knowledge, often of a technical nature. Many Westerners starting out in international development fall into the trap of overvaluing their own expertise. Development structures and practices can reinforce this tendency, as we have seen. Keeping the myth alive can dampen honest critical reflection.

When we place people in the category of "aid hero," we place high expectations on them. A recent example of this is Greg Mortenson, whose work became well known through *Three Cups of Tea*, a 2006 book he coauthored with David Relin.[2] The book told the story of Mortenson's quest to build a school for a remote mountain village in Pakistan after the villagers found him lost in the mountains and nursed him to health. Despite various setbacks, he persisted and managed to raise the resources to build the school and then went on to build schools in other villages. The success of his book also helped him to fund raise for his charity, the Central Asia Institute, which established schools in remote areas of Pakistan and Afghanistan.

Many people and organizations, including many Pakistanis and Afghans, as well as numerous international NGOs, have worked in the same region to build schools and promote education, often under dangerous conditions. So we can ask why Mortenson became so well known for his work, which was after all similar to the work of others who haven't received so much attention.

Mortenson's work received notice partly because his story resonated with the Western public. And it resonated because it was, in the most classic sense, a good story, a real-life hero's quest. But like most good stories, it was at best only a partial and selective reflection of reality, altered for dramatic and emotive effect. Several people took issue with Mortenson's rendition of events, which led the television program *60 Minutes* to air a full one-hour investigative report on Mortenson and his charity in April 2011. They argued not only that his initial story was partially fabricated but also that his charity had mismanaged funds and that Mortenson was putting more money into promoting himself and his books than into building schools.

The more serious charges of possible fraud and financial mismanagement aside, the problems that the Central Asia Institute faced in running its schools were similar to problems that many others have faced. Not all the schools had been well planned, had managed to secure qualified teachers, or were located in accessible places. Before the April 2011 scandal surfaced, I had asked a friend working for an NGO running schools in Afghanistan what he thought of Mortenson's work. He sighed and told me that he hadn't seen the schools that Mortenson had built, but he worried about the public response, that people got the idea that the problems were simpler than they really were. Effective schools require so much more than buildings: finding qualified teachers, developing curriculum, and coordinating with the government so that they outlast their start-up funding, none of which are trivial concerns. Protecting children from physical and sexual abuse within the schools was another issue: Save the Children had completed research on boys' and girls' schools in Afghanistan that showed both types of abuse were shockingly common. None of these issues were mentioned in Mortenson's book, although his foundation must have encountered them.

In many ways, Mortenson was playing to public understanding just as any savvy international development charity does, presenting issues in a simple and emotive way that makes it easy and desirable for people to give funds, funds that are after all necessary for building and running schools. But the flip side of this is that as people are told what they want to hear, the space to have frank discussion that may be needed to work effectively is reduced. As much as Mortenson may have placed himself in the role of aid hero, it was the popular belief in the development myth that held him there.

Mortenson is not the only Westerner who started an organization to bring schools to other lands. John Wood wrote of his own experiences in his book *Leaving Microsoft to Change the World*.[3] He recounts how he went on a hiking trip to Nepal and visited a school that had a library with only a few books, which they kept locked away. The teachers asked him to bring books with him if he ever returned. Struck by their need, he decided he would raise money to furnish the school with a proper library. He did and found the experience so rewarding that he decided to quit his job and continue. He established an NGO that got initial funding from a foundation focused specifically on social entrepreneurs. The fact he had worked for Microsoft allowed him to reinvent himself as one who was turning his business acumen and work ethic to the nonprofit world.

There is no way of judging the quality of Wood's efforts from his book, although the speed of his organization's growth and its achievements in numeric terms are impressive. As of October 2012, his NGO, Room to Read, had opened 1,556 schools and 13,599 libraries and estimates it has benefited 6.7 million children.[4] Whether the NGO is well run or poorly run, it is clearly improving access to books and education. Still, it is by no means groundbreaking. There is some hubris that seems to come with assuming that his skills from Microsoft are particularly well suited to the task at hand. Some crucial factors that are lacking in Wood's account are the in-depth knowledge of the context and the listening and responsiveness to feedback. Without contextual knowledge, even Wood himself is not in a great position to judge the success of the schools he has established or to mitigate against the risks. The schools may be there, but do the teachers show up every day? What's the quality of the education? And what other organizations were already working on this issue before his came along? Would it have been more effective if he had helped one of them out rather than start something new?

Lurking not so deeply in accounts such as Wood's is the hero myth. William Easterly observed, "We all love the fantasy of being the chosen one. Is part of the explanation for the Big Plan's Western popularity that it stars the rich West in the leading role, that of the chosen people to save the Rest?"[5] Easterly is skeptical of Western-led Big Plans such as the Millennium Development Goals, championed by high-profile Westerners such as Jeffrey Sachs. John Wood, by contrast, presents himself as a social entrepreneur, someone who is using his business skills and strong work ethic in aid of development. Social entrepreneurship is often touted as an alternative to the Big Plans and big bureaucracies that Easterly criticizes. However, if it's Western led and Western centric, I suspect that such efforts risk replicating many of the failings of old-style, top-down development.

My misgivings derive in part from experience. At the age of eighteen, fresh from high school, I had my very first experience working in international development. I signed up to volunteer for a small, well-intentioned Canadian NGO. A businessman who had turned his hand to international charity started it after a near-death experience inspired him to shift his priorities. He had all the directness and practical bent of a businessman. He had a good heart and a genuine desire to help. But he didn't have much knowledge about the places he was sending people to or about development processes.

I was sent off to the small island nation of Grenada, where I was dumped on an Anglican priest and his family who were affiliated with the NGO. They were bemused. What were they to do with me? My sole qualification was that I was a Canadian volunteer who had managed to gather some funds to support the trip. I had assumed that there was some need I was going to fill and that the organization knew what it was doing. I was just glad to go and honestly hadn't asked many questions, either of them or of myself. It was quite a shock to arrive and discover that there was no Master Plan in which my services were an essential component.

In the end, as such things often go, it was a very good learning experience for me. I quickly learned that many of the ideas I had about the world and my place in it were very silly. I ended up filling in for a teacher on maternity leave and was probably at least marginally better than if there had been no teacher. I made friends; there was the mutual benefit of cultural exchange. And I now know better than to assume that Western businesspeople have an inherent instinct for international development.

Overemphasizing the importance of visionary individuals in development also poses another danger. It can deepen the problem of fragmented, uncoordinated development efforts. Those who aspire to be seen as a visionary agent of change can set up their own NGO and do their own thing. As Jim Shute puts it,

> Almost every week I read in the paper about someone who retired, went on a cruise, got off the ship, and saw people in poverty and then said, "I have to do something about this." And then, instead of supporting professionals already doing good work, they just

start up a new organization themselves. These efforts, while based on altruistic instincts, are usually fragmented, scattered, ill thought through, and have little promise of funding, durability, or lasting results.

Even when people are local, their efforts are not always well directed. Some small communities are packed full of NGOs all seeming to run the same programs but often without much evident change. Too many visionaries can spoil the development broth, adding in so many different kinds of ingredients that the whole thing becomes an inedible onion marshmallow sausage stew of progress. One expat development worker recalls,

> I was working in Vietnam, in the mountain areas. It was a tiny district, and there were so many projects, so uncoordinated. We were doing livestock there, there must have been twenty projects doing livestock. Then an NGO came in and said, "We want to coordinate." They did a survey. There were seventy-eight different projects there, all doing the same thing. And then that was it. . . . We still all reported to our donors and had to sound good to our donors. There was a question on that survey, "How many trainings have you been to?" So the same people had been to the same trainings about twenty times, because we paid them to go to trainings, and if you were linked to the district official, it's the best way to make money, and those who aren't connected don't go to any of them.

People who are really committed to their work will be concerned about this. But then they are also constrained by the reality of their funding environment, which requires them to put effort toward showing donors the fruits of their agency's work. Short-term efforts at seeking a solution, like the survey, end up being largely symbolic in their attempts to address the issue because they don't follow through. People who aren't committed to that area for the long term are unlikely to be able to find a solution, because they won't be able to follow through. And if the solution requires agencies cooperating, it will be an uphill battle. Many NGOs are fiercely independent for a variety of reasons, including competition for funding, differing ideologies, fears of political interference, and the personalities of the leaders. Coordination can end up taking so much time and effort for so little result that it barely seems worth it.

Negotiators

Unlike aid heroes, negotiators are fully clued in to both the context and their own role within it. Their visions usually come from experience, whether personal or professional, and are grounded in much deeper understanding of a situation. It is probably easiest to understand what negotiation looks like by considering examples of those who have done it with some success. And so we will consider the stories of two women, Mary Abukutsa and Vicki Wilde. Mary is a professor who grew up in rural Kenya. Vicki is American but her background is international. As an "air force brat" she grew up in France, went to elementary school in Asia, and traveled all over the place. Both women are smart and determined, and both absolutely love their work. And as fate would have it, each, through her work, has supported the work of the other. We'll consider these two overlapping stories in turn.

Mary Abukutsa, Professor of Horticulture at Jomo Kenyatta University of Agriculture and Technology

Mary grew up in Kakamega, in western Kenya. The daughter of a school-teacher and a farmer, young Mary was allergic to animal proteins and could not eat meat or animal products. Her mother fed her nutritious vegetables that were indigenous to the area. Long known and eaten by many rural Kenyans are such plants as African nightshade, spider plant, vegetable amaranth, jute mallow, slender leaf, vine spinach, and African kale. These native vegetables were widely seen as poor people's last resort when they couldn't afford meat or the introduced crops that had become a staple part of people's diets. Mary's mother was struggling to make ends meet, but still for Mary, these vegetables provided an excellent source of nutrition.

Mary was a top student, and her father and teachers wanted her to go on to study medicine. But she had different ideas. She decided to study agriculture as influenced by her mother's struggle to ensure food security in the household. She also felt that it had played a key role in her life and the lives of those around her. She earned a bachelor's of science in agriculture and a master's of science in agronomy, both from the University of Nairobi, both paid for through full scholarships. She then worked for several years at the Ministry of Agriculture, first as a district agricultural officer, then as an agricultural information officer. After several years, she joined a Kenyan university as a junior research fellow. In 1992, she got a scholarship to do a PhD, and she completed it at the University of London in 1995.

Mary originally wanted to focus her PhD research on African indigenous vegetables, but her supervisor was dismissive of the idea. "He called them 'weeds,'" Mary recalls. He was working on a research project on onions, and he wanted her to work on that. So she did, with the idea that she'd be able to apply what she learned once she got back home to Kenya. In fact, Mary had already launched a project to promote the use of African indigenous vegetables in 1991, just before she went off to London. She used the same outreach skills she'd developed during her time with the Ministry of Agriculture to teach farmers about the benefits of these native crops. She produced pamphlets and DVDs, held field days, and talked to the media. Mary saw these vegetables as a hugely undervalued resource that could be the source of food security, nutrition, and income for Kenyan farmers. If the nutritional value of native vegetable species was widely recognized, they could even have value as an export crop. This has, for example, happened with quinoa, the ancient staple grown in Peru and other Andean countries. Quinoa was long seen as "peasant food" until its high protein and nutritional content became more widely known. It is now a valued export crop.[6]

At first, Mary faced an uphill battle in convincing other people of her ideas. She returned from her PhD program in 1995 and looked for funding for her research. She wanted to do research on indigenous vegetables in part to document and promote their use. But when she sought initial funding from the International Foundation for Science in 1996, it wrote back to her, "Your proposal is fantastic, but we can't fund it because these are weeds. Why not research on economically valuable crops like tomatoes?"

Mary responded by doing preliminary research to demonstrate the nutritional value of the crops. She remembers, "Even the university administrators, even the farmers—they said, 'We're just eating them because there is no alternative,' but they didn't know how beneficial they were. I started in it alone, but I brought in other players, and we brought many people on board." She eventually got funding from a number of international sources. One of the first was Biodiversity International, formerly the International Plant Genetic Resources Institute, which is one of the Consultative Group on International Agricultural Research (CGIAR) centers. Its mission is to promote agricultural biodiversity to increase food security and improve livelihoods.

Once she managed to convince some people, the momentum started to shift. Mary says information helped fuel this. It was easy to gather the empirical evidence showing the levels of calcium, iron, and other key nutrients of the indigenous vegetables and compare them with those of exotic vegetables. The indigenous vegetables compared very well, having more nutritional value than many commonly consumed vegetables. She said another key to changing the status quo was to use a multidisciplinary approach, bringing in social scientists and examining the whole marketing chain to see why traders weren't buying and selling these vegetables. There were no quality seed, no information on how to grow them, no information on their nutritional value, and people producing them for market had poor marketing strategies. Compounding this, the vegetables tended to be highly perishable. Once farmers and traders helped Mary to identify these limits through market and household surveys, she set about trying to address them systematically. She and her collaborators and students produced information on how to grow the vegetables and made it available to farmers. They also produced and packaged good quality seed and made it available to the farmers in collaboration with seed companies like the Kenya Seed Company and community-based organizations. They worked with other organizations like Farm Concern International to help farmers link to markets. The vegetables are now sold in Kenyan supermarkets like Nakumatt and Tuskys, major supermarket chains that operate across Kenya.

Mary also managed to stir up interest in indigenous vegetables in the two Kenyan public universities she worked in. When she started, few people were talking about and researching them. But by introducing them into the curricula, she increased students' exposure to the topic. Now more of them are choosing to study indigenous rather than introduced crop species. When Mary started tracking students' research, 20 percent of them chose to study indigenous crops, and by the time we spoke, it had risen to 70 percent. The universities also became more supportive of the work and have recently introduced an emphasis on indigenous fruit species as well. The government, through the Ministry of Agriculture and the Kenya Agricultural Research Institute, has also set up departmental sections on indigenous crops. Mary often consults for them pro bono. Farmer awareness and recognition is still not 100 percent, but, as she says, they've come a long way.

For Mary, the broader system of international donors and agencies has been a source of funding, ideas, and recognition, although it has not been problem free. She sees herself and her work as "100 percent part of the development system" as she focuses on ultimately improving farmers' nutritional and economic status. Her research is practical rather than purely academic, and she puts a lot of effort and emphasis on outreach. She's been involved in several internationally funded mentorship programs for African women agricultural scientists, mentoring younger women who are starting out as agronomists. She has also taken part in an EU-funded pan-African project to promote

African indigenous vegetables in markets. More recently, her achievements have been recognized in a number of international competitions. The Technical Centre for Agricultural and Rural Cooperation (CTA), based in the Netherlands, awarded Mary top prize in its 2009 Women in Science competition. Then she won recognition as the top woman scientist in the African Union's 2010 competition in the Earth and Life Sciences category. These awards have helped her to promote her own work as they boost her status and give her work more international exposure. When Hillary Clinton came to visit Kenya in 2009, Mary was selected by the African Women in Agricultural Research and Development (AWARD) program, where she was serving as a mentor, to meet her. She presented her work and argued that American and international consumers would benefit from the high nutritional value of exported African indigenous vegetables.

Mary's story shows that at least the international aid system can support locally driven efforts at development. But it wasn't automatic; it took quite a bit of convincing and cajoling on Mary's part. And it still isn't the default, as Mary and many others have noted. She argues,

> We have potential that's not been exploited, human resource potential. Let the Africans solve their own problems, let the Kenyans solve their own problems. And from my experience, some of those brought to help are less experienced than those here in Kenya. OK, if you're providing some aid, it can assist in the short term, but for sustainability there is need to fully involve the local people. That's what we're looking for; we're looking for sustainability, long-term solutions, we're not looking for aid just to put out a fire. There is dire need for proper human resource development, not just money for food to eat at a given time. I'd rather we conduct research and come up with lasting solutions to malnutrition, food insecurity, and poverty, and I believe African indigenous vegetables have unexploited potential to contribute to the solutions we are seeking.

Vicki Wilde, Director, Gender and Diversity, CGIAR

Vicki Wilde's role, more clearly within the international system, is essentially complementary to Mary's. Vicki's lifework, in many ways, has been to facilitate and create spaces for people like Mary to do what they want to do. She also pushes for the kind of international aid that Mary envisions—one that listens and supports local initiative.

When Vicki was still in high school, she got interested in women's rights. It really started when her guidance counselor told her she couldn't be an astronaut because she was a girl. She studied development in graduate school at the City University of New York (CUNY). She describes her program as very activist oriented, which fit her own inclinations. Her commitment to working in international development was strengthened when she won a Congressional Fellowship on Women in Public Policy to work as a legislative aide on issues of importance to women and children. She remembers, "I was studying development on one hand and looking at top policy on development on the other and looking at how women's rights were being traded for political favor, and how extremely vulnerable they were to that, they had no voice, no say—that definitely was an eye-opening experience."

After grad school, in 1989, she got her first job break with a two-week contract to write a pamphlet for the FAO in Rome. From that she got work as a consultant on gender issues in community forestry projects, and as she says, it went from there. She found she had a natural skill for advocating for and facilitating communication in different rural development projects:

> I loved talking to farmers and extension workers, and I loved developing methods that worked for improving communication between farmers and women and village chiefs and hearing all the different voices. And eventually I was specializing in participatory approaches for looking at food security issues, community forestry, extension, irrigation—a whole bunch of things. And always with the focus on gender—just making sure that we paid a lot of attention to what the women had to say, as well as what the men wanted to say in their own right. And the more I did this and listened to these men and women, the more I came to believe it was essential to coming up with development approaches that would be effective on the ground.

She continued on in the same vein, involved in a variety of initiatives to bring gender understanding into development projects, and even in the distribution of food aid, and to improve feedback in development planning. Then in 1999, she took on her current position, in charge of gender and diversity initiatives across all fifteen CGIAR centers internationally. Her work has focused on how to make agricultural research and development institutions more responsive to needs on the ground. One key to that is to have women inside the organizations, especially in leadership positions, and to have women-friendly policies. This has also led her to focus on internal human resource and policy issues within the CGIAR system: "Our motto was that we can't achieve on the outside what we don't practice on the inside."

As the worldwide Gender and Diversity Program matured and changed, Vicki wanted to apply what she saw as its most successful aspects more specifically to Africa, where she saw the need is greatest. Unlike most of the world, agricultural production and food security in Africa has been decreasing over the years. With funds from the Rockefeller Foundation, she set up a small fellowship program for women in East Africa as a three-year pilot. Mary Abukutsa was one of the first fellowship winners in this program, later going on to become a mentor. It was a roaring success. Vicki says, "It just so exceeded our hopes; it worked so beautifully."

This led to the AWARD program, funded by the Gates Foundation, USAID, and others. Operating in eleven countries, AWARD aims to get more women into areas of influence within the agricultural research and extension system, with the hope that they will be better at responding to the needs of rural women farmers, people who, like Mary's mother, are just trying to make ends meet and support their families: "Right now less than one in four agricultural researchers, and one in seven agricultural research managers, in Africa are women; we know rural women just aren't getting extension, access to land; they're not getting what they need."

Vicki's extremely proud of the AWARD program. In many ways, it is the culmination of all her previous work and learning:

> This is my dream. In fact, this is literally my dream. When I was asked by the Gates Foundation to write this proposal, I didn't involve any consultants. I just stayed for days in my pajamas writing up my dream all day and night. I had nothing to lose. I thought, based on all the experience I've had before, I'm going to write down what I think would really work. Of course I didn't get everything. Of course compromises are part of it.

When we spoke, AWARD was in year four and doing very well. It was designed to reach and support women at various stages of their careers and education, as early as post-bachelor's. There were no age restrictions, so it was open to women who have finished raising their families. It reached women in universities, the government, and NGOs. It had managed to gain support from men, who were involved as mentors. It promoted leadership and activism among its recipients, who in turn were speaking to young boys and girls in schools about working in science. Vicki explains,

We're still learning a lot, but it's going super well—it's very exciting. So I'm one of those development workers that every single day
I get success stories, e-mails saying, "You changed my life, I'm so
inspired that I've started this new program, or wrote this paper, or
gave this speech"—every day.

Despite having been able to leverage such success, Vicki is still in many
ways swimming against the stream. She finds that despite the rhetoric, gender
remains a marginal issue in most development organizations, both international and national. Musing on why this is in agricultural research and development particularly, she says,

You know the first tendency of any organization is reproduction of
the status quo—if you're really going to be more gender responsive,
you can't just tinker around the edges; at the end of the day, gender
issues are power issues and resource issues and influence issues, and
what technology for who. And the tendency of organizations is to
go the path of least resistance, and I think one of the results of that
is that women remain underserved. That's not a popular statement
at all, because people want easy solutions, and they want it in a way
that's not expensive or doesn't create much upheaval.

Her ultimate hope is that programs such as AWARD will change the playing
field by changing the players, bringing more African women into the game.

Is It a Particular Kind of Person?

I argued in the introduction to part 3 that it can be misleading to equate a
development persona—cynic, satisficer, do-gooder, or positive realist—with
a personality type. In practice, we can move among the types, depending on
our situations, our understandings, and the choices we make. But of all these
personas, negotiators often seem so rare and committed that they seem to be ex-
traordinary people. The terms "champion" and "social entrepreneur" have been
used to describe people with strong social commitment, vision, and the ability
to develop effective and often innovative responses to social issues. In short,
these terms are almost synonymous with the negotiator persona. Those writing
about champions or social entrepreneurs often describe them as rare individuals who should be sought out and supported, rather than expecting that we can
cultivate the qualities of negotiation in most people.[7]

So, do Mary and Vicki represent a special and particular kind of person? And does negotiation require such a person, a visionary leader? Well, both yes and no. In essence, negotiation is more about a mind-set than a person. It comes from a felt need to change something and the sense of agency to do it. While particular personalities may be more predisposed to it, this mind-set also comes out of cumulative experience and from the way one chooses to identify oneself.

Mary and Vicki both identify themselves as part of the development system but also as activists or advocates. They are clearly engaged with the issues they are addressing. And based on what they find out as they go along, they adjust. Mary has tried to understand and address the barriers to people benefiting from indigenous vegetables. And from necessity, she has learned the art of persuasion. Of her team, Vicki says,

> We're putting a lot of time into a rigorous monitoring and evaluation system; I think it will be groundbreaking. And we do change things based on what doesn't work—we're not so bureaucratic that we can't do it. I ensure my whole team knows that we run things on adaptive management. We take the feedback very, very seriously.

In Kenya, Uganda, and Afghanistan, I encountered similar stories from those working within their home countries based on the needs they see and then trying to draw on the international system as a resource for ideas, education, legitimacy, legal backing through international conventions, and financial resources. As they try to pursue their objectives, they have to learn the system, as well as about the problems they're trying to address. Having people like Vicki within the international system who listen to them and can leverage the bureaucracy to work for them makes a difference.

Gilbert Onyango, a trained lawyer who lives and works in Nairobi, Kenya, had an idea that he was in the process of realizing when he spoke with me in early 2011. He had just founded and registered the East African Centre for Human Rights (EACHRights), which will focus on promoting economic, social, and cultural rights in East Africa. He got the idea while undergoing a four-month Chevening Fellowship at the University of Nottingham, United Kingdom. He was inspired by his experiences over the previous nine years working for an NGO addressing issues of child rights. He was also part of the broader civil society movement that lobbied for a new Kenyan constitution. With the constitution recently passed into law, he sees new opportunities to use rights-based approaches to leverage greater government responsiveness to the people in Kenya and across Africa more broadly. The underlying premise of his venture is that there is an opportunity to use international rights conventions and the constitution itself to hold the government to account and to advocate for change.

When we spoke, he was still developing the idea by talking with people and seeing how it should play out in terms of activities. He had also just enrolled himself at the International Institute of Social Studies in The Hague, Netherlands, where he will pursue an MA in development studies and will specialize in human rights, development, and social justice.

> I think that gap between development and human rights in Africa must be bridged for greater accountability, transparency, and nondiscrimination. This is because violations of human rights and systemic failures are a result of poor governance, so we must bring out that linkage. . . .
>
> For example, the government policy is water for all by 2015—but are we holding the government accountable? And what does it mean to the common citizen? And how can the citizens participate and know that they can influence the leadership? This is the link between citizens and the realization of their economic and social rights.

Although he does not know Gilbert, David Dryonyi in Uganda has come to some similar conclusions about development needs in his own country and is taking a similar approach. He ran for office in the 2011 national elections for his home district in the West Nile region. But the official count was not in his favor. He questions the result but has accepted it and decided he can serve his people and keep his campaign promises by setting up a community development NGO. This he had done together with his campaign manager. David explains,

> I read a book a while back by Alex de Waal—I think it was *Famine Crimes*. He argues there are two kinds of accountability: social accountability and political accountability. He argues that social accountability is a wish list—we want this and this—but it doesn't hold government sufficiently obliged to provide; they'll provide if they have something left over. And many Ugandans think like that, but that's very different from a political accountability of the people—that look, we elected you to do a particular job, and if it's

not improving, we'll kick you out. They need to come up with so-lutions to a specific problem, that can only be driven from bottom up—which means that people need to have their own suggestions to their problems, their own solutions, and then follow up with their representatives and hold them to account for it. I don't think that's happening. And I'd say that the missing link is the people.

Both Gilbert and David have drawn some of their ideas and inspiration from international sources, and Gilbert is also interested in leveraging inter-national rights conventions that Kenya has signed on to. But their problem analysis and sense of what might work as a solution is based on long-term contextual knowledge. The ability of people like Mary, Gilbert, and David to gain support depends on their own persuasive skills but also on the policies and overall receptivity of donors. Ian Smillie says,

> You just have to keep at it. This is what BRAC did—they're very opportunistic, and they use that word but not in the negative sense. They use opportunities. I asked the founder of BRAC about this, and he recalled a question that someone had once asked Na-poleon: "What do you look for in a general?" And Napoleon said, "Luck, above all, luck." But luck, what is luck? It is about being ready for an opportunity, to be able to recognize it and take advan-tage of it: like an opening in the enemy lines or a new investment opportunity.

People like BRAC's founder, Fazle Hasan Abed, and Mary Abukutsa have, through their own persistence, managed to thrive despite the challenges. But the overall prognosis on the development system's ability to identify and nurture local talent is less impressive. The rhetoric is not new. Development agencies have been talking of the need for people and governments to lead in their own development back since the early postcolonial period of the 1960s and 1970s. But, forty years later, donors and Northern NGOs still often treat their Southern counterparts as less able versions of themselves. Knowledge of reporting requirements and the latest development theories is highly prized, while local knowledge is often discounted. Ian recalls,

> I was talking to a young Somali in Canada. He and his friends are raising money for a hospital in Somaliland—they fund the running costs of the hospital. There are Somalis in the US and the UK also

contributing. They have to transfer their money for the hospital through hawalas.[8] He's not a development expert, but he knows Somalia. He can't get the time of day from CIDA or Canadian NGOs; they treat him as though he's some kind of fool or worse. They tell him, "These aren't our priorities—we want to focus on sustainability and long-term development." But surely, if you have a group of Somali expatriates who want to do something useful in Somalia, they should be taken seriously and treated with respect as development actors.

Although development agencies have often failed to support local initiatives, there is a strong argument to be made that these are the heart of effective development.[9] Ricardo Ramirez and Wendy Quarry argue that successful development depends crucially on key people whom they call champions: "Champions are individuals or organizations with a sincere respect for the views of the people with whom they work and with people's ability to solve many of their own problems."[10] Describing some early champions in the field of communication for development, they write,

> They all decided to get things done no matter what. They did not have an ounce of naivety: they were very political in their outlook and knew that they were only able to shift things a little. . . . They understood the big picture, they understood the development industry, and they acted notwithstanding its straitjacket. Most important, they stayed in place for a long time and got to know the context well. This allowed them to zero in on what mattered most to rural and marginal communities.[11]

Ramirez and Quarry argue that such champions are very rare and hard to find but can mean the difference between shining success and mediocrity or failure in an initiative. In their own work, when they are not themselves deeply familiar with the context, they see part of their task as identifying local champions with whom they can partner and support.

This idea is also the center point of the work of Ashoka, a foundation that is dedicated to identifying and supporting people who have already started making positive social change. Ashoka designates successful candidates as "Ashoka fellows" and provides them with financial support and the legitimacy of formal recognition and networking opportunities. Rather than use the term "champion," they call such people "social entrepreneurs," but otherwise Ramirez and Quarry's description still serves well. Social entrepreneurs may be found in any sector, whether government, NGO, or for-profit business, but what characterizes them is their innovation and dogged commitment to a particular cause. For Ashoka, those people who are seen to best epitomize the social entrepreneur are those who are savvy at working with the system as it is, with all its flaws, while holding no illusions to its limitations. They are people who are clear about what they want and will follow through until they get it done.

William Easterly, in his book *The White Man's Burden*, distinguishes between planners and searchers. Planners pontificate and rationalize from afar, concocting grand but impossible theories to save the world.[12] Searchers are practical and pragmatic, embedded in the nitty-gritty of a situation and able to experiment until they find a solution that works. Easterly argues that pretty much all effective human activity is done by searchers. The international development industry is terminally ineffective because of its misdirected accountability, which allows planners to dominate despite their weak track record. With donors so far removed from the results of their largesse, they can be sold on the rhetoric of Big Plans and shielded from the uncomfortable fact that these never work. This is part of the reason why negotiators—or searchers—seem to be constantly swimming against the stream of the broader development system.

Everyone writing about the change-makers, whether they are called social entrepreneurs or champions or searchers or negotiators, agrees on the fact that such people are pretty rare and special. But one of the nicest surprises in writing this book was how many inspiring people I met along the way, people who in one way or another fit these labels. I didn't seek them out. I was interested in everyone's experiences, whether good, bad, or indifferent, whether I felt the person seemed effective in his or her work or not. And yet, without looking, I met many people who seemed to me to be exceptional, people whose existence made me feel a little bit more hopeful for the world. Maybe, just maybe, they are not as rare as we think. And maybe by controlling the context and recognizing the power of our own choices, we can increase the possibility of finding ourselves in a situation that brings this out in us, and we can bring inspiration to others.

No matter how remarkable, such individuals are never effective because of their own efforts alone. Change-makers within a place depend on sympathetic facilitators within the international system. The two are in fact mutually dependent. Sympathetic facilitators working at an international level cannot hope to achieve much without linking to or joining with locally engaged people and groups. These roles are complementary, and it is not unusual for one person to migrate between the two. Many individuals have shifted from locally engaged activist in their own country to act as an international support to people doing similar work in other countries.

The Role of Negotiation in International Development

At their best, negotiators can challenge and change ideas and practices within international development. But even negotiators are unlikely to succeed in radically transforming the overall sector. In international development, as in any human institution, the status quo is maintained through the constant and ongoing reproduction of understandings, relationships, and dynamics. Even ideas that seem intrinsically radical and transformative, ideas such as participatory development, become absorbed into the development status quo, perhaps changing it incrementally but not transforming its core.

Negotiators may not be able to fundamentally transform the international development system, but they can nonetheless be powerful and reach broadly. BRAC's programming is one example of powerful reach. As of 2009, it operated over 47,000 schools serving 1.4 million children from poor families in Bangladesh.[13] This is just one branch of its extensive network in Bangladesh, and it has a growing international presence. The Grameen Bank, also in Bangladesh, serves millions of people and has inspired many more microcredit programs around the world. These are ripples that have turned into great waves.

The stories of people like Mary and Vicki show us what is possible in taking international development work a little further. That's an important source of inspiration for those of us who are lost in the woods of day-to-day details and struggles. They also help us to understand the potential complementarities between those working within the international side of the development system and those working within a particular context.

Feeling inspired, you may be wondering about the best way of emulating such examples in your own work. There are certainly factors that you have control over. It also depends on your own goals and priorities in your work. Do you have a particular issue or area that you feel deeply committed to for as long as it takes to achieve change? If that is the case, you are much more likely to be a negotiator. If you are interested in exploring and working with opportunities as they arise, at least for the time being, then you can still be actively engaged in your work. In either case, critical reflection and engagement are crucial to keep you grounded, lest you veer off into myth.

Most people who are driven, passionate, and critical find themselves at various moments skeptical or overwhelmed. It doesn't mean they have a personal deficiency. In terms of the long-term prognosis of those people doing good work, it's much better than blind or passive alignment. As long as they're struggling and they still care about the outcomes of what they're doing, chances are they'll learn from it and see their way through, or if they can't, they'll choose to leave development or change their role. There are some really difficult situations in development: the expectation that we should all be "success stories" at all times is not realistic or helpful. It is the long haul that counts, and people have to respond to the particular situation they find themselves in.

There may not be a surefire recipe for becoming a negotiator. But there are ways of improving your odds of doing solid, useful work within your career. As we saw in chapter 7, one fundamental choice is making a long-term commitment, whether to a place, an issue, an organization, or all three. Another is to link up with the right people who have compatible goals and philosophies and complementary knowledge and skills. Visionaries and innovators often prefer to head up their own NGOs, as they find more latitude to work on their own terms, but they are also there in the big organizations. It may be harder to operate, but there are more resources and often more status and convening power. For those with the right personality and patience, these strengths can be considerable.

The best ideas and "visions" come from solid experience and observation. There's absolutely no need for all those coming into development to attempt to transform it with their latest insights, insights gleaned after a few weeks or months. Development doesn't really need any more heroes. The people who listen and learn and genuinely care, who can handle complexity and recognize the challenges, whether they're best characterized as critically engaged team players or visionary leaders, are the people who are most likely to contribute to sensible, responsible, and effective development work. The system may not always recognize them or thank them for it, especially as they're starting out, but when they find their balance, these people tend to be very happy in their work.

Notes

1. Muhammad Yunus, *Banker to the Poor: Micro-lending and the Battle Against World Poverty* (New York: PublicAffairs, 2003).

2. Greg Mortenson and David Oliver Relin, *Three Cups of Tea: One Man's Mission to Promote Peace . . . One School at a Time* (New York: Viking, 2006).

3. John Wood, *Leaving Microsoft to Change the World: An Entrepreneur's Odyssey to Educate the World's Children* (New York: Harper, 2007).

4. Room to Read, *Our Story 2012*, cited October 18, 2012, http://www.roomtoread.org.

5. William Easterly, *The White Man's Burden: Why the West's Efforts to Aid the Rest Have Done So Much Ill and So Little Good* (New York: Penguin, 2007).

6. "Quinoa Selection: Foreign Interest Grows in an Old Highland Staple," *The Economist*, May 12, 2012.

7. David Bornstein, *How to Change the World: Social Entrepreneurs and the Power of New Ideas* (Oxford: Oxford University Press, 2007).

8. *Hawala* is a traditional form of money transfer used through the Middle East, parts of Africa, and parts of Asia. It is based on trust and reciprocal agreements across a network of moneylenders.

9. Dominic Hounkonnou, "Listen to the Cradle: Building From Local Dynamics" (doctoral dissertation, University of Wageningen Communication and Innovation Studies, October 2005).

10. Ricardo Ramirez and Wendy Quarry, *Communication for Another Development* (London: Zed Books, 2008), 62.

11. Ibid., 84.

12. Easterly, *The White Man's Burden*.

13. Mahmuda Aldeen, *BRAC's Non-formal Primary Education Programme: Scope, Growth, Achievements and Factors Contributing to Its Success*, May 6, 2009, Articles on Education of Bangladesh, cited March 3, 2012, http://www.bdeduarticle.com/non-formal-education/27-uncatagorized/58-bracs-non-formal-primary-education-programme-scope-growth-achievements-and-factors-contributing-to-its-success.

11

Opting Out

When you are negotiating, it is always necessary to know at what point you're willing to walk away. The same is true of working in international development. Whether one stays working in this field or leaves it is a choice; a choice that is best made consciously and with careful consideration. With this in mind, it is helpful to understand the options open to those who are development minded but have chosen to stay out of the mainstream or to leave altogether.

People working in international development face inevitable limitations and frustrations. A majority navigate their way through and feel that international development does, overall, contribute something useful to the world. But as we've seen throughout this book, the funding conditions, management practices, and internal cultures of development agencies can be stifling and sometimes downright discriminatory. There may be more effective means of fighting poverty and contributing to social justice than through the formal mechanisms of international development. Some people go into international development and find that they dislike the nature of the work, the organizational culture, or the bureaucracy or find themselves doubting that it adds up to a net benefit to those they are hoping to help. And so they decide to leave. They still can contribute, possibly with greater effect, through other mechanisms. While some move on to other issues and priorities, many of those who leave international development do stay engaged with the issues that motivated them in the first place.

This chapter first examines some of the reasons why people leave international development and then looks at some of the ways that those who leave continue to engage with development issues.

Reasons for Leaving

People leave development work for a variety of reasons. Some never intended to stay. Some feel disillusioned with development institutions, finding them too hierarchical, bureaucratic, or inefficient. Some feel that the systemic challenges and complexities that development work faces ultimately undermine the value of their work. Others leave for more personal reasons: either they just can't find a position in the international development world that suits them or meets their expectations of what they thought they would be doing, or else they seek a more settled lifestyle. In the first part of this chapter, we look at some of the most common reasons why people decide to leave international development.

Just Visiting

I spoke with a woman from Ireland who doesn't identify herself as a "development worker" because she's never intended to stay working in international development. Eighteen years since she took her first overseas posting, she is still working in international development. She was working as the country director of an NGO in Afghanistan when we spoke. Professionally, however, she identifies herself more as a social worker. She explains that when she started working in international development, it was seen as a largely temporary and voluntary activity that people did for a few years before returning to their regular career. She finds it interesting, though, and she has kept taking "one last posting." Her friends don't believe her anymore when she says she's on the verge of leaving.

While she may have taken the art of "almost leaving" to new levels, many people do come into development work on a temporary basis. Some find enough in the work to keep them around for longer than they'd originally meant to stay, perhaps even for a lifetime. But others leave more or less when they intended, and the fact of their leaving is more indicative of their initial intention than any particular reaction to the realities of development work as they encounter it.

It is almost a truism that those who go abroad for development work—usually Westerners who are working in developing countries—gain more than they give. Still, in the field, the temporary flow of people who dip in and out of development work, especially with limited experience, can add to the overall instability of development systems. Carina Andersson used to supervise the placement of Swedish volunteers in African partner organizations and recalls,

> The volunteers were often nice young or old people who wanted to do good and [were] placed to work with a local organization that often didn't know what to do with them. . . . And there were often misunderstandings, different expectations, and cultural collisions,

and the volunteers were in many cases driving Toyota 4x4s to and from the office, which no one else was allowed to drive. . . . I think it's good to have Swedes come out to work, but with clear roles and responsibilities. Nowadays it's rather uncommon to work as a volunteer in someone else's office. Swedish NGOs more often have their own offices where they work from. Of late, it has become more common to send young people with a four- or six-month attachment with NGOs; as interns, they're basically there to get an experience, not to really work as such. . . . You know, I get so many requests from Swedish people who want to come and help: "Can we do something? I really want to go to Africa now." And I think it's fantastic, but it's so difficult to see exactly what they should do.

System Limits: "Winning the Battle but Losing the War"

Many people within international development worry about the overall limits and inconsistencies of the international development system. For most, these limits constrain effectiveness, but the system remains a tool, however inadequate, to address global poverty and related issues. For some, however, the inadequacies of international development to achieve its stated aims combined with the likelihood that it will have unintended and possibly harmful effects on the people and communities it is supposed to benefit mean that it is best not to engage. Postdevelopment critics have argued this point for many decades.[1]

People experiencing system limits often take one of two commonly argued points of view. One point of view suggests that while many small-scale development projects are successful, they have a limited impact and do not add up to broader sustainable change in the lives of people. So an NGO may set up a school or run a small income-generating project and have success within a community, but that doesn't necessarily add up to transformative change in the lives of people in the village, and it certainly doesn't reach to all the neighboring communities. One former development worker muses, "Especially when you see the immediate effects, it seems like it's working. I remember reading this quote that all these NGOs are islands of success floating in a sea of failure." Macrolevel issues such as international trade agreements really set limits on the economic prospects of a country and its people. Development projects can seem more like a distraction.

On its own, this perspective usually isn't enough to deter people from working in international development. It suggests their work will have a limited impact, but still a positive one. And the value of the work on the lives of people whom it touches may be quite significant—it is more the overall scope that may be limited.

However, some people further worry that even these small-scale projects have unintended effects that may actually weaken the people and local systems that they seek to help. This more serious concern can lead someone to decide to opt out of development work. A former development worker explains,

> The organization I worked for built a school for untouchables in India. It started as an elementary school but then it ballooned into a community center. . . . A side effect of having this successful project was that there was very little incentive for government to invest in the community because the foreign NGO is there. And a friend told me there is a local school that is now less supported by the government because all the students are going to this private school.
>
> And then they started giving handouts to people. Which is very harmful. But because of the status of the organization, they'd get requests from donors. And there aren't really any economically viable occupations in the village. And so what happened, when students finish and come out into the village, they can read and know a bit about the world, but there's really nothing for them to do. They don't want to do the manual labor their parents are doing. So apart from providing literacy, there was very little the school system was adding to the prosperity of the community. So you're building this school without understanding the system of the community.

Some of the most reflective and conscientious development workers also worry about the consequences of working in cultures that are not their own. As they struggle to understand, the level of complexity may be unmanageable. One former development worker explains,

> I tend to think that people in development are more on a personal journey—and for some people that journey is a kind of a side thing, because the person is an engineer or accountant and they're doing a job—so they'd describe the other stuff as culture shock. But if you're not really experienced as an expert in some field, or you're just terminally uncomfortable, you can find yourself feeling that you're not that suited, or you're not doing much good, and the whole development enterprise carries the seeds of self-destruction.

Sometimes you feel that it cannot but fail. [Perhaps] that's too strong, but [one feels] that there are countervailing forces. If this is development—people, money, per diems, travel, things, systems—they interact with environments, whether it's a government or a hospital or a grassroots community. Then there's all this stuff going on, and it's almost like an undertow, so there's a culture clash, that dissonance between what's coming in and what's there, that's just natural, and then the dysfunctions that are inherent in this whole thing—because those systems and things coming in have their own dysfunctions—say the models are taken from the West—they aren't perfect. And then the environment it's coming into has its own weaknesses—if you're in Kenya, people talk about tribalism, corruption—everything has its weaknesses. The system coming in is being tested in a new way, and then the thing that supposedly needs help—a society, government, or community that's identified as needing development assistance—they've got their own shit. And then they come into conflict, that's on the sociological level, then the individual development worker comes in as a microcosm of that. Here I am, coming in, I may think that I am a well-developed [Western] boy, but no, I have my own shit. I think I've got these skills—but they've never been tested in this way, and nothing is absolute, and then I'm interacting with this environment and these people, and they're interacting with me.

When people feel that they may not have the skills to grapple with development issues, they are out of place and risk doing harm, and they may well consider leaving development. This likelihood is increased if they feel that the formal institutions of development as a whole are weak at assessing and addressing systemic issues.

Disappointment With the Institutions

Many people working in international development are troubled by the policies and power dynamics within institutions that privilege some people over others. Westerners, white people, people with credentials from Ivy League colleges—various forms of social status and privilege are seen to be recognized and rewarded within development institutions. This is far from universal, and many institutions make efforts to create positive, equitable work environments. But it is still prevalent enough that many people find it shocking. And given many of the ideals of social justice and equity that are associated with development, many people find such inequalities hypocritical. The most obvious and glaring power imbalance is still that between the donors and those who receive funds. The target beneficiaries of development often appear as afterthoughts.

One former World Bank employee explains of the culture of the bank:

> I found it is an incredibly elitist institution that had a professional class, gleaned from the Ivy Leagues (read: wealthy, mostly Western European/American), and a sort of underclass made up of technical and supply workers who kind of represented the rest of the world. To put it cynically, a perfect microcosm of the model of economic development championed by the World Bank.
>
> I'm sure these aren't surprising revelations. . . . However, it was amazing how apparent this was on the day-to-day level.

Another former development worker recalls,

> I was at a conference with some big name speakers—Jeffrey Sachs, some people from DFID. There were about eight people on this panel, six were donors, and two were representatives from African states. And you could see how the discussion was dominated by white donors. It was an interesting display of power. The African delegates were very timid.

These apparent contradictions between the egalitarian rhetoric of development and its hierarchical practice are troubling, and they cause people to question how such institutions can possibly address the systemic complexities of development. The natural conclusion to this critique, argued by numerous people including Graham Hancock, Arturo Escobar, and, more recently, Dambisa Moyo, is that development institutions are parasitic and ought to be disbanded.[2]

Of course, many of those working within development make similar observations and have similar critiques. For some people, it is why they would never work for certain institutions—they may prefer to stay within NGOs rather than the World Bank, for example. Others see these dynamics as less pervasive or as just a side effect of bureaucratization and feel that they can still maneuver and work within big development agencies. The limitations and contradictions of the development system are significant and should be taken seriously by anyone who works or seeks to work in development. How to best respond to these issues I leave as a personal issue for readers to address on their own terms. Seeking to align with or strengthen alternatives or to walk away completely are absolutely valid options.

Can't Find the Right Niche

Many people who come into development have visions of themselves spending time with people in a village somewhere, getting to know them, understanding their ideas and problems, and helping them out, as we saw in chapter 6. Sometimes people do have these experiences in their work, but it is typically earlier in their career, if at all. Many development workers, and especially those working as expatriates, spend all or most of their time in meetings and writing reports, with occasional but brief field visits.

When she chose to pursue a career in international development, Harriet Menter had visions of working directly with communities. But after her studies and some time working for the International Center for Tropical Agriculture (CIAT), she began to work as an officer at DFID. Her job was largely desk based with meetings and occasional field visits. When she was working at DFID's Malawi office, she worked with orphans in her own time, and she found this to be more rewarding than her formal work. She decided to leave international development and pursue community work in the United Kingdom, her home country. She now works in environmental education, working with vulnerable and low-income children and families, encouraging the use of community gardens and green spaces. She loves her job and can't imagine going back to international development, although she has great admiration for many of her former colleagues.

Personal and Lifestyle

In chapter 6, we looked at some of the lifestyle issues around working in international development. Just as with the privilege and power dynamics within some of the big bureaucratic agencies, the lifestyle enjoyed by expatriate aid workers, especially those working for donors and the UN, is often seen to be excessive and wasteful. Aside from the damage it might have on local systems, the expat lifestyle abroad can just feel empty. One disenchanted expat in Kampala explains,

> What's important to me has totally shifted. I feel like this lifestyle, there's something very pathological about it. I almost feel like real life is when you're home and you're in a community and you see the same people every day. . . . I think a lot of expats keep themselves always moving on and moving on and so they never have to

deal with the real issues in life. And I think we live in a privileged place where we can have luxuries, and I've personally gotten disconnected from what's important to me; I've missed a huge part of my family's lives, and I'm not willing to miss any more. And in Uganda, in three and a half years, my friends have turned over three or four times, and I find it empty. On a superficial level, it's glossy and empty and extremely lonely—you can go to the pool all year around and go out. . . . I think even if you have family it's lonely; I don't have family. So I'm just like, you know what, maybe I'm completely off my rocker, but I want to be somewhere for a while where I'm not in an expat community. . . . There's this sense of not belonging anywhere; at the end of the day, you know, I don't belong anywhere. And I want to develop ties somewhere and set down some roots.

Uganda's a family duty station, and there are a lot of families here, but my friends with family, they still feel disconnected, and they feel they're living an artificial life here. I don't think it's different in other countries.

People sometimes choose to leave international development to get away from the superficiality of the expat lifestyle abroad, or to satisfy the need to settle with family, or to ensure that children have access to good schooling and health care. Sometimes it is because their parents are getting older. One development worker says,

For the expat, you think about your parents and should I go on this mission or not? Something could happen to you while you're away, who's going to look after them? Or what if they worry all the time? Do you have the right to inflict that on them? I think a lot of expats think of that, and it kind of spoils the fun. I think for a lot of us it happened that while we were away, someone we loved died or fell sick, and there was nothing we could do. I think that's a big deal for a lot of people.

And so family ties and changing life priorities can bring some people out of international development as they seek to establish a life for themselves at home. Some people may manage to stay in the development field if such jobs exist in their home area, but for others finding a job at home means a complete career change.

To Stay or to Go?

Most people who leave international development don't have a single reason. There are layers of unease around various aspects of development work that culminate to a tipping point at which they decide to leave or that they perhaps combine with a personal reason.

The concerns that drive some people to leave international development are often shared by those who choose to continue working within it. The difference often seems to come down to whether people feel they can be at least somewhat effective within international development, despite its limitations. Ian Smillie explains,

> People do ask me, "Why do you stay in it, if you're so critical?" Well, I stay in it because of things like BRAC, which I see do work. But I've stopped doing evaluation work for CIDA. A lot of problems in their projects lay in the design, rather than the implementation. But CIDA didn't want to know that. If you told them they had some responsibility for a failure, they'd ask you to take it out. A major failing in the development world is the unwillingness to acknowledge failure and to learn from it. So failures are repeated. I've written books about international development, some positive, some critical. . . . There's a role for people who are curmudgeonly but not totally negative.

One former development worker agrees that most of her former colleagues were dedicated, and many shared her concerns:

> Those people who have those issues but still stay in international development, I think the main reason they stay is that they're really committed, and even though it's really flawed as a system, it's the only one we've got. That accounts for a lot of people. And then, to be honest, some people just really enjoy the lifestyle—you get to go to another country every three years, you get a housekeeper, and great holidays.

Meanwhile, those who leave their employment in international development often remain engaged in other ways, and they remain affected by their experiences. The second part of this chapter considers some alternative ways of engaging.

Other Ways of Engaging

People who leave international development work often continue to engage with development and social justice issues in a range of ways. These alternative approaches, outside or on the edges of the international development sector, can help people to avoid many of the political, institutional, and lifestyle issues characteristic of the international development sector.

Active Citizenship

Even brief exposure to other places and cultures can lead people to a different sense of themselves, their own societies, and the world. Lynne Mitchell, who is the director of the University of Guelph's Centre for International Programs, recalls,

> I did my degree in crop science. When I graduated, all my colleagues were going off to sell fertilizer for large chemical companies. I didn't want to, so I applied to CUSO, went to Thailand on a two-year placement, and of course, when I came back, the whole world looked different.

Lynne's experience eventually led her into working in international education. Through this, she's seen that personally transformative experiences can translate to broader social benefits. She's seen the positive effect that international experience has on students and, through them, on Canadian society as a whole:

> I get parents who ask me why should I send a son or daughter on an exchange program. I say two reasons—they'll distinguish themselves on their transcripts, they may be more energized, they may get some interesting credentials, they'll make more money eventually. The other reason is that they'll make friends with people and feel like they can call another part of the world home. We have statistics that they, when they come home, will be more likely to vote, more likely to be engaged in the community, a better citizen, a better neighbor.

Likewise, many people who have worked in another part of the world feel that they have a better understanding of global issues and of the fragility and interconnectedness of humanity worldwide.

Many people who choose to work in international development start out with an interest in international political issues, but their commitment may grow with greater exposure to suffering and injustices. People see firsthand that the particular features of a society, whether positive or negative, can never be taken for granted. Societies are human creations, and their fortunes can change. They also see the gap between their initial understanding of the world and the understanding wrought by greater experience, and they realize that most people at home share their initial, rather simplistic, ideas.

Community Development at Home

Some people working in international development have dreams of returning to their home country and engaging in development work there, usually at the community level. Sogol Zand, an Iranian, is one of these. She's been working in Afghanistan, researching issues related to women and development. Of the future, she says,

> My dream would be to go back to Iran and to have an NGO doing community development, something like this. . . . And a part of it is that I think I owe it to people in Iran, because I think I come from a country that I haven't seen myself. I was born into a fairly upper-middle-class family, and until some years ago, I hadn't even been to poor parts of Tehran. . . . And one of the reasons I chose to be in Afghanistan is because language-wise it's close, and culturally, it is somehow close to Iran, so the experience I get could be some-how used when I go back.

Similarly, Bai Mankay Sankoh, who has been working with the World Food Programme in Rome and Uganda, says he would like to eventually go back home to his country of Sierra Leone and contribute to development there. Tariq Ihsan is from Pakistan but has spent many years working in Afghanistan. He feels at home with the people there, but his family is in Pakistan, and he feels he should be with them. He predicts, however, that he won't be able to stay out of development work, in some form or another:

> When I talked to my son and wife about spending time on the farm, they were very happy. But after a few weeks, I had an idea about doing development in the villages around our farm—I can't detach myself from it, I'll keep doing it.

Emanuele Lapierre-Fortine is a young Canadian just finishing her master's degree. She has some international experience and some Canadian experience and contemplates a career in which she does both. She says,

> I think in both [international and Canadian development work], the key is knowing the area and the context, and that's where I don't feel comfortable working for very short periods overseas. I feel like in Canada, it would be a bit easier to know the context. You're immersed in it every day, hear the daily news, and have a better understanding of how the government and different institutions work, so you can respond to that. I think some skill sets are similar; it depends what you're doing.

Emanuele cautions, however, that context varies: even neighboring villages can have different characteristics, and culture varies among social groups even within the same country.

Sometimes working on development in one's own country still means engaging with the international development system for funding, but not necessarily. It certainly opens up more possibilities in terms of organization, operation, and the financial base. Many of those who have worked in their own countries and internationally note that the basic skills and concepts are the same.

It is also hard to think of a country in the world in which there are not substantive issues of poverty and social exclusion to address. For example, one American development worker had been working in India but came back home to the United States because she had a young family. She describes her work there:

> I went back to the States and went to Baltimore—which is a shithole, like a developing country—really poor, no industry, no anything, everything falling apart. And in the middle of it you have this fabulous hospital and medical school. And I was working with African Americans and worked on, interestingly, obesity and nutrition, and I went from that to Nepal, where women didn't have enough to eat. But seeing the poverty in Baltimore, being part of the urban poor is worse—it's worse than being in a developing country. I only looked at it in terms of what were people eating? And of course, they were eating what they could afford, and what was culturally appropriate. If you asked people if they would eat differently if they could afford it, they all said yes. But they didn't

have money, or family support, they were very poorly educated . . . to the point that for me, a middle-class first-generation American for whose parents education was everything, it was just a shock. And these were two-hundred-pound sixteen-year-old girls, and this was before the Internet, they had such poor information. It was pretty bad, the conditions people lived in, their cockroach-infested apartments—you'd go to their homes, and you wouldn't really want to sit down.

She went from working in India, a country that has no shortage of extreme poverty, to Baltimore and was shocked by the deprivation people faced there. She said it was worse than a developing country. This is a point worth emphasizing, especially for those who come from the United States feeling that they are exporting the benefits of their country to other places.

Business

It is often argued that business is a valid means of development. In fact, proponents argue, it can be more effective than funded development initiatives because it must respond to real markets, so it is more responsive to clients and beneficiaries than to top-down development projects. Furthermore, it will sustain itself as long as there is market demand and without dependence on short-term donor funding, and it doesn't have distorting and inflationary effects. Some people who work in international development decide to switch over to the private sector, sometimes even starting their own businesses as a way of creating employment in addition to the service they provide.

Many development initiatives are aimed at creating income-generating opportunities for marginal groups and stimulating markets. But these often depend on subsidies that collapse as soon as the development agents leave. Starting businesses directly, the success of which depend on their ability to generate income, avoids this issue. Ian Clark, from Ireland, initially came to Uganda as a missionary. He came back and began a private hospital in Kampala. The hospital targets mainly those Ian classifies as the Ugandan "middle-income" group. Since he opened it, the hospital has grown, and he's introduced an insurance scheme for individuals and employers and also opened a nurses' training college, which eventually became a university. Ian says that the hospital has three bottom lines: "to be commercially viable, to have social impact, and the third is advocacy—setting an example, changing policy." Simon Amajuru, from Uganda, also runs a business, as we saw in chapter 9. Its main social value, he says, is through the employment that it provides.

Many people working in development are concerned about the sustainability of development initiatives and believe that they can learn and borrow from private sector practices. The idea of social enterprise is also growing in popularity.

Although purely profit-driven private business can seem soulless and blind to the needs of those without sufficient buying power, social enterprise promises the efficiencies of the business world while still making social benefit an explicit aim. An American development worker whom I spoke with in Uganda explains,

> I love social enterprise, the growth of social enterprise—particularly private. I think we should explore that. I'm sure like any other thing it will turn out to have its limitations that we don't see now. But I like it a lot, and that we can use more methods from the private sector—I think we can maintain some of the values while using more private sector methods. In fact, if you look at Iraq, we've sort of taken the worst of the private sector characteristics and the worst of the development implementation and put it together. Can't we reverse that? And part of the reason I'm excited about social enterprise is that it does seem to reverse that—to take some of the best of the private sector and the best of the motivation of the [development] industry.

For example, Acumen Fund, founded by Jacqueline Novogratz in 2001, is "a non-profit global venture fund that uses entrepreneurial approaches to solve the problems of global poverty."[3] Much like the Ashoka Foundation seeks out and supports social entrepreneurs, Acumen Fund invests in promising social entrepreneurial business models in the areas of agriculture, water, energy, health, and housing. For example, in Pakistan, Acumen Fund has provided capital to Pharmagen Healthcare Limited, which uses reverse osmosis to provide clean drinking water to the urban poor in Lahore at a price of 1.5 rupees a liter. Because public water supplies are often contaminated and bottled water is too expensive for many people, this offers a compromise. In Kenya, they have invested $2.1 million in the Western Seed Company, owned by Salaam Ismail. This company is selling hybrid maize seeds to Kenyan smallholders with the potential to greatly increase their crop yields.

The idea of using for-profit business approaches to tackle development raises questions about the role of the government versus the private sector, especially when dealing with issues that are normally seen as public social investments such as health and education. Still, in countries where approaches to work with and through the public sector have not worked, more people seem willing to consider private sector approaches. Novogratz, who worked in international development prior to starting Acumen, argues that this approach is a useful complement to traditional aid.

Activism and Advocacy

Development NGOs often act as both implementers and watchdogs of development policies. But these two roles don't always sit well together. For some people, there are more appropriate vantage points from which to observe and critique international development efforts. Two obvious ones are within universities and within more radically political or independent organizations that focus purely on advocacy rather than development implementation. These organizations sit on the edge of the development world. Some people working here see themselves as part of development, while others emphasize their independence and outsider status. The work of Pat Mooney provides one fascinating example of international research and advocacy on the fringes of the development establishment.

Pat Mooney heads the ETC Group in Ottawa, Canada, which he cofounded back in 1977 as the Rural Advancement Foundation International (RAFI). He identifies himself as part of global civil society rather than international development, which he sees as representing the political status quo. His early work experience was in international development, but he found that development NGOs were not critical or effective lobbyists either on their own behalf or on behalf of the poor for whom they claimed to be advocating.

Pat first got involved in international development as a youth representative for the FAO back in 1966. The idea for forming RAFI came in the late 1970s, when Pat was working for Oxfam, when farmers in Sri Lanka and Kenya told Pat about losing their old varieties of seeds. Pat recalls,

> When I was in Kenya . . . a guy told me about an old Kenyan wheat variety that was grown in the prairies in Canada. I thought that was ridiculous, and I looked it up. And he was right! It was genetic material that was from a [Kenyan] variety, and what was more interesting is that thirteen different seed varieties from the global South were in the Canadian seed varieties—so the South was literally feeding the North.

RAFI was formed to research and advocate around issues of plant genetic biodiversity and germoplasm conservation. In 1981, RAFI got agreement to negotiate in the FAO, and in 1983, it got agreement to establish a commission on plant genetic resources. It took until 2004 for it to establish a treaty that set out terms governing the conservation and management of plant germoplasm internationally. As Pat explains, the issue was that germoplasm was being exported from the global South to the North without any compensation to the former and without heed to the rapid loss of genetic biodiversity. Among other things, this treaty makes it possible to stop private companies from patenting traditional varieties, such as quinoa or basmati rice. Such treaties are crucial to safeguard the potential of the work of people like Mary Abukutsa, from chapter 10, so it benefits African farmers rather than private corporations.

From this, Pat and RAFI became concerned about the impact of biotechnology on food production and farmers' livelihoods. They were among the first to recognize the social and economic implications of biotechnology. As Pat explains,

> Our first study we did was in 1981. We didn't know about biotechnology as such, but we saw that pesticide companies were buying seed companies, our conclusion was that they'd focus their research on making pesticide-resistant plant varieties that liked the company's herbicides; it was just economic logic. . . . And when the first biotech seeds came onto the market in '95, they were all herbicide-tolerant varieties, all the genetically modified crops, so we were absolutely right about it.

RAFI raised awareness about the issue and got other civil society organizations on the alert. They also lobbied governments to make sure they had policies in place to address these issues. Their view was that although these issues were international in scope, countries in the global South were particularly attractive to transnational companies because they often didn't have effective policy or watchdog organizations.

RAFI changed its name to ETC in 2001, but its work has continued in much the same vein. More recently, it has been tracking the implications of nanotechnology and synthetic biology.[4]

ETC's advocacy involves working in partnership with organizations from the global South. It also advises Southern governments, especially during international agricultural and environmental conferences, where delegates from the South are often at a relative disadvantage in terms of not having the same resources to prepare. The role ETC has taken up has basically come from the needs that Pat and his colleagues see as most pressing and have chosen to respond to. In his estimation, this work is essentially more political in nature than traditional international development work:

> Are we a development organization or not? I mean, I have nothing against that, but our work is entirely on this research, writing, lobbying, politicking, but it is overwhelmingly with our partners in the South; we have partners in the North as well, but it's overwhelmingly focused in the South because that's where most of the abuse is taking place, not the only place. And we find ourselves in the position of sort of providing advice to governments and providing advice to partners . . . and organizing training workshops and stuff like that and then helping to put together political strategies.

Pat has moved in this direction because he feels it is more effective. Of international development he says,

> International development through aid agencies and so on, it's not going to ever be anything that's going to work, you know?
>
> The cynical reality of capitalist politics is that we're never going to give up power in any useful way, and it's always going to be manipulation of others with our money. And again, that doesn't mean that there can't be good things here and there, that's not at all what I'm saying, and it doesn't mean that I don't want to try to fight to make things better, or at least less bad in some cases and better in others, but it's a hard battle. Two trillion dollars later, after fifty years. . . . I've seen lots of the good side of it, too—things that have been helpful to us, for sure. And I guess I still think that it's better that it's there, at least some of it, through the NGOs and otherwise, it is better than if it didn't exist at all, but not a whole lot.

While Pat has made a career out of his research and advocacy, others who leave international development but remain politically engaged in the issues may do their advocacy in a voluntary capacity, as individual citizens.

Maintaining a Different Identity

While Pat chooses to identify himself as outside the international development system, his organization does get money from donors and engages in activity that some people would classify as development. The lines are blurred, but some people prefer to identify themselves as outside the international development system, even when there are these links. This approach may help people to keep a critical edge or ensure that they are still engaging on their own terms.

For example, Lorenzo Delesgues is a French/Italian citizen who fell in love with Central Asia and Afghanistan, mainly through studying its poetry and literature. He has worked in development in Afghanistan, but he doesn't characterize himself as a development worker:

> I'm someone who's interested in the region, more than develop-
> ment—like I wouldn't go and do development anywhere, because
> I don't think you come to do development. I don't see myself as
> someone who is bringing something that the others don't really
> know. I just have some ideas that I try to apply in places I really
> love. But I really need to know the place before I start to work in
> it. I would feel uncomfortable working in Morocco, or China, or
> Ethiopia, because I don't know them. . . . So no, I don't think I'm
> doing international development, although what I'm doing has an
> impact on international development somehow. I have more the
> impression to act as a citizen of a country that I'm not a citizen of.

Together with his Afghan colleague and friend Yama Torabi, Lorenzo formed an NGO called Integrity Watch Afghanistan, focused on issues of corruption and transparency in various aspects of Afghan public service and in the delivery of development projects. The two were codirectors until Lorenzo left the organization under Yama's full directorship in early 2011.

Like ETC, Integrity Watch Afghanistan has depended financially on support from sympathetic donors and can be seen in many ways as part of the development world. But, also like Pat, Lorenzo acts foremost as a concerned citizen rather than as a development professional. He has been concerned by the influx of expat development workers coming into Afghanistan after the events of 9/11. Most of the new arrivals were following the funding and had limited understanding of and commitment to Afghanistan and its people. His concern with the systemic shortcomings of international development that are so evident in Afghanistan means that for him the distinction between his own identity and intentions and the overall development system is an important one.

Other people work as consultants or contractors both internationally and in their home countries. This again gives them a distance from international development that can be professionally useful. Because they are not exclusively dependent on international development work for income, such people can be more selective about which contracts they take and the terms under which they work.

Conclusion

The examples in this and the previous two chapters show that working in international development and finding other ways of engaging is not an either–or proposition. Many people working in international development also take on other roles and responsibilities, as citizens, friends, and activists.

Still, whether to engage your efforts in the international development system at all is another question. We've seen throughout this book some of its limitations and inconsistencies. For those who sincerely want to contribute to positive social change through their work, it is thus a completely legitimate question as to whether working in international development is the best approach.

Some people do find themselves caught up in the system, wondering how to get out. Many of the skills that people use in international development travel well back to their home countries. These include community development, facilitation, management, and cross-cultural communication, as well as the application of particular technical skills, such as engineering or nursing. Still, people often run into problems getting recognition for their international skills and experience when they try to come back home. This is important for young development workers to keep in mind when thinking about their long-term careers. Even for those who think they'll always stay in international development, it is advisable for them to keep alternatives open by refreshing and presenting their skills in a way that will keep them employable back home. This then means they are staying international by choice.

For people from countries that are high recipients of aid, leaving international development is perhaps a more philosophical distinction. Major sectors of the economy can seem to be permeated with aid, and it may be hard to operate without it. Government agencies and ministries may be aid dependent, and most civil service positions that have the resources to do anything get those resources through aid. And so economically, doing without this aid is difficult. And yet, many people would like the aid system to leave altogether. It can represent a form of dependence and foreign interference that they believe they'd ultimately be better off without. In practical terms this poses something of a catch-22. Many people I spoke with for this book, whether Ugandan, Kenyan, or Afghan, who worked in the aid system or had work that was funded by aid, felt their work had value, and yet wished that their countries were independent of aid.

These broader issues about whether the aid system should exist at all, and if so, in what form, are the focus of perennial debate and have not been tackled in this book in any substantive way. This book doesn't posit that the international development/aid system is a net positive or a net negative. I question whether it is possible to make a definitive claim about this based on the available evidence and given the broad-ranging and sometimes contradictory activities that this system has supported. Our point of departure has been that this system exists, and as it exists, should, and how should, individuals who want to be engaged in positive international change engage with it? This is essentially a personal question, and so the answer, in the end, must also be a personal one.

Notes

1. Majid Rahnema and Victoria Bawtree, eds., *The Post-Development Reader* (London: Zed Books, 1997).

2. Graham Hancock, *The Lords of Poverty* (New York: Atlantic Monthly Press, 1989); Arturo Escobar, *Encountering Development: The Making and Unmaking of the Third World* (Princeton, NJ: Princeton University Press, 2011); Dambissa Moyo, *Dead Aid: Why Aid Is Not Working and How There Is a Better Way for Africa* (London: Penguin, 2010).

3. Acumen Fund, *Acumen Fund*, 2012, cited January 7, 2012, http://www.acumenfund .org.

4. ETC is concerned that advances in technology that allow a wide variety of products, including fuel and plastics, to be manufactured from biomass have opened up competition for the world's biomass and the land to produce it. This means that transnational companies can buy up land in Africa and elsewhere to produce fuel and consumer goods, putting the interests and desires of the world's rich into direct competition with the basic food security of the poor. Pat explains,

> The most shocking fact I know is 23.8 percent of the world's biomass has been commodified, which means that what, 76.2 percent of the world's terrestrial biomass has not been commodified and remains to be monopolized. And what they're saying is that they can monopolize that—and they're saying they can take the remainder and use synthetic biology to take any biomass you want, whether it's bits of cows, or cow dung or stuff left over in the field, or food crops or trees or shrubs or dirt pretty much and turn that into plastic or fuel or anything they want. So the whole thing is up for grabs, and to us that's terribly threatening to food production in the global South and to the environment.

12

Conclusion

If you have come to help me, you are wasting your time.
But if you have come because your liberation is bound up with
mine, then let us work together.
   —*Lilla Watson*

And now that you don't have to be perfect, you can be good.
   —*John Steinbeck,* East of Eden

In an imperfect world, development workers should claim all the power
and responsibility they have to act ethically and effectively within the situations that they find themselves. Those working in international development
are faced with a multitude of gaps and inconsistencies among what the international development system claims to be about, what it seems to strive for,
and how it functions.

Throughout this book, we have explored how the international development system works and how we as individuals can make choices and cultivate
skills and insights to be more effective within it. In the first part of this final
chapter, we revisit how the international development system can work either
as a trap, in which development workers feel constrained and helpless, or as
a tool that they can skillfully use to attain the goals they are committed to.
The second part of this chapter is an exploration of our dream of the deeper
structural change that could be possible through a widespread commitment to
development ethics.

The International Development System: Trap or Tool?

International Development in Context
International development is a fairly recent policy innovation.[1] It came into
existence in the 1950s and 1960s. Today it is already an established staple of

international relations. It is hard to imagine the world without it, and it is unlikely to disappear anytime soon.

International development exists within, and is often overshadowed by, the broader political, social, and economic context. Official bilateral and multilateral aid reflects a contradictory global order in which rich countries are much more willing to give tokens to small countries than to make changes in their own societies, economies, and trade relations that would create a more even global playing field. The United States, the world's biggest contributor to greenhouse gases responsible for global warming, is persistently reluctant to commit itself to emissions reductions, but it provides funding to African countries that are responsible for only a tiny fraction of greenhouse gases to reduce their own emissions. These are the political realities within which overseas development assistance funds are granted.

Politics and economics within recipient countries can also overshadow development work, so that development efforts often seem like trying to build a house in a marsh. Development efforts can be focused within a community or region, or even across the nation, but then comes a civil war or a natural disaster or some other major turmoil, and everything that was built up comes tumbling down.

Whenever resources are being introduced into a resource-scarce environment, there are politics. We've seen examples of how aid funding in Kenya, Uganda, and Afghanistan has fueled government corruption in each of these countries. In Afghanistan, the corruption has reached such a level that donors have felt compelled to act, but it is now so pervasive that reversing the situation is very difficult. Afghanistan is now ranked as one of the most corrupt countries in the world according to Transparency International.[2] The issue is a matter not just of theft but also of social control. Aid subcontractors working in conflict areas give up to 20 percent of their contracts to insurgents in exchange for "protection."[3]

In this sense, the development sector itself can seem to be entrapped and compromised by larger political and economic factors. Individual development workers can feel that they are unwittingly feeding into negative dynamics that they cannot get out of.

But even on this broad scale, this is only one side of the story. The Organisation for Economic Co-operation and Development (OECD) acts as a peer group of donors and has done much to track issues of aid effectiveness and aid coordination and to reduce blatantly self-interested behavior on the part of donors, such as the tying of aid. Agreements such as the 2005 Paris Declaration on Aid Effectiveness and the 2011 Busan Partnership for Effective

Development Co-operation have been seen as solid steps forward in this direction. More donors are pooling their funds and engaging with governments on coordinated "sector-wide approaches."[4] Various NGOs and civil society organizations have fought for aid policy that is driven by development principles rather than by political and economic interest. And sometimes, in some places, they have been successful. Countries such as Sweden, Norway, and Denmark, although not perfect, perform relatively well in terms of using their national development agencies to pursue principled development aims.[5] Such efforts and spaces often open and close with political cycles within donor countries. The point is that they exist, and they open up opportunities for principled work.

Advice for Weathering the Broader Context

At the broadest level, there is often not much that an individual development worker can do. Unfavorable government policies, ruling despots, widespread corruption, war, and natural disaster are facts that individuals can rarely do much about. The key is to recognize that these are not the only forces prevailing at the larger levels and not to get too fatalistic. The very existence of some of our international institutions and agreements is a wonderful opportunity, even if they may not always yield the results we hope for. For example, the Universal Declaration of Human Rights, signed in 1948, is an amazing document. The nations of the world have signed on to some very hopeful statements that affirm a shared vision of a peaceful, just, and prosperous human community living in harmony with the natural world. That may not be where we are now, but it is a step. The fact that nations dedicate billions of dollars each year to development efforts that, at least rhetorically, are aimed to improve social justice because of a sense of unity and shared responsibility is cause for hope. And so without being naive about the challenges before us, as individual development practitioners, we must never become blind to these positive signs and opportunities but should seek to leverage and build on them in whatever ways we can.

Development Organizations

As we saw in chapter 4, development organizations come in a variety of flavors, including bilateral donors; multilateral donors; international financial institutions; research centers; international, national, and local nongovernmental organizations; aid contractors; and consultants. Each of these organizational types has its strengths and weaknesses. And within each type, there is a huge range in terms of the commitment of the staff and the quality and effectiveness of their work.

One definitive feature of international development work, no matter what its form, is the geographic distance between the sources of funding and the target beneficiaries of that funding. Funders may be government donors, multilateral donors, development banks, private foundations or trusts, individuals, churches, member organizations and societies, or service organizations such as the Rotary Club. The relationship between donors and recipients is almost always characterized by a large physical, communication, and perceptual gap. This is the greatest structural weakness of the international development system. In practical terms, accountability is always to the funders, because they are the ones with the power to stop or continue funding. And funders have different perspectives, interests, and values from recipients. They live in different worlds.

The gap between funders and recipients can be problematic for two reasons. One, as we've already discussed, is that funders may have interests other than development in mind. They may be more focused on furthering their own political, economic, religious, or ideological agendas than on actually helping out. And if they are genuinely interested in helping out, there is the risk that they might impose their ideas of what development is on the beneficiaries of their largesse. Finally, even if the funders are genuinely interested in supporting beneficiaries so that the latter can pursue their own development priorities, they are usually in a poor position to monitor how well that is happening.

If the funders give the development organizations receiving funds enough freedom to do their work, and if the development organizations are principled and well run, then there is space for good work to happen. There can be alignment among the funders, the beneficiaries, and the various intermediary institutions delivering and using the funds. But if the funders place conditions on funding or take away funding, the organizations are compromised. And if the organizations are poorly run, whether because of ill intent or incompetence, the funders may be unaware and the beneficiaries have little recourse. After all, most feedback to funders comes from the implementing organizations, which obviously have a vested interest in looking good.

In chapter 4, we came across the story of a little boy who could no longer go to school because he was in charge of looking after rabbits that had been donated to his family by a church organization. The funders, in this case Western churchgoers, probably thought they were helping the boy and his family by donating the rabbits. There is no way they could have known otherwise without going down to check on the situation firsthand.

The only form of funding where there is a direct link between the ability of the organization to gain funds and the response of the beneficiaries is from social enterprises where the beneficiaries are contributing to the service costs. Social enterprise is no panacea, as markets often don't respond well to poor people with very limited purchasing power or to those in remote areas or areas with low population densities. Still, some development organizations have gained financial independence and stability by such "self-financing."

In most instances, good development depends on deserved trust, principled action, and alignment of intention all the way across the aid chain, from funders to intermediary and implementing organizations to the recipients. Where this sort of alignment exists, excellent development work can be done. Throughout the development system, there are potential allies, principled people within institutions small and large who can help support well-motivated and well-thought-out development initiatives. In chapter 10, for example, we saw how the founder of Grameen Bank, Muhammad Yunus, was able to draw on resources from the World Bank to support the expansion of microcredit within Bangladesh. Despite Yunus's misgivings about the World Bank, he was able to work with it to support an agenda he believed in.

Advice for Finding Opportunities in the Workplace

Development workers may find themselves trapped in the system, caught up in reporting requirements, the fight for institutional survival, and the need to respond to a host of other issues that divert their energy from effective work. Effective practitioners manage to work despite these shortcomings and draw on the institutions and resources available within international development to help them further their work. Obviously, we would rather be more like Yunus than like a passive cog in the machine. Three pieces of advice in this regard are as follows: (1) choose your workplace with care, (2) cultivate relationships with like-minded people, and (3) seek out resources.

Choose Your Workplace With Care

One of the biggest choices we make as development workers is what role to take on. This is primarily about deciding what type of organization to work for or else perhaps to work independently or start a new organization. Most people take on more than one position throughout their careers. Changing positions and organizations gives us a chance to explore and see what fits us best. Some of this also comes down to strategy and whether we prefer working on tangible grassroots projects or with higher-level strategic issues.

What type of organization is best? Much of this also depends on your own temperament and goals. Some people can manage the slow pace, bureaucracy, and complexities of the larger organizations. And it is true that the biggest, most staid organizations often have the greatest resources and the broadest mandates. If you can find your way within them and stay true to your goals, you're a useful ally across the board, because you can partner with smaller organizations that are more active but lack resources and clout. Some people enjoy the independence of working as a consultant. Others prefer the relative independence of the NGO sector. As we saw back in chapter 3, each type of organization has its strengths and drawbacks.

No matter what type of organization, some are better run and stick better to their mandates than others. Even from one department or work group or country office to another, the dynamics vary and are often driven by personalities and localized interpersonal relations. So deciding where to work also requires considering these specifics.

Cultivate Relationships With Like-Minded People

Development processes are highly dependent on relationships, which take time to deepen. Effective development practitioners depend on alliances with like-minded people with complementary skills and positions. While local people may have a better knowledge of context, sometimes they aren't accorded the recognition and credit that they deserve. We saw this with Ajay's experiences in chapter 6, and the same can be said of the Honduran farmers conducting seed trials, as discussed in chapter 7. Sally Humphries's long association with FIPAH, the Honduran NGO working with farmer groups, combined with her role as a Canadian university professor, boosted FIPAH's international credibility and support. The research that she and her graduate students conducted analyzed and documented FIPAH's work and so provided further evidence of its validity and legitimacy.

Sally and FIPAH together did more than either of them could alone. Kenyan civil society was bolstered by the support of the UN and international community in its efforts for constitutional reform. The work of Mary Abukutsa and Vicki Wilde has been mutually complementary, and both have done much to support both the role of women in agricultural research and, through that, the priorities and needs of women farmers, addressing previously neglected issues such as affordable household nutrition.

On a more personal level, many development workers have noted the important role that mentoring has played in their careers, both receiving advice and support from mentors as they were starting out and, later, mentoring others. Mentors often help guide their junior colleagues through the vagaries of the development world, providing a sounding board while they grapple with the ethical and practical dilemmas of what is right and possible within the institutions that always seem rather more chaotic than they had imagined. Within the system, where the structures are not as concrete or clear-cut as they seem, it is in other people that we can trust, rely on, and come back to. And many people take pleasure in mentoring because they understand that it is through building up their junior colleagues and trying to instill good practices that they can, in some sense, leave a legacy and maintain the heart of what they feel is most important about their work.

Seek Out Resources

Relationships with allies and mentors are crucial resources for committed development practitioners. Other resources can provide further points of leverage for effective development work. Despite talk of the need for better coordination, development practitioners often behave as if they are working on something brand new that no one has ever thought of or attempted to work on before. Development agencies commonly suffer from institutional amnesia, due perhaps to frequent changes in personnel. Small NGOs striving to win funding from the same set of donors may be focused more on proving their own competitive edge than on cooperating to solve the problem to which they are all committed.

If effectively solving development issues is the goal, rather than survival or promoting one's own importance, then it makes sense to identify and build on previous and existing efforts. Research papers, existing organizations, community efforts, conventions, and legal agreements are all resources that can be leveraged and built on. The key point is simply to take the time and effort to look. There is no need to reinvent the wheel or be an aid hero. Don't assume that you need to innovate and start from scratch; assume the opposite.

Ourselves

We have more control over ourselves, our own perceptions, and our own behavior than over any other aspect of the international development system. But if we fail to exercise that control thoughtfully, we can trap ourselves in unfulfilling and ineffective work. As we saw in part 3, our style of work is determined by two key factors: the first is critical awareness and the second is engagement. When we lack critical awareness, we can have blind faith in either the development system or ourselves. When we have critical awareness but lack engagement, we become cynics. But when we have both in fair measure, we have a decent chance of finding opportunities to be effective.

Advice for Developing a Reflective Practice

When we go into development work, there is no guarantee that we will manage to line up the circumstances that we need to work effectively. But by committing to reflective practice, we increase our odds of doing so and reduce the risk of doing damage. One key aspect of reflective practice is humility, given the historical hubris of international development institutions. While advice for and examples of reflective practice have been scattered throughout this book, three key ones to remember are (1) develop clarity about your own aspirations, (2) develop clarity about your own ethical commitment, and (3) deepen critical awareness over time.

Develop Clarity About Your Own Aspirations

Most people come into international development work with an idea of what they want to accomplish. Many people are driven by that idea. They want to combat poverty, improve social justice, and contribute to positive social change in some form or another. And for most people, over the course of their careers, this basic motive remains unchanged. With the course of experience, what does change is their understanding of what they should do, what they can do, and what they are willing to do to pursue it.

Through experience, development workers change in their understandings of the nature of the world and why things are the way they are, what might lead to some more desirable state, and how their work might fit into that. The balance in their own lives also shifts: the degree of commitment they feel to their jobs versus their families and personal lives and the lifestyle they aspire to. These shifts in commitment shift the possibilities of what sort of work they can undertake. As they gain seniority in their careers, the possibilities of what they can do often expand.

For example, in chapter 5 we met Claudia Hudspeth. Committed to improving public health, she came to the insight that in the health sector, it was easy to know what needed to be done but much harder to make the systems work so that it actually happened. In chapter 11, we saw that Harriet Menter discovered that for her, working directly with children in communities was more rewarding than being a bureaucrat in a donor agency.

Some people find themselves in situations where they cannot fully follow their own aspirations. It may be because they have not fully clarified what their aspirations are, the situation doesn't allow it, they cannot get into the position they would need, or the tools are not available to do so. It is hard to stay motivated in such situations, and one is likely to feel trapped. So developing clarity about aspirations also means finding a realistic, balanced way to pursue them, if not in the short term, then in the long term.

Develop Clarity About Your Own Ethical Commitment

Because many people in development come up against situations of ethical compromise, it is worth taking time to think through how you want to respond if your organization makes a decision you disagree with, perhaps a compromise in mandate or quality because of funding considerations, or it has a bias against national staff that you don't think is justified, or it employs a colleague who is so grossly incompetent that he is endangering others, or it decides to stay quiet on an important issue because of concerns about maintaining good relations. Even if you decide, at a junior level, that you are not able to effectively counteract whatever issues you come across, you can always choose to voice an objection, leave, or perhaps bide your time and develop your career to the point where you have enough positional power to counteract. When we find ourselves in the midst of these situations, we may often feel unprepared and overwhelmed, and we may find that when no one else seems very concerned, we second-guess ourselves. If it comes down to it, what matters to you? What can you compromise on without having major moral qualms, and what are you willing to stand up for?

Deepen Critical Awareness Over Time

Development practitioners need to constantly exercise judgment and discernment in their work. As we saw in part 3, the most effective development workers are those who maintain a tempered optimism and critical awareness. Anyone working in international development is feeding on, and often continuing, all the habits and understandings and dynamics that went on before them. It is a tall order to step entirely outside of automatic or conditioned behavior, and doing so is not something that most of us can realistically aspire to. And this is why actively revisiting one's own expectations and intentions is so important. We have to decide carefully where to put our energy and attention.

The complexity of development means that learning to work within it effectively takes more than just critical awareness; it takes awareness over time. Development processes are usually about social change, and depending on the nature of that change, it can take decades to manifest results. Writers are often given the advice to "write what you know." The same advice could apply to development workers: if we're working in a context that we're already familiar with, because we grew up there or spent a long time there, it can be easier to interpret events that might seem surprising to an outsider. Understanding the relationship between action and effect usually requires an in-depth knowledge of context, since cause-effect relationships in social change are rarely linear or direct. Time, and how we invest our time over our work lives, is thus one of the greatest resources that we each possess.

If we're working on tangible projects such as constructing fishponds, drilling boreholes, or providing emergency relief, we can see immediate results. Sometimes those results last and they benefit people. Sometimes they don't—the roads fall into disrepair, the ponds silt over. But over a longer time, and with some luck, it may be possible to weave some of these changes into the structures and policies of existing institutions. In chapter 7, we saw how the persistence of Sally Humphries and FIPAH meant they were eventually able to get government recognition and support for their efforts to promulgate seed varieties that grew better in highland areas under the conditions that most poor farmers were facing.

Critical awareness over time comes in part from a long-term commitment to one's work, coupled with an ongoing willingness to revisit one's assumptions and aspirations. Sometimes, in the rush of deadlines and to-do lists, practitioners find it difficult to set aside the time and space to do this on a periodic basis. The Internet is one space where development workers are increasingly venting and reflecting on their experiences aloud, often anonymously and often in a critical or satirical vein. There is an increasing number of blogs about aid work, some deliberately focused on critical reflection and sharing ideas and experiences.[6]

Simply reading books and articles about working in development or in humanitarian relief can help us in reflecting on our own work. These books might include firsthand accounts or more analytical or research-based pieces, including aid ethnographies. The more analytical books can help us to think through some of the international development concepts and discourses that we tend to otherwise adopt and get caught up in without necessarily having fully analyzed their implications. One excellent book in this regard is Gilbert Rist's *The History of Development*.[7] Some of these books are listed in the reference list at the end of this book. Another option is to enroll in formal education, usually graduate school, partway into one's career as a way of stepping out and making sense of one's experiences.

For those who manage to find a place within the system that fits with their skills and aspirations, who are careful and patient in how they spend their time and about the relationships they cultivate, and who are critically engaged in their work and their institutions, the fruit of their efforts still depends, to some degree, on luck and serendipity. But they have greatly improved their odds. And as long as they maintain that engagement, they can continue to adjust and further improve their odds of being effective.

A Wish for Wise Professionalism

This book has focused on what we, as individual development practitioners, can do to improve our chances of being effective in our work and to narrow the gaps between intention and action within our own practice. I have focused on the individual because repeated calls for broad reform of the international development system have been made to limited effect. The interests, perceptions, and actions that hold the international development system in its current formation have their own momentum. They are not easily undone. No one has found the spot from which, as Archimedes said, he or she could use a lever to shift the world. And so it is better to face the world we find ourselves in and to do what we can actually do within it.

Nonetheless, social norms and practices do change, and there is no reason to assume that the international development sector is immune to this. Although none of us may be in a position to transform the development system single-handedly, the sum of our collective actions could be a powerful force. To date, however, efforts at reform have been fairly unimpressive. Much as if we mix together all the colors from a paint set and end up with an uninspired shade of blah, the sum of our collective action is a messy mix of all the different approaches we saw in part 3 of this book. The drifters, cynics, and those who are using the system for their own interests; the uncritically aligned who work on faith rather than evidence; and the aid heroes who are caught up in their own myths counterbalance those who are critically engaged and seeking to use the system effectively or negotiate structural changes to improve it.

If we were able to clarify and align our purposes a little bit more, at least those of us with the intention to do so, the result could be a potent groundswell, a force for greater and deeper changes within international development. Trends within international development currently provide us with two openings through which we could achieve this. The first is the increasing diversity of approaches and international movements around and beyond the borders of the international development system. The second is the increasing number of educational programs devoted to preparing people to work in international development.

Shifting Borders and Parallel Movements

Lilla Watson, in one of the opening quotes to this chapter, says, "If you have come to help me, you are wasting your time. But if you have come because your liberation is bound up with mine, then let us work together." This quote resonates with grassroots citizens' movements and community development efforts that are focused on redefining development away from charity and toward solidarity. As the world becomes ever more interconnected and we face urgent global problems such as climate change, it becomes easier for us to recognize that our fates are bound together, and so we must work together. That is where the notion of global citizenship comes from. And from this notion, our sense of self and our place in the world shifts and new possibilities arise.

The world is not the same place that it was in the 1950s, when international development began. Some aid recipient countries have become donors. China, India, and Brazil are all economic forces to be reckoned with, and each now provides aid to other countries, along with substantial sums of foreign direct investment, as part of its own foreign policy. We can debate these changes, whether they are good or bad. But they do, at the very least, move us farther away from the postcolonial order on which the international development system was founded.

Even more significant than this, in terms of breaking out of old hierarchies and patterns, is the emergence of identity-driven and issues-driven global citizens' movements. Many of these have been fueled by the spread of the Internet, cellular phones, and new social media. Avaaz.org, for example, began in 2007, and describes itself as a member-driven, member-funded "global web movement to bring people-powered politics to decision-making everywhere."[8] As of 2012, it claimed almost 17 million members worldwide and has campaigned on issues such as climate change, press freedom, government corruption, the child sex trade, and basically any issue that enough of its members decide is worth taking action on. It claims to have played a decisive role in political decisions by demonstrating widespread public support at key moments. For example, in 2011, Avaaz members supported indigenous protestors in Bolivia who wanted to stop the construction of a highway through the Amazon. In response to the public pressure, the Bolivian president repealed an earlier approval and stopped the project.[9]

Over the past decade, many national and regional indigenous rights movements have linked together and recognized commonalities in their struggles. By doing so, they have also managed to gain recognition at the United Nations. In 2002, the United Nations Permanent Forum on Indigenous Issues was established, and in 2007, the UN Declaration on the Rights of Indigenous Peoples was adopted by the General Assembly. Both of these came about largely because indigenous movements have been able to organize and lobby more effectively. By working together and with other civil society groups, they have been able to influence the outcome of specific issues, such as the construction project in the Amazon.

New technologies have also allowed organizations such as Kiva to innovate fund-raising. Kiva provides an Internet platform that allows individuals to lend money to microcredit agencies around the world. The agencies in turn lend the money to small entrepreneurs. Individuals eventually get their money back as loans are repaid, and they are free to invest it again.[10]

All of these movements and approaches are parallel to international development, operating largely outside its institutions but often working on similar issues and often linking to them for resources or recognition. Development NGOs such as Oxfam identify themselves as part of the global citizens' movements and actively participate in platforms such as the World Social Forum.[11]

Transformation of the international development system, insofar as it happens, happens as old boundaries shift and the old institutions have to adapt. New donors influence old donors. New citizens' movements influence both NGOs and governments. As those outside of the traditionally defined development system address some similar issues in their own ways, this is likely to provoke a response and adjustment within the old system. Connections and collaborations between the critically engaged practitioners from the inside and those working outside of development institutions have been, and will continue to be, the source of much of the most dynamic, interesting, and effective development work.

New Possibilities for an Ethics of Practice

If professional ethics were instilled deeply in the educational curriculum that prepares development workers and then promulgated within the institutions where they work, could this be a path forward? Dedicated practitioners have often distilled practical and ethical lessons from their own experiences, as we've seen throughout this book. Yet these lessons have, by and large, failed to penetrate into the institutional culture of development agencies. If those lessons were widely included in educational curricula for those studying to become development workers, the result could be a cadre of principled but savvy workers with enough critical mass to really challenge and even change the prevailing institutional ethos. Think back to the story of Dave in chapter 5. He wasn't able to successfully challenge his bosses from excluding Kenyans from senior positions in his organization. Although this practice is discriminatory and unwarranted, prevailing norms throughout international development still permit it. It will be a great moment when our shared norms and principles of equity are clear and strong enough that it would be difficult for any organization to formally ban national staff from positions just on the basis that they are national, even if they are qualified.

Back in 1993, Robert Chambers wrote *Challenging the Professions.*[12] He argued against hierarchies of knowledge that he saw as unjustified and that mainly served to maintain power relationships. According to Chambers, formal expertise was overrated within international development. Informal and local forms of knowledge are more relevant to development problems but have often been overlooked. This means that discriminatory practices of hiring, to take just one example, are not just ethically questionable but also undermine the quality of development work. Chambers and others wrote about participatory development and did much to begin forging the ideal of an ethical development practitioner: one focused on process, and one who listened, learned, and facilitated.

The ideals of participatory development have resonated with many of those who have studied and worked in development. But participatory development has also been criticized for failing to go deep enough, for giving an unfair and ineffective system an appealing makeover without changing the deeper substance. As we have seen in this book, this criticism isn't entirely deserved. There are numerous instances where people have taken these values on and lived them. The problem is more that such people are still a minority. And although international development is no longer new, an ethics of practice is still not fully developed.

Des Gasper argues for development ethics that provide "a broader, looser professional forum [than traditional professional ethics] . . . since 'development theory, planning and practice' do not define a single profession or well-bounded set of professions and agents—but with comparable functions to narrower professional ethics."[13] He argues that any form of ethical code within international development that seeks to be prescriptive will generally fall down quickly, as circumstances arise in which it is clearly unsuited. Hence, ethical practice must be based on some universal principles, which practitioners can then draw on using their own discretion.[14] And ethical principles must come back to the rationale for doing development work in the first place.

At the time that *Challenging the Professions* came out, the idea of a development professional per se was not common. Chambers was talking about those who had claim to specific kinds of expertise within international development: engineers, social workers, agronomists, and so forth. Since then, the international development sector has continued to grow, and there have been many more college and university programs dedicated to the study of international development, aiming to prepare students to work within it. These educational programs offer an opening to strengthen the emergence of development ethics by giving it space in their curricula. Students of international development have long been exposed to critiques of the development system and its weaknesses. But what has been largely absent is an ethics of practice.

As development studies programs have become more numerous, so too is it more common to come across people who identify themselves as development professionals. This, again, may provide an opening for a greater emphasis on the sort of quasi-professional ethics Des Gasper favors. On the other hand, it could be yet another means of reinforcing long-standing hierarchies. An American working on political development in Uganda reflects on changes between 2000, when she started this work, and 2011, when we spoke:

> Back then, it was just professionals applying their skills helping other people—it wasn't a profession, if you know what I mean. And you know, the longer I've been in the field, the more prevalent it has been for people to enter development as development professionals—and I'm undecided as to whether that's good or bad.

Formalizing development ethics in any particular configuration across the board could, ironically, become another way of reinforcing existing hierarchies in development through a facade of moral authority. After all, this is one of the main charges against participatory development.[15]

But there is a valid need to recognize that working in international development is different from working within a given profession under different circumstances. The funding structures, political relationships, and cultural differences that circumscribe international development lend it different characteristics that need to be understood if work is to be ethical. There is a positive need for recognizing an ethics of practice and for cultivating a shared professional identity and ethos within international development. In fact, it is those who come as subject matter experts without an understanding of international development and who assume that their professional expertise can carry over to any situation, and that any special status conferred on them is based on merit rather than historically gained entitlements, who run the greatest risk of working ineffectively with unintended consequences.

Throughout the aid system, the rhetoric of equal partnership is often belied by the intrinsically unequal relationship between giver and recipient. As individual practitioners working within the aid system, we must both live with this discordance and attempt to bridge it. The spread of formal development studies provides us an opportunity for bringing ethics—and particularly the ethics of practice—to the forefront and tying it back to our notions of why we are doing what we are doing.

To the degree that we can share such conversations and consciousness together and begin to embed our thoughts about principled practice into formal studies, there is hope that we can begin to address some of these gaps even at the structural level. And that means that those who choose to practice international development and head out into the jumbled, often hierarchical, often predatory world will be better equipped to act with integrity, to do less harm, and to do more good.

Notes

1. Carol Lancaster, *Foreign Aid: Diplomacy, Development, Domestic Politics* (Chicago: University of Chicago Press, 2006).

2. Transparency International, *Corruption Perceptions Index 2011*, 2011, cited February 8, 2012, http://cpi.transparency.org/cpi2011/results/#CountryResults.

3. International Crisis Group, *Aid and Conflict in Afghanistan* (London: International Crisis Group, 2011), 20.

4. Roger C. Riddell, *Does Foreign Aid Really Work?* (New York: Oxford University Press, 2007).

5. Center for Global Development, 2012 Commitment to Development Index, cited October 28, 2012, http://www.cgdev.org/section/initiatives/_active/cdi/.

6. Some examples of such blogs include Stuff Expat Aid Workers Like (http://stuffexpataidworkerslike.com/), Aid Watch (aidwatchers.com, discontinued May 2011), and La Vida id Loca (http://lavidaidloca.wordpress.com/).

7. Gilbert Rist, *The History of Development: From Western Origins to Global Faith*, 3rd ed. (London: Zed Books, 2009).

8. Avaaz.org, Homepage, 2012, cited November 1, 2012, http://www.avaaz.org.

9. Avaaz.org, *Highlights: Success Stories From the Avaaz Movement Worldwide*, 2012, cited November 1, 2012, http://www.avaaz.org/en/highlights.php.

10. See www.kiva.org.

11. The World Social Forum began in 2001 and is an annual meeting that is held as a citizens' alternative to the World Economic Forum. According to its Charter of Principles,

The World Social Forum is an open meeting place for reflective thinking, democratic debate of ideas, formulation of proposals, free exchange of experiences and interlinking for effective action, by groups and movements of civil society that are opposed to neo-liberalism and to domination of the world by capital and any form of imperialism, and are committed to building a planetary society directed towards fruitful relationships among Mankind and between it and the Earth.

12. Robert Chambers, *Challenging the Professions: Frontiers for Rural Development* (London: Intermediate Technology Development Group, 1993).

13. Des Gasper, *Ethics and the Conduct of International Development Aid: Charity and Obligation* (The Hague: Institute of Social Studies, ORPAS, 1999), 7.

14. See the International Development Ethics Association's website at http://www.development-ethics.org/ for further attempts to expound on ethical issues and standards around development.

15. Bill Cooke and Uma Kothari, eds., *Participation: The New Tyranny?* (London: Zed Books, 2001).

References

Acumen Fund. *Acumen Fund*, 2012, cited January 7, 2012.

Aga Khan Development Network. *Rural Development in Pakistan*, 2007, cited February 6, 2012, http://www.akdn.org/rural_development/pakistan.asp.

AGRA. *Agra: Growing Africa's Agriculture*, 2012, cited February 2, 2012, www.agra-alliance.org.

Aldeen, Mahmuda. *BRAC's Non-formal Primary Education Programme: Scope, Growth, Achievements and Factors Contributing to Its Success*, May 6, 2009, Articles on Education of Bangladesh, cited March 3, 2012, http://www.bdeduarticle.com/non-formal-education/27-uncatagorized/58-bracs-non-formal-primary-education-programme-scope-growth-achievements-and-factors-contributing-to-its-success.

Avaaz.org. *Highlights: Success Stories From the Avaaz Movement Worldwide*, 2012, cited November 1, 2012, http://www.avaaz.org/en/highlights.php.

Barrett, Christopher, and Daniel Maxwell. *Food Aid After 50 Years: Recasting Its Role*. New York: Routledge, 2005.

Bieckmann, Frans, and Anna Meijer van Putten. "Goalposts: What Next for the MDGs?" *The Broker*, October 6, 2010, cited February 3, 2012, http://www.thebrokeronline.eu/Articles/Goalposts-What-next-for-the-MDGs.

Black, Stephanie. *Life and Debt*. Documentary movie produced by Stephanie Black, Tuff Gong Pictures, 2001.

Boone, Jon, and Jason Burke. "Afghanistan Faces $7bn Annual Budget Shortfall, World Bank Warns." *The Guardian*, November 22, 2011.

Bornstein, David. *How to Change the World: Social Entrepreneurs and the Power of New Ideas*. Oxford: Oxford University Press, 2007.

Bowman, Tom. *In Afghanistan, the Civil Service "Surge" That Isn't*. Washington, DC: NPR, 2010.

BRAC. *BRAC*, 2012, cited February 15, 2012, http://www.brac.net/.

Center for Army Lessons Learned. *Commander's Guide to Money as a Weapons System: Tactics, Techniques and Procedures*. Fort Leavenworth, KS: US Army, 2009.

Center for Global Development. *2012 Commitment to Development Index*, cited October 28, 2012, http://www.cgdev.org/section/initiatives/_active/cdi/.

Chambers, Robert. *Challenging the Professions: Frontiers for Rural Development*. London: Intermediate Technology Development Group, 1993.

Cooke, Bill, and Uma Kothari, eds. *Participation: The New Tyranny?* London: Zed Books, 2001.

Cornwell, Susan. "Angry US House Lawmaker Cuts Aid to Afghanistan." *Reuters*, June 28, 2010.

Crewe, Emma, and Elizabeth Harrison. *Whose Development? An Ethnography of Aid*. London: Zed Books, 1999.

Crocker, David. *International Development Ethics*. Paper presented at the Twentieth World Congress of Philosophy, Boston, MA, August 10–15, 1998.

Curtis, Polly, and Tom McCarthy. "Kony 2012: What's the Real Story?" *The Guardian*, March 8, 2012.

Daño, Elenita C. *Unmasking the New Green Revolution in Africa: Motives, Players and Dynamics*. Penang, Malaysia: Church Development Service, Third World Network, African Centre for Biosafety, 2007.

Denny, Charlotte. "Suharto, Marcos and Mobutu Head Corruption Table With $50bn Scams." *The Guardian*, March 26, 2004.

Department of Social Services and Poverty Alleviation. *The Population Register Update: Khayelitsha, 2005*. Cape Town: Government of the Western Cape, 2006.

Easterly, William. "The Cartel of Good Intentions: The Problem of Bureaucracy in Foreign Aid." *Policy Reform* 5, no. 4 (2002): 223–50.

———. "Foreign Aid for Scoundrels." *The New York Review of Books*, November 25, 2010.

———. *The White Man's Burden: Why the West's Efforts to Aid the Rest Have Done So Much Ill and So Little Good*. New York: Penguin, 2007.

Easterly, William, and Laura Freschi. *Save the Poor Beltway Bandits!* NYU Development Research Institute, May 7, 2012, cited October 20, 2012, http://nyudri.org/2012/05/07/save-the-poor-beltway-bandits/.

Escobar, Arturo. *Encountering Development: The Making and Unmaking of the Third World*. Princeton, NJ: Princeton University Press, 2011.

Farrington, J., and A. Martin. "Farmer Participation in Agricultural Research: A Review of Concepts and Practices." In *Agricultural Administration Unit Occasional Paper #9*. London: ODI, 1988.

Filkins, Dexter. "The Afghan Bank Heist: A Secret Investigation May Implicate Dozens of High-Ranking Government Officials." *The New Yorker*, February 14, 2011.

Food and Agriculture Organization. *The Farming Systems Approach to Development and Appropriate Technology Generation*. Rome: FAO, 1995.

Gambrell, Jon. "IMF Stops Payment to Afghanistan Due to Lax Financial Oversight." *Huffington Post*, June 17, 2011.

Gasper, Des. *Development Aid: Charity and Obligation*. The Hague: Institute of Social Studies, ORPAS, 1999.

"Global Homicide: Murder Rates Around the World." DataBlog. *The Guardian*, October 13, 2009, http://www.guardian.co.uk/news/datablog/2009/oct/13/homicide-rates-country-murder-data.

GRAIN. *A New Green Revolution for Africa?* Barcelona, Spain: GRAIN, 2007.

Haidt, Jonathan. *The Happiness Hypothesis: Finding Modern Truth in Ancient Wisdom*. New York: Basic Books, 2006.

Hancock, Graham. *The Lords of Poverty: The Power, Prestige, and Corruption of the International Aid Business*. New York: Atlantic Monthly Press, 1989.

Heron, Barbara. *Desire for Development: Whiteness, Gender, and the Helping Imperative*. Waterloo, ON: Wilfrid Laurier University Press, 2007.

Homeland Security and Governmental Affairs Subcommittee on Contracting Oversight, *Memorandum Re. Hearing: "Afghanistan Contracts: An Overview"* (Washington, DC: Homeland Security and Governmental Affairs, December 16, 2009), 5.

Hounkonnou, Dominic. "Listen to the Cradle: Building From Local Dynamics." Doctoral diss., University of Wageningen Communication and Innovation Studies, October 2005.

IDA Resource Mobilisation. *Aid Architecture: An Overview of the Main Trends in Official Development Assistance Flows*. Washington, DC: International Development Association, 2007.

IMF. *Program Note: Islamic Republic of Afghanistan*, April 9, 2012, cited April 20, 2012, http://www.imf.org/external/np/country/notes/afghanistan.htm.

Independent Inquiry Committee Into the United Nations Oil-for-Food Programme. *Report on Programme Manipulation*. Washington, DC: Independent Inquiry Committee Into the United Nations Oil-for-Food Programme, 2005.

International Crisis Group. *Aid and Conflict in Afghanistan*. London: International Crisis Group, 2011.

Invisible Children. *Kony 2012 Part II: Beyond Famous* [online video], Invisible Children, March 5, 2012, cited April 2, 2012, http://www.youtube.com/watch?v=Y4MnpzG5Sqc.

Jackson, Ashley. *Quick Impact, Quick Collapse: The Dangers of Militarized Aid in Afghanistan*. Kabul: Oxfam, 2010.

Kneen, Brewster. *Invisible Giant: Cargill and Its Transnational Strategies*, 2nd ed. London: Pluto Press, 2002.

Kothari, Uma. "Authority and Expertise: The Professionalisation of International Development and the Ordering of Dissent." *Antipode* 37, no. 3 (2005): 425–46.

———. "From Colonial Administration to Development Studies: A Post-colonial Critique of the History of Development Studies." In *A Radical History of Development Studies: Individuals, Institutions and Ideologies*, edited by Uma Kothari, 47–66. Cape Town: David Philip, 2005.

Lancaster, Carol. *Foreign Aid: Diplomacy, Development, Domestic Politics*. Chicago: University of Chicago Press, 2006.

Lewis, David, and David Mosse, eds. *Development Brokers and Translators: The Ethnography of Aid and Agencies*. Sterling, VA: Kumarian Press, 2006.

"The List: The World's Most Powerful Development NGOs." *Foreign Policy*, July 1, 2008.

Maren, Michael. *The Road to Hell: The Ravaging Effects of Foreign Aid and International Charity*. New York: Free Press, 2002.

———. *Save the Children: A Different Kind of Child Abuse*, December 12, 1996, cited March 2, 2012, http://michaelmaren.com/1996/12/save-the-children-a-different-kind-of-child-abuse/.

Maslach, Christina, and Wilmar B. Schaufeli. "Historical and Conceptual Development of Burnout: Recent Developments in Theory and Research." In *Professional Burnout: Recent Developments in Theory and Research*, edited by Christina Maslach and Tadeusz Marek, Series in Applied Psychology: Social Issues and Questions, 1–16. Philadelphia: Taylor & Francis, 1993.

Mortenson, Greg, and David Oliver Relin. *Three Cups of Tea: One Man's Mission to Promote Peace . . . One School at a Time*. New York: Viking, 2006.

Mosse, David. *Cultivating Development: An Ethnography of Aid Policy and Practice*. London: Pluto Press, 2004.

Moyo, Dambissa. *Dead Aid: Why Aid Is Not Working and How There Is a Better Way for Africa*. London: Penguin, 2010.

Musa, Saif Ali, and Abdalla A. R. M. Hamid. "Psychological Problems Among Aid Workers Operating in Darfur." *Social Behavior and Personality* 36, no. 3 (2008): 407–16.

NGO Branch of the United Nations Department of Economic and Social Affairs. *At Your Service*, 2012, cited June 10, 2012, http://csonet.org/.

Nordland, Rod. "Afghan Bank Commission Absolves President's Brother in Fraud Case." *New York Times*, May 29, 2011.

OECD. "50 Years of Official Development Assistance," cited October 28, 2012, http://webnet .oecd.org/dcdgraphs/ODAhistory/.

———. *Development: Aid to Developing Countries Falls Because of Global Recession*, April 4, 2012, cited June 2, 2012, http://www.oecd.org/document/3/0,3746,en_21571361_ 44315115_50058883_1_1_1_1,00.html.

———. *Development Aid: Total Official and Private Flows*, April 4, 2012, cited June 2, 2012, http://www.oecd-ilibrary.org/development/development-aid-total-official-and-private -flows_20743866-table5.

———. *Development Co-operation Directorate (DCD-DAC)*, cited January 15, 2012, http://www .oecd.org.

———. *ODA by Country at 2009 Prices and Exchange Rates (Net Disbursements)*, 2011, cited August 16, 2011, http://www.oecd.org/dataoecd/31/35/47452831.xls.

Okwonga, Musa. "Stop Kony, Yes. But Don't Stop Asking Questions." *The Independent*, March 7, 2012.

Oxfam. *Food Aid or Hidden Dumping? Separating Wheat From Chaff*. Oxfam, 2005.

———. *Oxfam: About Us*, 2012, cited February 15, 2012, http://www.oxfam.org/en/about.

Paterson, Anna, and James Blewett. *Putting the Cart Before the Horse? Privatisation and Economic Reform in Afghanistan*. Kabul: Afghanistan Research and Evaluation Unit, 2006.

Penketh, Anne. "Kenya Tells Former Envoy Clay He Is 'Persona Non Grata.'" *The Independent*, February 6, 2008.

Priesner, Stefan. "Gross National Happiness—Bhutan's Vision of Development and Its Challenges." In *Gross National Happiness*, edited by Sonam Kinga et al., 24–52. Thimphu: Centre for Bhutan Studies, 1999.

"Quinoa Selection: Foreign Interest Grows in an Old Highland Staple." *The Economist*, May 12, 2012.

Rahnema, Majid, and Victoria Bawtree, eds. *The Post-Development Reader*. London: Zed Books, 1997.

Ramirez, Ricardo, and Wendy Quarry. *Communication for Another Development*. London: Zed Books, 2008.

Richardson, Michael. "Q&A/Jeffrey Sachs: IMF Prescribes 'Wrong Medicine.'" *New York Times*, January 15, 1998.

Riddell, Roger C. *Does Foreign Aid Really Work?* New York: Oxford University Press, 2007.

Rist, Gilbert. *The History of Development: From Western Origins to Global Faith*, 3rd ed. London: Zed Books, 2009.

Room to Read. *Our Story 2012*, cited October 18, 2012, http://www.roomtoread.org.

Ryan, Halford Ross. *The Inaugural Addresses of Twentieth-Century American Presidents*. Santa Barbara, CA: Praeger, 1993.

Sachs, Jeffrey. "The African Green Revolution." *Scientific American*, May 2008.

Salamon, Lester M. "The Rise of the Nonprofit Sector: A Global Associational Revolution." *Foreign Affairs*, July/August 1994.

Schön, Donald A. *The Reflective Practitioner: How Professionals Think in Action*. New York: Basic Books, 1984.

Scott, James C. *Seeing Like a State: How Certain Schemes to Improve the Human Condition Have Failed*. New Haven, CT: Yale University Press, 1999.

Sen, A. *Development as Freedom*. London: Oxford University Press, 1999.

Shiva, Vandana. "The Green Revolution in the Punjab." *The Ecologist* 21, no. 2 (1991): 57–60.

Shukla, Archna. "First Official Estimate: An NGO for Every 400 People in India." *Indian Express*, July 7, 2010.

Smillie, Ian. *The Alms Bazaar*. Ottawa: International Development Research Centre, 1995.

———. *Freedom From Want: The Remarkable Success Story of BRAC, the Global Grassroots Organization That's Winning the Fight Against Poverty*. Sterling, VA: Kumarian Press, 2009.

Soussan, Michael. *Backstabbing for Beginners: My Crash Course in International Diplomacy*. New York: Nation Books, 2008.

South African Police Service. *Crime in the Khayelitsha (Wc) Police Precinct From April to March: 2003/2004–2008/2009*. Cape Town: Government of Cape Town, 2009.

Transparency International. *Corruption Perceptions Index 2011*, 2011, cited February 8, 2012, http://cpi.transparency.org/cpi2011/results/#CountryResults.

"Uganda Shaken by Fund Scandal." *Washington Times*, June 15, 2006.

United Nations. "Growth in United Nations Membership, 1945–Present," 2012, cited October 20, 2012, http://www.un.org/en/members/growth.shtml.

———. *United Nations*, cited February 8, 2012, http://www.un.org/en/.

United Nations Department of Economic and Social Affairs. *Record Number of NGOs Seeking Participation in the UN*, January 31, 2011, cited January 6, 2012, http://www.un.org/en/development/desa/news/ecosoc/ngos-applications-ecosoc.html.

United Nations Development Programme. *Human Development Report 1990: Concept and Measurement of Human Development*. New York: United Nations Development Programme, 1990.

———. Overview: What We Do, 2012, cited February 15, 2012, http://www.undp.org/content/undp/en/home/ourwork/overview.html.

Uphoff, N., M. Esman, and A. Krishna. *Reasons for Success: Learning From Instructive Experiences in Rural Development*. West Hartford, CT: Kumarian Press, 1998.

Ura, Karma. *The Bhutanese Development Story*. Thimphu: Centre for Bhutan Studies, 2005.

Verma, Rita. "Intercultural Encounters, Colonial Continuities and Contemporary Disconnects in Rural Aid: An Ethnography of Development Practitioners in Madagascar." In *Inside the Everyday Lives of Development Workers: The Challenges and Futures of Aidland*, edited by Anne-Meike Fechter and Heather Hindman, 59–82. Sterling, VA: Kumarian Press, 2010.

Véron, R. "The 'New' Kerala Model: Lessons for Sustainable Development." *World Development* 29, no. 8 (2001): 1455.

Wallace, Tina, Lisa Bornstein, and Jennifer Chapman. *The Aid Chain: Coercion and Commitment in Development NGOs*. Bourton-on-Dunsmore: Practical Action, 2007.

Whitney, Jake. "Going Too Far: Jake Whitney Interviews Michela Wrong." *Guernica*, June 9, 2009.

Wilder, Andrew. "Losing Hearts and Minds in Afghanistan." *Middle East Institute Viewpoints*, 2009.

Wilder, Andrew, and Stuart Gordon. "Money Can't Buy America Love." *Foreign Policy*, December 1, 2009.

Willetts, Peter. *The Growth in the Number of NGOs in Consultative Status With the Economic and Social Council of the United Nations*, City University, 2002, cited November 6, 2011, http://www.staff.city.ac.uk/p.willetts/NGOS/NGO-GRPH.HTM#graph.

Wood, John. *Leaving Microsoft to Change the World: An Entrepreneur's Odyssey to Educate the World's Children.* New York: Harper, 2007.

World Bank. *World Bank Group: Working for a World Free of Poverty.* Washington, DC: World Bank, 2006.

"The World Bank and the Environment: When the Learning Curve Is Long." *The Economist,* June 25, 2009.

Wrong, Michela. *It's Our Turn to Eat: The Story of a Kenyan Whistle-Blower.* New York: Harper, 2009.

Yunus, Muhammad. *Banker to the Poor: Micro-lending and the Battle Against World Poverty.* New York: PublicAffairs, 2003.

Zimbardo, Philip, Christina Maslach, and Craig Hanley. "Chapter 11: Reflections on the Stanford Prison Experiment: Genesis, Transformations, Consequences." In *Obedience to Authority: Current Perspectives on the Milgram Paradigm,* edited by Thomas Blass. London: Psychology Press, 2000.

Index

About the Book

Despite the labyrinthine bureaucracies, frustrating inefficiencies, and disorienting complexities of the "development business," many individuals and groups find their way through and contribute to positive change. How do they do it? What ethical and practical dilemmas do they face, and what strategies do they find most effective for overcoming them? Sarah Parkinson draws on the experiences of more than 150 practitioners to provide insights on how the international development system functions—and seasoned, down-to-earth advice about how to successfully confront its challenges.

Sarah Parkinson is a consultant on the monitoring and evaluation of development projects.